Sweet Bird of Youth and Other Plays

Tennessee Williams was one of the most influential American playwrights of the twentieth century. Born Thomas Lanier Williams III in 1911 in Columbus, Mississippi, he later changed his name to 'Tennessee' after the state of his father's birth. Williams was diagnosed with diphtheria at the age of seven, causing him to spend much of his adolescence at home. Tennessee's older sister, Rose, suffered from schizophrenia and later underwent a prefrontal lobotomy, after which she was incapacitated. In 1938, Williams entered the University of Iowa and completed his course, at the same time holding down a large number of part-time jobs. Writing continually during this period, Williams soon made his name as a play-wright, producing shows in Boston and on Broadway in New York. Whilst living in New Orleans Williams met Frank Merlo, with whom he had a long-term relationship until Frank's premature death in 1961. Tennessee Williams died at his New York City residence, the Hotel Elysee, in 1983.

In 1940 Williams received the Rockefeller Fellowship for his play *Battle of Angels* (later rewritten as *Orpheus Descending*) and, with *The Glass Menagerie* in 1944 won the New York Drama Critics' Circle Award, which established him as an important playwright. He won the Pulitzer Prize twice: in 1948 for *A Streetcar Named Desire*; and in 1955 for *Cat on a Hot Tin Roof*. His plays have enjoyed great success both on stage and on screen, some memorable productions of which starred actors Marlon Brando, Vivien Leigh, Katharine Hepburn, Elizabeth Taylor and Paul Newman. Among his many plays Penguin publishes *The Glass Menagerie* (1944), *A Streetcar Named Desire* (1947), *Summer and Smoke* (1948), *The Rose Tattoo* (1951), *Cat on a Hot Tin Roof* (1955), *Baby Doll* (1957), *Something Unspoken* (1958), *Suddenly Last Summer* (1958), *Sweet Bird of Youth* (1959), *Period of Adjustment* (1960), *The Night of the Iguana* (1961), *The Milk Train Doesn't Stop Here Anymore* (1963; revised 1964) and *Small Craft Warnings* (1972). Penguin also publishes Tennessee Williams's *Memoirs*.

TENNESSEE WILLIAMS

Sweet Bird of Youth and Other Plays

Sweet Bird of Youth
Period of Adjustment
The Night of the Iguana

Edited by
E. Martin Browne

PENGUIN BOOKS

PENGUIN CLASSICS

Published by the Penguin Group
Penguin Books Ltd, 80 Strand, London WC2R ORL, England
Penguin Group (USA) Inc., 375 Hudson Street, New York, New York 10014, USA
Penguin Group (Canada), 90 Eglinton Avenue East, Suite 700, Toronto, Ontario, Canada M4P 2Y3
(a division of Pearson Penguin Canada Inc.)
Penguin Ireland, 25 St Stephen's Green, Dublin 2, Ireland (a division of Penguin Books Ltd)
Penguin Group (Australia), 250 Camberwell Road, Camberwell, Victoria 3124, Australia
(a division of Pearson Australia Group Pty Ltd)
Penguin Books India Pvt Ltd, 11 Community Centre, Panchsheel Park, New Delhi – 110 017, India
Penguin Group (NZ), 67 Apollo Drive, Rosedale, North Shore 0632, New Zealand
(a division of Pearson New Zealand Ltd)
Penguin Books (South Africa) (Pty) Ltd, 24 Sturdee Avenue, Rosebank, Johannesburg 2196, South Africa

Penguin Books Ltd, Registered Offices: 80 Strand, London WC2R ORL, England

www.penguin.com

Sweet Bird of Youth first published 1959
Period of Adjustment first published in Great Britain by Martin Secker & Warburg Ltd 1961
The Night of the Iguana first published in Great Britain by Martin Secker & Warburg Ltd 1963
These selected plays first published together in Penguin Classics 2009

008

Sweet Bird of Youth copyright © 1959, 1962, renewed 1987, 1990 by The University of the South
The Foreword, which appeared in *The New York Times* on 8 March 1959, copyright © 1959
The New York Times, is reprinted with permission
Period of Adjustment copyright © 1960, 1961, renewed 1988, 1989 by The University of the South
The Night of the Iguana copyright © 1948, renewed 1976 by The University of the South
All rights reserved

The moral right of the author has been asserted

Set in Dante MT 10.5/13 pt
Typeset by Palimpsest Book Production Limited, Grangemouth, Stirlingshire
Printed in England by Clays Ltd, St Ives plc

978-0-141-19108-9

www.greenpenguin.co.uk

MIX
Paper from
responsible sources
FSC® C018179

Penguin Books is committed to a sustainable
future for our business, our readers and our planet.
This book is made from Forest Stewardship
Council™ certified paper.

Contents

Sweet Bird of Youth   vii
(with a Foreword by the author)

Period of Adjustment   85

The Night of the Iguana   181

Sweet Bird of Youth

To Cheryl Crawford

Relentless caper for all those who step
The legend of their youth into the noon

Hart Crane

Foreword*

When I came to my writing desk on a recent morning, I found lying on my desk top an unmailed letter that I had written. I began reading it and found this sentence: 'We are all civilized people, which means that we are all savages at heart but observing a few amenities of civilized behaviour.' Then I went on to say: 'I am afraid that I observe fewer of these amenities than you do. Reason? My back is to the wall and has been to the wall for so long that the pressure of my back on the wall has started to crumble the plaster that covers the bricks and mortar.'

Isn't it odd that I said the wall was giving way, not my back? I think so. Pursuing this course of free association, I suddenly remembered a dinner date I once had with a distinguished colleague. During the course of this dinner, rather close to the end of it, he broke a long, mournful silence by lifting to me his sympathetic gaze and saying to me, sweetly, 'Tennessee, don't you feel that you are blocked as a writer?'

I didn't stop to think of an answer; it came immediately off my tongue without any pause for planning. I said, 'Oh, yes, I've always been blocked as a writer but my desire to write has been so strong that it has always broken down the block and gone past it.'

Nothing untrue comes off the tongue that quickly. It is planned speeches that contain lies or dissimulations, not what you blurt out so spontaneously in one instant.

It was literally true. At the age of fourteen, I discovered writing as an escape from a world of reality in which I felt acutely uncomfortable. It immediately became my place of retreat, my cave, my refuge. From

* Written prior to the Broadway opening of *Sweet Bird of Youth* and published in the *New York Times* on Sunday, 8 March 1959.

what? From being called a sissy by the neighbourhood kids, and Miss Nancy by my father, because I would rather read books in my grandfather's large and classical library than play marbles and baseball and other normal kid games, a result of a severe childhood illness and of excessive attachment to the female members of my family, who had coaxed me back into life.

I think no more than a week after I started writing I ran into the first block. It's hard to describe it in a way that will be understandable to anyone who is not a neurotic. I will try. All my life I have been haunted by the obsession that to desire a thing or to love a thing intensely is to place yourself in a vulnerable position, to be a possible, if not a probable, loser of what you most want. Let's leave it like that. That block has always been there and always will be, and my chance of getting, or achieving, anything that I long for will always be gravely reduced by the interminable existence of that block.

I described it once in a poem called 'The Marvellous Children'.

'He, the demon, set up barricades of gold and purple tinfoil, labelled Fear (and other august titles), which they, the children, would leap lightly over, always tossing backwards their wild laughter.'

But having, always, to contend with this adversary of fear, which was sometimes terror, gave me a certain tendency towards an atmosphere of hysteria and violence in my writing, an atmosphere that has existed in it since the beginning.

In my first published work, for which I received the big sum of thirty-five dollars, a story published in the July or August issue of *Weird Tales* in the year 1928, I drew upon a paragraph in the ancient histories of Herodotus to create a story of how the Egyptian queen, Nitocris, invited all of her enemies to a lavish banquet in a subterranean hall on the shores of the Nile, and how, at the height of this banquet, she excused herself from the table and opened sluice gates admitting the waters of the Nile into the locked banquet hall, drowning her unloved guests like so many rats.

I was sixteen when I wrote this story, but already a confirmed writer, having entered upon this vocation at the age of fourteen, and, if you're well acquainted with my writings since then, I don't have to tell you that it set the keynote for most of the work that has followed.

My first four plays, two of them performed in St Louis, were correspondingly violent or more so. My first play professionally produced and aimed at Broadway was *Battle of Angels* and it was about as violent as you can get on the stage.

During the nineteen years since then I have only produced five plays that are *not* violent: *The Glass Menagerie*, *You Touched Me*, *Summer and Smoke*, *The Rose Tattoo*, and, recently in Florida, a serious comedy called *Period of Adjustment*, which is still being worked on.

What surprises me is the degree to which both critics and audience have accepted this barrage of violence. I think I was surprised, most of all, by the acceptance and praise of *Suddenly Last Summer*. When it was done off Broadway, I thought I would be critically tarred and feathered and ridden on a fence rail out of the New York theatre, with no future haven except in translation for theatres abroad, who might mistakenly construe my work as a castigation of American morals, not understanding that I write about violence in American life only because I am not so well acquainted with the society of other countries.

Last year I thought it might help me as a writer to undertake psychoanalysis and so I did. The analyst, being acquainted with my work and recognizing the psychic wounds expressed in it, asked me, soon after we started, 'Why are you so full of hate, anger, and envy?'

Hate was the word I contested. After much discussion and argument, we decided that 'hate' was just a provisional term and that we would only use it till we had discovered the more precise term. But unfortunately I got restless and started hopping back and forth between the analyst's couch and some Caribbean beaches. I think before we called it quits I had persuaded the doctor that hate was not the right word, that there was some other thing, some other word for it, which we had not yet uncovered, and we left it like that.

Anger, oh yes! And envy, yes! But not hate. I think that hate is a thing, a feeling, that can only exist where there is no understanding. Significantly, good physicians never have it. They never hate their patients, no matter how hateful their patients may seem to be, with their relentless, maniacal concentration on their own tortured egos.

Since I am a member of the human race, when I attack its behaviour towards fellow members I am obviously including myself in the attack, unless I regard myself as not human but superior to humanity. I don't. In fact, I can't expose a human weakness on the stage unless I know it through having it myself. I have exposed a good many human weaknesses and brutalities and consequently I have them.

I don't even think that I am more conscious of mine than any of you are of yours. Guilt is universal. I mean a strong sense of guilt. If there exists any area in which a man can rise above his moral condition, imposed upon him at birth, and long before birth, by the nature of his breed, then I think it is only a willingness to know it, to face its existence in him, and I think that, at least below the conscious level, we all face it. Hence guilty feelings, and hence defiant aggressions, and hence the deep dark of despair that haunts our dreams, our creative work, and makes us distrust each other.

Enough of these philosophical abstractions, for now. To get back to writing for the theatre, if there is any truth in the Aristotelian idea that violence is purged by its poetic representation on a stage, then it may be that my cycle of violent plays have had a moral justification after all. I know that I have felt it. I have always felt a release from the sense of meaninglessness and death when a work of tragic intention has seemed to me to have achieved that intention, even if only approximately, nearly.

I would say that there is something much bigger in life and death than we have become aware of (or adequately recorded) in our living and dying. And, further, to compound this shameless romanticism, I would say that our serious theatre is a search for that something that is not yet successful but is still going on.

The Characters

Sweet Bird of Youth was presented at the Martin Beck Theatre in New York on 10 March 1959 by Cheryl Crawford. It was directed by Elia Kazan; the stage settings and lighting were by Jo Mielziner, the costumes by Anna Hill Johnstone, and the music by Paul Bowles; production stage manager, David Pardoll. The cast was as follows:

CHANCE WAYNE	*Paul Newman*
THE PRINCESS KOSMONOPOLIS	*Geraldine Page*
FLY	*Milton J. Williams*
MAID	*Patricia Ripley*
GEORGE SCUDDER	*Logan Ramsey*
HATCHER	*John Napier*
BOSS FINLEY	*Sidney Blackmer*
TOM JUNIOR	*Rip Torn*
AUNT NONNIE	*Martine Bartlett*
HEAVENLY FINLEY	*Diana Hyland*
CHARLES	*Earl Sydnor*
STUFF	*Bruce Dern*
MISS LUCY	*Madeleine Sherwood*
THE HECKLER	*Charles Tyner*
VIOLET	*Monica May*
EDNA	*Hilda Brawner*
SCOTTY	*Charles McDaniel*
BUD	*Jim Jeter*
MEN IN BAR	*Duke Farley*
	Ron Harper
	Kenneth Blake
PAGE	*Glenn Stensel*

Synopsis of Scenes

Act One

SCENE ONE: A bedroom in the Royal Palms Hotel, somewhere on the Gulf Coast.

SCENE TWO: The same, later.

Act Two

SCENE ONE: The terrace of Boss Finley's house in St Cloud.

SCENE TWO: The cocktail lounge and Palm Garden of the Royal Palms Hotel.

Act Three

The bedroom again.

TIME: Modern, an Easter Sunday, from late morning till late night.

SETTING and 'SPECIAL EFFECTS': The stage is backed by a cyclorama that should give a poetic unity of mood to the several specific settings. There are non-realistic projections on this 'cyc', the most important and constant being a grove of royal palm trees. There is nearly always a wind among these very tall palm trees, sometimes loud, sometimes just a whisper, and sometimes it blends into a thematic music which will be identified, when it occurs, as the 'Lament'.

During the daytime scenes the cyclorama projection is a poetic abstraction of semi-tropical sea and sky in fair spring weather. At night it is the palm garden with its branches among the stars.

The specific settings should be treated as freely and sparingly as the sets for *Cat on a Hot Tin Roof* or *Summer and Smoke*. They'll be described as you come to them in the script.

Act One

Scene One

A bedroom of an old-fashioned but still fashionable hotel somewhere along the Gulf Coast in a town called St Cloud. I think of it as resembling one of those 'Grand Hotels' around Sorrento or Monte Carlo, set in a palm garden. The style is vaguely 'Moorish'. The principal set-piece is a great double bed which should be raked towards the audience. In a sort of Moorish corner, backed by shuttered windows, is a wicker tabouret and two wicker stools, over which is suspended a Moorish lamp on a brass chain. The windows are floor length and they open out upon a gallery. There is also a practical door frame, opening on to a corridor: the walls are only suggested.

On the great bed are two figures, a sleeping woman, and a young man awake, sitting up, in the trousers of white silk pyjamas. The sleeping woman's face is partly covered by an eyeless black satin domino to protect her from morning glare. She breathes and tosses on the bed as if in the grip of a nightmare. The young man is lighting his first cigarette of the day.

> [*Outside the windows there are heard the soft, urgent cries of birds, the sound of their wings. Then a coloured waiter,* FLY, *appears at the door on the corridor, bearing coffee-service for two. He knocks.* CHANCE *rises, pauses a moment at a mirror in the fourth wall to run a comb through his slightly thinning blond hair before he crosses to open the door.*]

CHANCE: Aw, good, put it in there.

FLY: Yes, suh.

CHANCE: Give me the Bromo first. You better mix it for me, I'm –

FLY: Hands kind of shaky this mawnin'?

CHANCE [*shuddering after the Bromo*]: Open the shutters a little. Hey, I said a little, not much, not that much!

I

[*As the shutters are opened we see him clearly for the first time: he's in his late twenties and his face looks slightly older than that; you might describe it as a 'ravaged young face' and yet it is still exceptionally good-looking. His body shows no decline, yet it's the kind of a body that white silk pyjamas are, or ought to be, made for. A church bell tolls, and from another church, nearer, a choir starts singing the 'Hallelujah Chorus'. It draws him to the window, and as he crosses he speaks.*]

I didn't know it was – Sunday.

FLY: Yes, suh, it's *Easter* Sunday.

CHANCE [*leaning out a moment, hands gripping the shutters*]: Uh-huh . . .

FLY: That's the Episcopal Church they're singin' in. The bell's from the Catholic Church.

CHANCE: I'll put your tip on the check.

FLY: Thank you, Mr Wayne.

CHANCE [*as FLY starts for the door*]: Hey. How did you know my name?

FLY: I waited tables in the Grand Ballroom when you used to come to the dances on Saturday nights, with that real pretty girl you used to dance so good with, Mr Boss Finley's daughter.

CHANCE: I'm increasing your tip to five dollars in return for a favour which is not to remember that you have recognized me or anything else at all. Your name is Fly – Shoo, Fly. Close the door with no noise.

VOICE OUTSIDE: Just a minute.

CHANCE: Who's that?

VOICE OUTSIDE: George Scudder.

[*Slight pause. FLY exits.*]

CHANCE: How did you know I was here?

[GEORGE SCUDDER *enters: a coolly nice-looking, business-like young man who might be the head of the Junior Chamber of Commerce but is actually a young doctor, about thirty-six or -seven.*]

SCUDDER: The assistant manager that checked you in here last night phoned me this morning that you'd come back to St Cloud.

CHANCE: So you came right over to welcome me home?

SCUDDER: Your lady friend sounds like she's coming out of ether.

CHANCE: The Princess had a rough night.

SCUDDER: You've latched on to a Princess? [*mockingly*] Gee.

CHANCE: She's travelling incognito.

SCUDDER: Golly, I should think she would, if she's checking in hotels with *you*.

CHANCE: George, you're the only man I know that still says 'gee', 'golly', and 'gosh'.

SCUDDER: Well, I'm not the sophisticated type, Chance.

CHANCE: That's for sure. Want some coffee?

SCUDDER: Nope. Just came for a talk. A quick one.

CHANCE: O.K. Start talking, man.

SCUDDER: Why've you come back to St Cloud?

CHANCE: I've still got a mother and a girl in St Cloud. How's Heavenly, George?

SCUDDER: We'll get around to that later. [*He glances at his watch.*] I've got to be in surgery at the hospital in twenty-five minutes.

CHANCE: You operate now, do you?

SCUDDER [*opening doctor's bag*]: I'm chief of staff there now.

CHANCE: Man, you've got it made.

SCUDDER: Why have you come back?

CHANCE: I heard that my mother was sick.

SCUDDER: But you said 'How's Heavenly?' not 'How's my mother?' Chance. [CHANCE *sips coffee*.] Your mother died a couple of weeks ago . . .

[CHANCE *slowly turns his back on the man and crosses to the window. Shadows of birds sweep the blind. He lowers it a little before he turns back to* SCUDDER.]

CHANCE: Why wasn't I notified?

SCUDDER: You were. A wire was sent you three days before she died, at the last address she had for you which was General Delivery, Los Angeles. We got no answer from that and another wire was sent you after she died, the same day of her death and we got no response from that either. Here's the Church Record. The church

3

took up a collection for her hospital and funeral expenses. She was buried nicely in your family plot and the church has also given her a very nice headstone. I'm giving you these details in spite of the fact that I know and everyone here in town knows that you had no interest in her, less than people who knew her only slightly, such as myself.

CHANCE: How did she go?

SCUDDER: She had a long illness, Chance. You know about that.

CHANCE: Yes. She was sick when I left here the last time.

SCUDDER: She was sick at heart as well as sick in her body at that time, Chance. But people were very good to her, especially people who knew her in church, and the Reverend Walker was with her at the end.

[CHANCE *sits down on the bed. He puts out his unfinished cigarette and immediately lights another. His voice becomes thin and strained.*]

CHANCE: She never had any luck.

SCUDDER: Luck? Well, that's all over with now. If you want to know anything more about that, you can get in touch with Reverend Walker about it, although I'm afraid he won't be likely to show much cordiality to you.

CHANCE: She's gone. Why talk about it?

SCUDDER: I hope you haven't forgotten the letter I wrote you soon after you last left town.

CHANCE: No. I got no letter.

SCUDDER: I wrote you in care of an address your mother gave me, about a very important private matter.

CHANCE: I've been moving a lot.

SCUDDER: I didn't even mention names in the letter.

CHANCE: What was the letter about?

SCUDDER: Sit over here so I don't have to talk loud about this. Come over here. I can't talk loud about this. [SCUDDER *indicates the chair by the tabouret.* CHANCE *crosses and rests a foot on the chair.*] In this letter I just told you that a certain girl we know had to go through an awful experience, a tragic ordeal, because of past contact with you. I told you that I was only giving you this information so that you would know better than to come back to St Cloud, but you didn't know better.

CHANCE: I told you I got no letter. Don't tell me about a letter, I didn't get any letter.

SCUDDER: I'm telling you what I told you in this letter.

CHANCE: All right. Tell me what you told me, don't – don't talk to me like a club, a chamber of something. What did you tell me? What ordeal? What girl? Heavenly? Heavenly? George?

SCUDDER: I see it's not going to be possible to talk about this quietly and so I . . .

CHANCE [*rising to block* SCUDDER's *way*]: Heavenly? What ordeal?

SCUDDER: We will not mention names. Chance, I rushed over here this morning as soon as I heard you were back in St Cloud, before the girl's father and brother could hear that you were back in St Cloud, to stop you from trying to get in touch with the girl and to get you out of here. That is absolutely all I have to say to you in this room at this moment . . . But I hope I have said it in a way to impress you with the vital urgency of it, so you will leave . . .

CHANCE: Jesus! If something's happened to Heavenly, will you please tell me – what?

SCUDDER: I said no names. We are not alone in this room. Now when I go downstairs now, I'll speak to Dan Hatcher, assistant manager here . . . he told me you'd checked in here . . . and tell him you want to check out, so you'd better get Sleeping Beauty and yourself ready to travel, and I suggest that you keep on travelling till you've crossed the State line . . .

CHANCE: You're not going to leave this room till you've explained to me what you've been hinting at about my girl in St Cloud.

SCUDDER: There's a lot more to this which we feel ought not to be talked about to anyone, least of all to you, since you have turned into a criminal degenerate, the only right term for you, but, Chance, I think I ought to remind you that once long ago the father of this girl wrote out a prescription for you, a sort of medical prescription, which is castration. You'd better think about that, that would deprive you of all you've got to get by on. [*He moves towards the steps.*]

CHANCE: I'm used to that threat. I'm not going to leave St Cloud without my girl.

SCUDDER [*on the steps*]: You don't have a girl in St Cloud. Heavenly and I are going to be married next month. [*He leaves abruptly.*]

[CHANCE, *shaken by what he has heard, turns and picks up the phone, and kneels on the floor.*]

CHANCE: Hello? St Cloud 525. Hello, Aunt Nonnie? This is Chance, yes, Chance. I'm staying at the Royal Palms and I . . . what's the matter, has something happened to Heavenly? Why can't you talk now? George Scudder was here and . . . Aunt Nonnie? Aunt Nonnie?

[*The other end hangs up. The sleeping woman suddenly cries out in her sleep.* CHANCE *drops the phone on its cradle and runs to the bed.*]

CHANCE [*bending over her as she struggles out of a nightmare*]: Princess! Princess! Hey, *Princess Kos*! [*He removes her eyemask; she sits up gasping and staring wild-eyed about her.*]

PRINCESS: Who are you? Help!

CHANCE [*on the bed*]: Hush now . . .

PRINCESS: Oh . . . I . . . had . . . a *terrible* dream.

CHANCE: It's all right. Chance's with you.

PRINCESS: Who?

CHANCE: Me.

PRINCESS: I don't know who you are!

CHANCE: You'll remember soon, Princess.

PRINCESS: I don't know, I don't know . . .

CHANCE: It'll come back to you soon. What are you reachin' for, honey?

PRINCESS: Oxygen! Mask!

CHANCE: Why? Do you feel short-winded?

PRINCESS: Yes! I have . . . air . . . shortage!

CHANCE [*looking for the correct piece of luggage*]: Which bag is your oxygen in? I can't remember which bag we packed it in. Aw, yeah, the crocodile case, the one with the combination lock. Wasn't the first number zero . . . ? [*He comes back to the bed and reaches for a bag under its far side.*]

PRINCESS [*as if with her dying breath*]: Zero, zero. Two zeros to the right and then back around to . . .

CHANCE: Zero, three zeros, two of them to the right and the last one to the left . . .

PRINCESS: Hurry! I can't breathe, I'm dying!

CHANCE: I'm getting it, Princess.

PRINCESS: *HURRY!*

CHANCE: Here we are, I've got it . . .

[*He has extracted from the case a small oxygen cylinder and mask. He fits the inhalator over her nose and mouth. She falls back on the pillow. He places the other pillow under her head. After a moment, her panicky breath subsiding, she growls at him.*]

PRINCESS: Why in hell did you lock it up in that case?

CHANCE [*standing at the head of the bed*]: You said to put all your valuables in that case.

PRINCESS: I meant my jewellery, and you know it, you bastard!

CHANCE: Princess, I didn't think you'd have these attacks any more. I thought that having me with you to protect you would stop these attacks of panic, I . . .

PRINCESS: Give me a pill.

CHANCE: Which pill?

PRINCESS: A pink one, a pinkie, and vodka . . .

[*He puts the tank on the floor, and goes over to the trunk. The phone rings.* CHANCE *gives the* PRINCESS *a pill, picks up the vodka bottle, and goes to the phone. He sits down with the bottle between his knees.*]

CHANCE [*pouring a drink, phone held between shoulder and ear*]: Hello? Oh, hello, Mr Hatcher – Oh? But Mr Hatcher, when we checked in here last night we weren't told that, and Miss Alexandra Del Lago . . .

PRINCESS [*shouting*]: *Don't use my name!*

CHANCE: . . . is suffering from exhaustion, she's not at all well, Mr Hatcher, and certainly not in any condition to travel . . . I'm sure you don't want to take the responsibility for what might happen to Miss Del Lago . . .

PRINCESS [*shouting again*]: *Don't use my name!*

CHANCE: . . . if she attempted to leave here today in the condition she's in . . . do you?

PRINCESS: *Hang up!* [*He does. He comes over with his drink and the bottle to the* PRINCESS.] I want to forget everything, I want to forget who I am . . .

CHANCE [*handing her the drink*]: He said that . . .

PRINCESS [*drinking*]: Please shut up, I'm *forgetting*!

CHANCE [*taking the glass from her*]: Okay, go on, forget. There's nothing better than that, I wish I could do it . . .

PRINCESS: I can, I will. I'm forgetting . . . I'm forgetting . . .

[*She lies down.* CHANCE *moves to the foot of the bed, where he seems to be struck with an idea. He puts the bottle down on the floor, runs to the chaise, and picks up a tape recorder. Taking it back to the bed, he places the recorder on the floor. As he plugs it in, he coughs.*]

What's going on?

CHANCE: Looking for my toothbrush.

PRINCESS [*throwing the oxygen mask on the bed*]: Will you please take that away.

CHANCE: Sure you've had enough of it?

PRINCESS [*laughing breathlessly*]: Yes, for God's sake, take it away. I must look hideous in it.

CHANCE [*taking the mask*]: No, no, you just look exotic, like a Princess from Mars or a big magnified insect.

PRINCESS: Thank you, check the cylinder please.

CHANCE: For what?

PRINCESS: Check the air left in it; there's a gauge on the cylinder that gives the pressure . . .

CHANCE: You're still breathing like a quarter horse that's been run a full mile. Are you sure you don't want a doctor?

PRINCESS: No, for God's sake . . . no!

CHANCE: Why are you so scared of doctors?

PRINCESS [*hoarsely, quickly*]: I don't need them. What happened is nothing at all. It happens frequently to me. Something disturbs me . . . adrenalin's pumped in my blood and I get short-winded, that's all, that's all there is to it . . . I woke up, I didn't know where I was or who I was with, I got panicky . . . adrenalin was released and I got short-winded . . .

CHANCE: Are you okay now, Princess? Huh? [*He kneels on the bed, and helps straighten up the pillows.*]

PRINCESS: Not quite yet, but I will be. I will be.

CHANCE: You're full of complexes, plump lady.

PRINCESS: What did you call me?

CHANCE: Plump lady.

PRINCESS: Why do you call me that? Have I let go of my figure?

CHANCE: You put on a good deal of weight after that disappointment you had last month.

PRINCESS [*hitting him with a small pillow*]: What disappointment? I don't remember any.

CHANCE: Can you control your memory like that?

PRINCESS: Yes. I've had to learn to. What is this place, a hospital? And you, what are you, a male nurse?

CHANCE: I take care of you but I'm not your nurse.

PRINCESS: But you're employed by me, aren't you? For some purpose or other?

CHANCE: I'm not on salary with you.

PRINCESS: What are you on? Just expenses?

CHANCE: Yep. You're footing the bills.

PRINCESS: I see. Yes, I see.

CHANCE: Why're you rubbing your eyes?

PRINCESS: My vision's so cloudy! Don't I wear glasses, don't I have any glasses?

CHANCE: You had a little accident with your glasses.

PRINCESS: What was that?

CHANCE: You fell on your face with them on.

PRINCESS: Were they completely demolished?

CHANCE: One lens cracked.

PRINCESS: Well, please give me the remnants. I don't mind waking up in an intimate situation with someone, but I like to see who it's with, so I can make whatever adjustment seems called for . . .

CHANCE [*rising and going to the trunk, where he lights cigarette*]: You know what I look like.

PRINCESS: No, I don't.

CHANCE: You did.

PRINCESS: I tell you I don't remember, it's all gone away!

CHANCE: I don't believe in amnesia.

PRINCESS: Neither do I. But you have to believe a thing that happens to you.

CHANCE: Where did I put your glasses?

PRINCESS: Don't ask me. You say I fell on them. If I was in that condition I wouldn't be likely to know where anything is I had with me. What happened last night?

[*He has picked them up but not given them to her.*]

CHANCE: You knocked yourself out.

PRINCESS: Did we sleep here together?

CHANCE: Yes, but I didn't molest you.

PRINCESS: Should I thank you for that, or accuse you of *cheating?* [*She laughs sadly.*]

CHANCE: I like you, you're a nice monster.

PRINCESS: Your voice sounds young. Are you young?

CHANCE: My age is twenty-nine years.

PRINCESS: That's young for anyone but an Arab. Are you very good-looking?

CHANCE: I used to be the best-looking boy in this town.

PRINCESS: How large is the town?

CHANCE: Fair-sized.

PRINCESS: Well, I like a good mystery novel, I read them to put me to sleep and if they don't put me to sleep, they're good; but this one's a little too good for comfort. I wish you would find me my glasses . . .

[*He reaches over the headboard to hand the glasses to her. She puts them on and looks him over. Then she motions him to come nearer and touches his bare chest with her finger tips.*]

Well, I may have done better, but God knows I've done worse.

CHANCE: What are you doing now, Princess?

PRINCESS: The tactile approach.

CHANCE: You do that like you were feeling a piece of goods to see if it was genuine silk or phoney . . .

PRINCESS: It feels like silk. Genuine! This much I do remember, that I like bodies to be hairless, silky-smooth gold!

CHANCE: Do I meet these requirements?

PRINCESS: You seem to meet those requirements. But I still have a feeling that something is not satisfied in the relation between us.

CHANCE [*moving away from her*]: You've had your experiences, I've had mine. You can't expect everything to be settled at once . . . Two different experiences of two different people. Naturally there's some things that have to be settled between them before there's any absolute agreement.

PRINCESS [*throwing the glasses on the bed*]: Take that splintered lens out before it gets in my eye.

CHANCE [*obeying this instruction by knocking the glasses sharply on the bed table*]: You like to give orders, don't you?

PRINCESS: It's something I seem to be used to.

CHANCE: How would you like to *take* them? To be a slave?

PRINCESS: What time is it?

CHANCE: My watch is in hock somewhere. Why don't you look at yours?

PRINCESS: Where's mine?

[*He reaches lazily over to the table, and hands it to her.*]

CHANCE: It's stopped, at five past seven.

PRINCESS: Surely it's later than that, or earlier, that's no hour when I'm . . .

CHANCE: Platinum, is it?

PRINCESS: No, it's only white gold. I never travel with anything very expensive.

CHANCE: Why? Do you get robbed much? Huh? Do you get 'rolled' often?

PRINCESS: Get what?

CHANCE: 'Rolled'. Isn't that expression in your vocabulary?

PRINCESS: Give me the phone.

CHANCE: For what?

PRINCESS: I said give me the phone.

CHANCE: I know. And I said for what?

PRINCESS: I want to inquire where I am and who is with me.

CHANCE: Take it easy.

PRINCESS: Will you give me the phone?

CHANCE: Relax. You're getting short-winded again . . .

[*He takes hold of her shoulders.*]

PRINCESS: Please let go of me.

CHANCE: Don't you feel secure with me? Lean back. Lean back against me.

PRINCESS: Lean back?

CHANCE: This way, this way. There . . .

[*He pulls her into his arms. She rests in them, panting a little like a trapped rabbit.*]

PRINCESS: It gives you an awful trapped feeling this, this memory block . . . I feel as if someone I loved had died lately, and I don't want to remember who it could be.

CHANCE: Do you remember your name?

PRINCESS: Yes, I do.

CHANCE: What's your name?

PRINCESS: I think there's some reason why I prefer not to tell you.

CHANCE: Well, I happen to know it. You registered under a phoney name in Palm Beach but I discovered your real one. And you admitted it to me.

PRINCESS: I'm the Princess Kosmonopolis.

CHANCE: Yes, and you used to be known as . . .

PRINCESS [*sitting up sharply*]: No, stop . . . will you let me do it? Quietly, in my own way? The last place I remember . . .

CHANCE: What's the last place you remember?

PRINCESS: A town with the crazy name of Tallahassee.

CHANCE: Yeah. We drove through there. That's where I reminded you that today would be Sunday and we ought to lay in a supply of liquor to get us through it without us being dehydrated too severely, and so we stopped there but it was a college town and we had some trouble locating a package store, open . . .

PRINCESS: But we did, did we?

CHANCE [*getting up for the bottle and pouring her a drink*]: Oh, sure, we bought three bottles of vodka. You curled up in the back seat with one of those bottles and when I looked back you were blotto. I intended to stay on the old Spanish Trail straight through to Texas, where you had some oil wells to look at. I didn't stop here . . . I was stopped.

PRINCESS: What by, a cop? Or . . .

CHANCE: No. No cop, but I was arrested by something.

PRINCESS: My car. Where is my car?

CHANCE [*handing her the drink*]: In the hotel parking lot, Princess.

PRINCESS: Oh, then, this is a hotel?

CHANCE: It's the elegant old Royal Palms Hotel in the town of St Cloud.

[*Gulls fly past window, shadows sweeping the blind: they cry out with soft urgency.*]

PRINCESS: Those pigeons out there sound hoarse. They sound like gulls to me. Of course, they could be pigeons with laryngitis.

[CHANCE *glances at her with his flickering smile and laughs softly.*]

Will you help me, please? I'm about to get up.

CHANCE: What do you want? I'll get it.

PRINCESS: I want to go to the window.

CHANCE: What for?

PRINCESS: To look out of it.

CHANCE: I can describe the view to you.

PRINCESS: I'm not sure I'd trust your description. *WELL?*

CHANCE: Okay, *oopsa-daisy.*

PRINCESS: My God! I said help me up, not . . . toss me on to the carpet! [*Sways dizzily a moment, clutching the bed. Then draws a breath and crosses to the window.*]

[*The* PRINCESS *pauses as she gazes out, squinting into noon's brilliance.*]

CHANCE: Well, what do you see? Give me your description of the view, Princess?

PRINCESS [*facing the audience*]: I see a palm garden.

CHANCE: And a four-lane highway just past it.

PRINCESS [*squinting and shielding her eyes*]: Yes, I see that and a strip of beach with some bathers and then, an infinite stretch of nothing but water and . . . [*She cries softly and turns away from the window.*]

CHANCE: What? . . .

PRINCESS: Oh God, I remember the thing I wanted not to. The goddam end of my life! [*She draws a deep shuddering breath.*]

CHANCE [*running to her aid*]: What's the matter?

PRINCESS: Help me back to bed. Oh God, no wonder I didn't want to remember, I was no fool!

[*He assists her to the bed. There is an unmistakable sympathy in his manner, however shallow.*]

CHANCE: Oxygen?

PRINCESS [*drawing another deep shuddering breath*]: No! Where's the stuff? Did you leave it in the car?

CHANCE: Oh, the stuff? Under the mattress. [*Moving to the other side of the bed, he pulls out a small pouch.*]

PRINCESS: A stupid place to put it.

CHANCE [*sitting at the foot of the bed*]: What's wrong with under the mattress?

PRINCESS [*sitting up on the edge of the bed*]: There's such a thing as chambermaids in the world, they make up beds, they come across lumps in a mattress.

CHANCE: This isn't pot. What is it?

PRINCESS: Wouldn't that be pretty? A year in jail in one of those model prisons for distinguished addicts. What is it? Don't you know what it is, you beautiful, stupid young man? It's hashish, Moroccan, the finest.

CHANCE: Oh, hash! How'd you get it through customs when you came back for your come-back?

PRINCESS: I didn't get it through customs. The ship's doctor gave me injections while this stuff was winging over the ocean to a shifty young gentleman who thought he could blackmail me for it. [*She puts on her slippers with a vigorous gesture.*]

CHANCE: Couldn't he?

PRINCESS: Of course not. I called his bluff.

CHANCE: You took injections coming over?

PRINCESS: With my neuritis? I had to. Come on, give it to me.

CHANCE: Don't you want it packed right?

PRINCESS: You talk too much. You ask too many questions. I need something quick. [*She rises.*]

CHANCE: I'm a new hand at this.

PRINCESS: I'm sure, or you wouldn't discuss it in a hotel room . . .

[*She turns to the audience, and intermittently changes the focus of her attention.*]

For years they all told me that it was ridiculous of me to feel that I couldn't go back to the screen or the stage as a middle-aged woman. They told me I was an artist, not just a star whose career depended on youth. But I knew in my heart that the legend of Alexandra del Lago couldn't be separated from an appearance of youth . . .

There's no more valuable knowledge than knowing the right time to go. I knew it. I went at the right time to go. *RETIRED!* Where to? To what? To that dead planet the moon . . .

There's nowhere else to retire to when you retire from an art because, believe it or not, I really was once an artist. So I retired to the moon, but the atmosphere of the moon doesn't have any oxygen in it. I began to feel breathless, in that withered, withering country, of time coming after time not meant to come after, and so I discovered . . . Haven't you fixed it yet?

[CHANCE *rises and goes to her with a cigarette he has been preparing.*]

Discovered this!

And other practices like it, to put to sleep the tiger that raged in my nerves . . . Why the unsatisfied tiger? In the nerves' jungle? Why is anything, anywhere, unsatisfied, and raging? . . .

Ask somebody's good doctor. But don't believe his answer because it isn't . . . the answer . . . if I had just been old but you see, I wasn't old . . .

I just wasn't young, not young, young. I just wasn't young any more . . .

CHANCE: Nobody's young any more . . .

PRINCESS: But you see, I couldn't get old with that tiger still in me raging.

CHANCE: Nobody can get old . . .

PRINCESS: Stars in retirement sometimes give acting lessons. Or take up painting, paint flowers on pots, or landscapes. I could have painted the landscapes of the endless, withering country in which I wandered like a lost nomad. If I could paint deserts and nomads, if I could paint . . . hahaha . . .

CHANCE: Sh-Sh-sh-

PRINCESS: Sorry!

CHANCE: Smoke.

PRINCESS: Yes, smoke! And then the young lovers . . .

CHANCE: Me?

PRINCESS: You? Yes, finally you. But you come after the come-back. Ha . . . Ha . . . The glorious come-back, when I turned fool and came back . . . The screen's a very clear mirror. There's a thing called a close-up. The camera advances and you stand still and your head, your face, is caught in the frame of the picture with a light blazing on it and all your terrible history screams while you smile . . .

CHANCE: How do you know? Maybe it wasn't a failure, maybe you were just scared, just chicken, Princess . . . ha-ha-ha . . .

PRINCESS: Not a failure . . . after that close-up they gasped . . . People gasped . . . I heard them whisper, their shocked whispers. Is that her? Is that her? Her? . . . I made the mistake of wearing a very elaborate gown to the *première*, a gown with a train that had to be gathered up as I rose from my seat and began the interminable retreat from the city of flames, up, up, up the unbearably long theatre aisle, gasping for breath and still clutching up the regal white train of my gown, all the way up the forever . . . length of the aisle, and behind me some small unknown man grabbing at me, saying, stay, stay! At last the top of the aisle, I turned and struck him, then let the train fall, forgot it, and tried to run down the marble stairs, tripped of course, fell and rolled, rolled, like a sailor's drunk whore to the bottom . . . hands, merciful hands without faces, assisted me to get up. After that? Flight, just flight, not interrupted until I woke up this morning . . . Oh God it's gone out . . .

CHANCE: Let me fix you another. Huh? Shall I fix you another?

PRINCESS: Let me finish yours. You can't retire with the out-crying heart of an artist still crying out, in your body, in your nerves, in your what? Heart? Oh, no, that's gone, that's . . .

CHANCE [*He goes to her, takes the cigarette out of her hand and gives her a fresh one.*]: Here, I've fixed you another one . . . Princess, I've fixed you another . . . [*He sits on the floor, leaning against the foot of the bed.*]

PRINCESS: Well, sooner or later, at some point in your life, the thing that you lived for is lost or abandoned, and then . . . you die, or find something else. This is my something else . . . [*She approaches the bed.*] And ordinarily I take the most fantastic precautions against . . . detection . . . [*She sits on the bed, then lies down on her back, her head over the foot, near his.*] I cannot imagine what possessed me to let you know. Knowing so little about you as I seem to know.

CHANCE: I must've inspired a good deal of confidence in you.

PRINCESS: If that's the case, I've gone crazy. Now tell me something. What is that body of water, that sea, out past the palm garden and four-lane highway? I ask you because I remember now that we turned west from the sea when we went on to that highway called the Old Spanish Trail.

CHANCE: We've come back to the sea.

PRINCESS: What sea?

CHANCE: The Gulf.

PRINCESS: The Gulf?

CHANCE: The Gulf of misunderstanding between me and you . . .

PRINCESS: We don't understand each other? And lie here smoking this stuff?

CHANCE: Princess, don't forget that this stuff is yours, that you provided me with it.

PRINCESS: What are you trying to prove? [*Church bells toll.*] Sundays go on a long time.

CHANCE: You don't deny it was yours.

PRINCESS: What's mine?

CHANCE: You brought it into the country, you smuggled it through customs into the U.S.A., and you had a fair supply of it at that hotel in Palm Beach and were asked to check out before you were ready to do so, because its aroma drifted into the corridor one breezy night.

PRINCESS: What are you trying to prove?

CHANCE: You don't deny that you introduced me to it?

PRINCESS: Boy, I doubt very much that I have any vice that I'd need to introduce to you . . .

CHANCE: Don't call me 'boy'.

PRINCESS: Why not?

CHANCE: It sounds condescending. And all my vices were caught from other people.

PRINCESS: What are you trying to prove? My memory's come back now. Excessively clearly. It was this mutual practice that brought us together. When you came in my cabaña to give me one of those papaya cream rubs, you sniffed, you grinned, and said you'd like a stick too.

CHANCE: That's right. I knew the smell of it.

PRINCESS: What are you trying to prove?

CHANCE: You asked me four or five times what I'm trying to prove, the answer is nothing. I'm just making sure that your memory's cleared up now. You do remember me coming in your cabaña to give you those papaya cream rubs?

PRINCESS: Of course I do, Carl!

CHANCE: My name is not Carl. It's Chance.

PRINCESS: You called yourself Carl.

CHANCE: I always carry an extra name in my pocket.

PRINCESS: You're not a criminal, are you?

CHANCE: No ma'am, not me. You're the one that's committed a federal offence.

[*She stares at him a moment, and then goes to the door leading to the hall, looks out and listens.*]

What did you do that for?

PRINCESS [*closing the door*]: To see if someone was planted outside the door.

CHANCE: You still don't trust me?

PRINCESS: Someone that gives me a false name?

CHANCE: You registered under a phoney one in Palm Beach.

PRINCESS: Yes, to avoid getting any reports or condolences on the disaster I ran from. [*She crosses to the window. There is a pause followed by the 'Lament'.*] And so we've not arrived at any agreement?

CHANCE: No ma'am, not a complete one.

[*She turns her back to the window and gazes at him from there.*]

PRINCESS: What's the gimmick? The hitch?

CHANCE: The usual one.

PRINCESS: What's that?

CHANCE: Doesn't somebody always hold out for something?

PRINCESS: Are you holding out for something?

CHANCE: Uh-huh . . .

PRINCESS: What?

CHANCE: You said that you had a large block of stock, more than half-ownership in a sort of a second-rate Hollywood studio, and could put me under contract. I doubted your word about that. You're not like any phoney I've met before, but phoneys come in all types and sizes. So I held out, even after we locked your cabaña door for the papaya cream rubs . . . You wired for some contract papers we signed. It was notarized and witnessed by three strangers found in a bar.

PRINCESS: Then why did you hold out, still?

CHANCE: I didn't have much faith in it. You know, you can buy those things for six bits in novelty stores. I've been conned and tricked too often to put much faith in anything that could still be phoney.

PRINCESS: You're wise. However, I have the impression that there's been a certain amount of intimacy between us.

CHANCE: A certain amount. No more. I wanted to hold your interest.

PRINCESS: Well, you miscalculated. My interest always increases with satisfaction.

CHANCE: Then you're unusual in that respect, too.

PRINCESS: In all respects I'm not common.

CHANCE: But I guess the contract we signed is full of loopholes?

PRINCESS: Truthfully, yes, it is. I can get out of it if I wanted to. And so can the studio. Do you have any talent?

CHANCE: For what?

PRINCESS: Acting, baby, *ACTING*!

CHANCE: I'm not as positive of it as I once was. I've had more chances than I could count on my fingers, and made the grade almost, but not quite, every time. Something always blocks me . . .

PRINCESS: What? What? Do you *know*? [*He rises. The lamentation is heard very faintly.*] Fear?

CHANCE: No, not fear, but terror . . . otherwise would I be your god-dam caretaker, hauling you across the country? Picking you up when you fall? Well would I? Except for that block, be anything less than a star?

PRINCESS: *CARL!*

CHANCE: Chance . . . Chance Wayne. You're stoned.

PRINCESS: Chance, come back to your youth. Put off this false, ugly hardness and . . .

CHANCE: And be took in by every con-merchant I meet?

PRINCESS: I'm not a phoney, believe me.

CHANCE: Well, then, what is it you want? Come on, say it, Princess.

PRINCESS: Chance, come here. [*He smiles but doesn't move.*] Come here and let's comfort each other a little. [*He crouches by the bed; she encircles him with her bare arms.*]

CHANCE: Princess! Do you know something? All this conversation has been recorded on tape?

PRINCESS: What are you talking about?

CHANCE: Listen. I'll play it back to you. [*He uncovers the tape recorder; approaches her with the earpiece.*]

PRINCESS: How did you get that thing?

CHANCE: You bought it for me in Palm Beach. I said that I wanted it to improve my diction . . .

[*He presses the 'play' button on the recorder. The following in the left column can either be on a public address system, or can be cut.*]

(PLAYBACK)

PRINCESS: What is it? Don't you know what it is, you beautiful, stupid, young man? It's hashish, Moroccan, the finest.

PRINCESS: What a smart cookie you are.

CHANCE: How does it feel to be over a great big barrel?

CHANCE: Oh, hash! How'd you get it through customs when you came back for your come-back?

PRINCESS: I didn't get it through customs. The ship's doctor . . .

[*He snaps off the recorder and picks up the reels.*]

PRINCESS: This is blackmail, is it? Where's my mink stole?

CHANCE: Not stolen.

[*He tosses it to her contemptuously from a chair.*]

PRINCESS: Where is my jewel case?

CHANCE [*picking it up off the floor and throwing it on the bed*]: Here.

PRINCESS [*opening it up and starting to put on some jewellery*]: Every piece is insured and described in detail. Lloyd's in London.

CHANCE: Who's a smart cookie, Princess? You want your purse now so you can count your money?

PRINCESS: I don't carry currency with me, just travellers' cheques.

CHANCE: I noted that fact already. But I got a fountain pen you can sign them with.

PRINCESS: Ho, ho!

CHANCE: 'Ho, ho!' What an insincere laugh; if that's how you fake a laugh, no wonder you didn't make good in your come-back picture . . .

21

PRINCESS: Are you serious about this attempt to blackmail me?

CHANCE: You'd better believe it. Your trade's turned dirt on you, Princess. You understand that language.

PRINCESS: The language of the gutter is understood anywhere that anyone ever fell in it.

CHANCE: Aw, then you *do* understand.

PRINCESS: And if I shouldn't comply with this order of yours?

CHANCE: You still got a name, you're still a personage, Princess. You wouldn't want *Confidential* or *Whisper* or *Hush-Hush* or the narcotics department of the F.B.I. to get hold of one of these tape-records, would you? And I'm going to make lots of copies. Huh? Princess?

PRINCESS: You are trembling and sweating . . . you see this part doesn't suit you, you just don't play it well, Chance . . . [CHANCE *puts the reels in a suitcase.*] I hate to think of what kind of desperation has made you try to intimidate me, *ME? ALEXANDRA DEL LAGO?* with that ridiculous threat. Why it's so silly, it's touching, downright endearing, it makes me feel close to you, Chance. You were well born, weren't you? Born of good Southern stock, in a genteel tradition, with just one disadvantage, a laurel wreath on your forehead, given too early, without enough effort to earn it . . . where's your scrapbook, Chance? [*He crosses to the bed, takes a travellers' chequebook out of her purse, and extends it to her.*] Where's your book full of little theatre notices and stills that show you in the background of . . .

CHANCE: Here! Here! Start signing . . . or . . .

PRINCESS [*pointing to the bathroom*]: Or *WHAT?* Go take a shower under cold water. I don't like hot sweaty bodies in a tropical climate. Oh, you, I do want and will accept, still . . . under certain conditions which I will make very clear to you.

CHANCE: Here. [*Throws the chequebook towards the bed.*]

PRINCESS: Put this away. And your leaky fountain pen . . . When monster meets monster, one monster has to give way, *AND IT WILL NEVER BE ME.* I'm an older hand at it . . . with much more natural aptitude at it than you have . . . Now then, you put the cart a little in front of the horse. Signed cheques are payment, delivery comes first. Certainly I can afford it, I could deduct you, as my caretaker, Chance, remember that I was a star before big taxes . . .

and had a husband who was a great merchant prince. He taught me to deal with money . . . Now, Chance, please pay close attention while I tell you the very special conditions under which I will keep you in my employment . . . after this miscalculation . . .

Forget the legend that I was and the ruin of that legend. Whether or not I do have a disease of the heart that places an early terminal date on my life, no mention of that, no reference to it ever. No mention of death, never, never a word on that odious subject. I've been accused of having a death wish but I think it's life that I wish for, terribly, shamelessly, on any terms whatsoever.

When I say now, the answer must not be later. I have only one way to forget these things I don't want to remember and that's through the act of love-making. That's the only dependable distraction so when I say now, because I need that distraction, it has to be now, not later.

[*She crosses to the bed. He rises from the opposite side of the bed and goes to the window. She gazes at his back as he looks out of the window. Pause: 'Lament'.*]

PRINCESS [*finally, softly*]: Chance, I need that distraction. It's time for me to find out if you're able to give it to me. You mustn't hang on to your silly little idea that you can increase your value by turning away and looking out of a window when somebody wants you . . . I want you . . . I say now and I mean now, then and not until then will I call downstairs and tell the hotel cashier that I'm sending a young man down with some travellers' cheques to cash for me . . .

CHANCE [*turning slowly from the window*]: Aren't you ashamed, a little?

PRINCESS: Of course I am. Aren't you?

CHANCE: More than a little . . .

PRINCESS: Close the shutters, draw the curtain across them.

[*He obeys these commands.*]

Now get a little sweet music on the radio and come here to me and make me almost believe that we're a pair of young lovers without any shame.

Scene Two

[*As the curtain rises, the* PRINCESS *has a fountain pen in hand and is signing cheques.* CHANCE, *now wearing dark slacks, socks, and shoes of the fashionable loafer type, is putting on his shirt and speaks as the curtain opens.*]

CHANCE: Keep on writing, has the pen gone dry?

PRINCESS: I started at the back of the book where the big ones are.

CHANCE: Yes, but you stopped too soon.

PRINCESS: All right, one more from the front of the book as a token of some satisfaction. I said some, not complete.

CHANCE [*picking up the phone*]: Operator – Give me the cashier please.

PRINCESS: What are you doing that for?

CHANCE: You have to tell the cashier you're sending me down with some travellers' cheques to cash for you.

PRINCESS: Have to? Did you say have to?

CHANCE: Cashier? Just a moment. The Princess Kosmonopolis. [*He thrusts the phone at her.*]

PRINCESS [*into the phone*]: Who is this? But I don't want the cashier. My watch has stopped and I want to know the right time . . . five after three? Thank you . . . he says it's five after three. [*She hangs up and smiles at* CHANCE.] I'm not ready to be left alone in this room. Now let's not fight any more over little points like that, let's save our strength for the big ones. I'll have the cheques cashed for you as soon as I've put on my face. I just don't want to be left alone in this place till I've put on the face that I face the world with, baby. Maybe after we get to know each other, we won't fight over little points any more, the struggle will stop, maybe we won't even fight over big points, baby. Will you open the shutters a little bit, please? [*He doesn't seem to hear her. The 'Lament' is heard.*] I won't be able to see my face in the mirror . . . Open the shutters, I won't be able to see my face in the mirror.

CHANCE: Do you want to?

PRINCESS [*pointing*]: Unfortunately I have to! Open the shutters!

[*He does. He remains by the open shutters, looking out as the Lament in the air continues.*]

CHANCE: – I was born in this town. I was born in St Cloud.

PRINCESS: That's a good way to begin to tell your life story. Tell me your life story. I'm interested in it, I really would like to know it. Let's make it your audition, a sort of screen test for you. I can watch you in the mirror while I put my face on. And tell me your life story, and if you hold my attention with your life story, I'll know you have talent, I'll wire my studio on the Coast that I'm still alive and I'm on my way to the Coast with a young man named Chance Wayne that I think is cut out to be a great young star.

CHANCE [*moving out on the forestage*]: Here is the town I was born in, and lived in till ten years ago, in St Cloud. I was a twelve-pound baby, normal and healthy, but with some kind of quantity 'X' in my blood, a wish or a need to be different . . . The kids that I grew up with are mostly still here and what they call 'settled down', gone into business, married, and bringing up children; the little crowd I was in with, that I used to be the star of, was the snobset, the ones with the big names and money. I didn't have either . . . [*The* PRINCESS *utters a soft laugh in her dimmed-out area.*] What I had was . . . [*The* PRINCESS *half-turns, brush poised in a faint, dusty beam of light.*]

PRINCESS: *BEAUTY!* Say it! Say it! What you had was beauty! I had it! I say it with pride, no matter how sad, being gone, now.

CHANCE: Yes, well . . . the others . . . [*The* PRINCESS *resumes brushing hair and the sudden cold beam of light on her goes out again.*] . . . are all now members of the young social set here. The girls are young matrons, bridge-players, and the boys belong to the Junior

25

Chamber of Commerce and some of them, clubs in New Orleans such as Rex and Comus and ride on the Mardi Gras floats. Wonderful? No, boring . . . I wanted, expected, intended to get, something better . . . Yes, and I did, I got it. I did things that fat-headed gang never dreamed of. Hell, when they were still freshmen at Tulane or L.S.U. or Ole Miss, I sang in the chorus of the biggest show in New York, in *Oklahoma*, and had pictures in *Life* in a cowboy outfit, tossin' a ten-gallon hat in the air! *YIP . . . EEEEEE!* Ha-ha . . . And at the same time pursued my other vocation . . .

Maybe the one I was truly meant for, love-making . . . slept in the social register of New York! Millionaires' widows and wives and débutante daughters of such famous names as Vanderbrook and Masters and Halloway and Connaught, names mentioned daily in columns, whose credit cards are their faces . . . And . . .

PRINCESS: What did they pay you?

CHANCE: I gave people more than I took. Middle-aged people I gave back a feeling of youth. Lonely girls? Understanding, appreciation! An absolutely convincing show of affection. Sad people, lost people? Something light and uplifting! Eccentrics? Tolerance, even odd things they long for . . .

But always just at the point when I might get something back that would solve my own need, which was great, to rise to their level, the memory of my girl would pull me back home to her . . . and when I came home for those visits, man oh man how that town buzzed with excitement. I'm telling you, it would blaze with it, and then that thing in Korea came along. I was about to be sucked into the Army so I went into the Navy, because a sailor's uniform suited me better, the uniform was all that suited me, though . . .

PRINCESS: Ah-ha!

CHANCE [*mocking her*]: Ah-ha. I wasn't able to stand the goddam routine, discipline . . .

I kept thinking, this stops everything. I was twenty-three, that was the peak of my youth, and I knew my youth wouldn't last long. By the time I got out, Christ knows, I might be nearly thirty! Who would remember Chance Wayne? In a life like mine, you just can't stop, you know, can't take time out between steps, you've got to keep going right on up from one thing to the other; once you drop out, it leaves you and goes on without you and you're washed up.

PRINCESS: I don't think I know what you're talking about.

CHANCE: I'm talking about the parade. *THE* parade! The parade! The boys that go places, that's the parade I'm talking about, not a parade of swabbies on a wet deck. And so I ran my comb through my hair one morning and noticed that eight or ten hairs had come out, a warning signal of a future baldness. My hair was still thick. But would it be, five years from now, or even three? When the war would be over, that scared me, that speculation. I started to have bad dreams. Nightmares and cold sweats at night, and I had palpitations, and on my leaves I got drunk and woke up in strange places with faces on the next pillow I had never seen before. My eyes had a wild look in them in the mirror . . . I got the idea I wouldn't live through the war, that I wouldn't come back, that all the excitement and glory of being Chance Wayne would go up in smoke at the moment of contact between my brain and a bit of hot steel that happened to be in the air at the same time and place that my head was . . . that thought didn't comfort me any. Imagine a whole lifetime of dreams and ambitions and hopes dissolving away in one instant, being blacked out like some arithmetic problem washed off a blackboard by a wet sponge, just by some little accident like a bullet, not even aimed at you but just shot off in space, and so I cracked up, my nerves did. I got a medical discharge out of the service and I came home in civvies, then it was when I noticed how different it was, the town and the people in it. Polite? Yes, but not cordial. No headlines in the papers, just an item that measured one inch at the bottom of page five saying that Chance Wayne, the son of Mrs Emily Wayne of North Front Street, had received an honourable discharge from the Navy as the result of illness and was home to recover . . . that was when Heavenly became more important to me than anything else . . .

PRINCESS: Is Heavenly a girl's name?

CHANCE: Heavenly is the name of my girl in St Cloud.

PRINCESS: Is Heavenly why we stopped here?

CHANCE: What other reason for stopping here can you think of?

PRINCESS: So . . . I'm being used. Why not? Even a dead race horse is used to make glue. Is she pretty?

CHANCE [handing PRINCESS a snapshot]: This is a flashlight photo I took of her, nude, one night on Diamond Key, which is a little sandbar about half a mile off-shore which is under water at high tide. This was taken with the tide coming in. The water is just beginning to lap over her body like it desired her like I did and still do and will always, always. [CHANCE takes back the snapshot.] Heavenly was her name. You can see that it fits her. This was her at fifteen.

PRINCESS: Did you have her that early?

CHANCE: I was just two years older, we had each other that early.

PRINCESS: Sheer luck!

CHANCE: Princess, the great difference between people in this world is not between the rich and the poor or the good and the evil, the biggest of all differences in this world is between the ones that had or have pleasure in love and those that haven't and hadn't any pleasure in love, but just watched it with envy, sick envy. The spectators and the performers. I don't mean just ordinary pleasure or the kind you can buy, I mean great pleasure, and nothing that's happened to me or to Heavenly since can cancel out the many long nights without sleep when we gave each other such pleasure in love as very few people can look back on in their lives . . .

PRINCESS: No question, go on with your story.

CHANCE: Each time I came back to St Cloud I had her love to come back to . . .

PRINCESS: Something permanent in a world of change?

CHANCE: Yes, after each disappointment, each failure at something, I'd come back to her like going to a hospital.

PRINCESS: She put cool bandages on your wounds? Why didn't you marry this Heavenly little physician?

CHANCE: Didn't I tell you that Heavenly is the daughter of Boss Finley, the biggest political wheel in this part of the country? Well, if I didn't I made a serious omission.

PRINCESS: He disapproved?

CHANCE: He figured his daughter rated someone a hundred, a thousand per cent better than me, Chance Wayne . . . The last time I came back here, she phoned me from the drugstore and told me to swim out to Diamond Key, that she would meet me there. I waited a long time, till almost sunset, and the tide started coming in before I heard the put-put of an outboard motor-boat coming out to the sandbar. The sun was behind her, I squinted. She had on a silky wet tank suit and fans of water and mist made rainbows about her . . . she stood up in the boat as if she was water-skiing, shouting things at me an' circling around the sandbar, around and around it!

PRINCESS: She didn't come to the sandbar?

CHANCE: No, just circled around it, shouting things at me. I'd swim towards the boat, I would just about reach it and she'd race it away, throwing up misty rainbows, disappearing in rainbows and then circling back and shouting things at me again . . .

PRINCESS: What things?

CHANCE: Things like, 'Chance go away.' 'Don't come back to St Cloud.' 'Chance, you're a liar.' 'Chance, I'm sick of your lies!' 'My father's right about you!' 'Chance, you're no good any more.' 'Chance, stay away from St Cloud.' The last time around the sandbar she shouted nothing, just waved good-bye and turned the boat back to shore.

PRINCESS: Is that the end of the story?

CHANCE: Princess, the end of the story is up to you. You want to help me?

PRINCESS: I want to help you. Believe me, not everybody wants to hurt everybody. I don't want to hurt you, can you believe me?

CHANCE: I can if you prove it to me.

PRINCESS: How can I prove it to you?

CHANCE: I have something in mind.

PRINCESS: Yes, what?

CHANCE: O.K., I'll give you a quick outline of this project I have in mind. Soon as I've talked to my girl and shown her my contract, we go on, you and me. Not far, just to New Orleans, Princess. But no more hiding away, we check in at the Hotel Roosevelt there as Alexandra Del Lago and Chance Wayne. Right away the newspapers call you and you give a Press conference . . .

PRINCESS: Oh?

CHANCE: Yes! The idea briefly, a local contest of talent to find a pair of young people to star as unknowns in a picture you're planning to make to show your faith in *YOUTH*, Princess. You stage this contest, you invite other judges, but your decision decides it!

PRINCESS: And you and . . . ?

CHANCE: Yes, Heavenly and I win it. We get her out of St Cloud, we go to the West Coast together.

PRINCESS: And me?

CHANCE: You?

PRINCESS: Have you forgotten, for instance, that any public attention is what I least want in the world?

CHANCE: What better way can you think of to show the public that you're a person with bigger than personal interest?

PRINCESS: Oh, yes, yes, but not true.

CHANCE: You could pretend it was true.

PRINCESS: If I didn't despise pretending!

CHANCE: I understand. Time does it. Hardens people. Time and the world that you've lived in.

PRINCESS: Which you want for yourself. Isn't that what you want? [*She looks at him, goes to the phone, then speaks into phone.*] Cashier? Hello, Cashier? This is the Princess Kosmonopolis speaking. I'm sending down a young man to cash some travellers' cheques for me. [*She hangs up.*]

CHANCE: And I want to borrow your Cadillac for a while . . .

PRINCESS: What for, Chance?

CHANCE [*posturing*]: I'm pretentious. I want to be seen in your car on the streets of St Cloud. Drive all around town in it, blowing those long silver trumpets and dressed in the fine clothes you bought me . . . Can I?

PRINCESS: Chance, you're a lost little boy that I really would like to help find himself.

CHANCE: I passed the screen test!

PRINCESS: Come here, kiss me, I love you. [*She faces the audience.*] Did I say that? Did I mean it? [*Then to* CHANCE *with arms outstretched.*] What a child you are . . . Come here . . . [*He ducks under her arms, and escapes to the chair.*]

CHANCE: I want this big display. Big phoney display in your Cadillac around town. And a wad of dough to flash in their faces and the fine clothes you've bought me, on me.

PRINCESS: Did I buy you fine clothes?

CHANCE [*picking up his jacket from the chair*]: The finest. When you stopped being lonely because of my company at that Palm Beach Hotel, you bought me the finest. That's the deal for tonight, to toot those silver horns and drive slowly around in the Cadillac convertible so everybody that thought I was washed up will see me. And I have taken my false or true contract to flash in the faces of various people that called me washed up. All right, that's the deal. Tomorrow you'll get the car back and what's left of your money. Tonight's all that counts.

PRINCESS: How do you know that as soon as you walk out of this room I won't call the police?

CHANCE: You wouldn't do that, Princess. [*He puts on his jacket.*] You'll find the car in back of the hotel parking lot, and the left-over dough will be in the glove compartment of the car.

PRINCESS: Where will you be?

CHANCE: With my girl, or nowhere.

PRINCESS: Chance Wayne! This was not necessary, all this. I'm not a phoney and I wanted to be your friend.

CHANCE: Go back to sleep. As far as I know you're not a bad person, but you just got into bad company on this occasion.

PRINCESS: I am your friend and I'm not a phoney. [CHANCE *turns and goes to the steps.*] When will I see you?

CHANCE [*at the top of the steps*]: I don't know – maybe never.

PRINCESS: Never is a long time, Chance, I'll wait.

[*She throws him a kiss.*]

CHANCE: So long.

[*The* PRINCESS *stands looking after him as the lights dim and the curtain closes.*]

Act Two

Scene One

The terrace of Boss Finley's house, which is a frame house of Victorian Gothic design, suggested by a door frame at the right and a single white column. As in the other scenes, there are no walls, the action occurring against the sky and sea cyclorama.

The Gulf is suggested by the brightness and the gulls crying as in Act One. There is only essential porch furniture, Victorian wicker but painted bone white. The men should also be wearing white or off-white suits: the tableau is all blue and white, as strict as a canvas of Georgia O'Keeffe's.

[*At the rise of the curtain,* BOSS FINLEY *is standing in the centre and* GEORGE SCUDDER *nearby.*]

BOSS FINLEY: Chance Wayne had my daughter when she was fifteen.

SCUDDER: That young.

BOSS: When she was fifteen he had her. Know how I know? Some flashlight photos were made of her, naked, on Diamond Key.

SCUDDER: By Chance Wayne?

BOSS: My little girl was fifteen, barely out of her childhood when – [*calling offstage*] Charles –

[CHARLES *enters*]

BOSS: Call Miss Heavenly –

CHARLES [*concurrently*]: Miss Heavenly. Miss Heavenly. Your daddy wants to see you.

[CHARLES *leaves.*]

BOSS [*to* SCUDDER]: By Chance Wayne? Who the hell else do you reckon? I seen them. He had them developed by some studio in

Pass Christian that made more copies of them than Chance
Wayne ordered and these photos were circulated. I seen them.
That was when I first warned the son-of-a-bitch to git out of St
Cloud. But he's back in St Cloud right now. I tell you –

SCUDDER: Boss, let me make a suggestion. Call off this rally, I mean
your appearance at it, and take it easy tonight. Go out on your boat,
you and Heavenly take a short cruise on *The Starfish* . . .

BOSS: I'm not about to start sparing myself. Oh, I know, I'll have me
a coronary and go like that. But not because Chance Wayne had
the unbelievable gall to come back to St Cloud. [*Calling offstage*]
Tom Junior!

TOM JUNIOR [*offstage*]: Yes, sir!

BOSS: Has he checked out yet?

TOM JUNIOR [*entering*]: Hatcher says he called their room at the
Royal Palms, and Chance Wayne answered the phone, and
Hatcher says . . .

BOSS: Hatcher says – who's Hatcher?

TOM JUNIOR: Dan Hatcher.

BOSS: I hate to expose my ignorance like this but the name Dan
Hatcher has no more meaning to me than the name of Hatcher,
which is none whatsoever.

SCUDDER [*quietly, deferentially*]: Hatcher, Dan Hatcher, is the assistant
manager of the Royal Palms Hotel, and the man that informed
me this morning that Chance Wayne was back in St Cloud.

BOSS: Is this Hatcher a talker, or can he keep his mouth shut?

SCUDDER: I think I impressed him how important it is to handle this
thing discreetly.

BOSS: Discreetly, like you handled that operation you done on my
daughter, so discreetly that a hillbilly heckler is shouting me questions about it wherever I speak?

SCUDDER: I went to fantastic lengths to preserve the secrecy of that
operation.

TOM JUNIOR: When Papa's upset he hits out at anyone near him.

BOSS: I just want to know – Has Wayne left?

TOM JUNIOR: Hatcher says that Chance Wayne told him that this old
movie star that he's latched on to . . .

SCUDDER: Alexandra Del Lago.

TOM JUNIOR: She's not well enough to travel.

BOSS: Okay, you're a doctor, remove her to a hospital. Call an ambulance and haul her out of the Royal Palms Hotel.

SCUDDER: Without her consent?

BOSS: Say she's got something contagious, typhoid, bubonic plague. Haul her out and slap a quarantine on her hospital door. That way you can separate them. We can remove Chance Wayne from St Cloud as soon as this Miss Del Lago is removed from Chance Wayne.

SCUDDER: I'm not so sure that's the right way to go about it.

BOSS: Okay, you think of a way. My daughter's no whore, but she had a whore's operation after the last time he had her. I don't want him passin' another night in St Cloud. Tom Junior.

TOM JUNIOR: Yes, sir.

BOSS: I want him gone by tomorrow – tomorrow commences at midnight.

TOM JUNIOR: I know what to do, Papa. Can I use the boat?

BOSS: Don't ask me, don't tell me nothin' –

TOM JUNIOR: Can I have *The Starfish* tonight?

BOSS: I don't want to know how, just go about it. Where's your sister?

[CHARLES *appears on the gallery, points out* HEAVENLY *lying on the beach to Boss and exits.*]

TOM JUNIOR: She's lyin' out on the beach like a dead body washed up on it.

BOSS [*calling*]: Heavenly!

TOM JUNIOR: Gawge, I want you with me on this boat trip tonight, Gawge.

BOSS [*calling*]: Heavenly!

SCUDDER: I know what you mean, Tom Junior, but I couldn't be involved in it. I can't even know about it.

BOSS [*calling again*]: Heavenly!

TOM JUNIOR: Okay, don't be involved in it. There's a pretty fair doctor that lost his licence for helping a girl out of trouble, and he won't be so goddam finicky about doing this absolutely just thing.

SCUDDER: I don't question the moral justification, which is complete without question . . .

TOM JUNIOR: Yeah, complete without question.

SCUDDER: But I am a reputable doctor, I haven't lost my licence. I'm chief of staff at the great hospital put up by your father . . .

TOM JUNIOR: I said, don't know about it.

SCUDDER: No, sir, I won't know about it . . . [BOSS *starts to cough.*] I can't afford to, and neither can your father . . .

[SCUDDER *goes to gallery writing prescription.*]

BOSS: Heavenly! Come up here, sugar. [*To* SCUDDER] What's that you're writing?

SCUDDER: Prescription for that cough.

BOSS: Tear it up, throw it away. I've hawked and spit all my life, and I'll be hawking and spitting in the hereafter. You all can count on that.

[*Auto horn is heard.*]

TOM JUNIOR [*leaps up on the gallery and starts to leave*]: Papa, he's drivin' back by.

BOSS: Tom Junior.

[TOM JUNIOR *stops.*]

TOM JUNIOR: Is Chance Wayne insane?

SCUDDER: Is a criminal degenerate sane or insane is a question that lots of law courts haven't been able to settle.

BOSS: Take it to the Supreme Court, they'll hand you down a decision on that question. They'll tell you a handsome young criminal degenerate like Chance Wayne is the mental and moral equal of any white man in the country.

TOM JUNIOR: He's stopped at the foot of the drive.

BOSS: Don't move, don't move, Tom Junior.

TOM JUNIOR: I'm not movin', Papa.

CHANCE [*offstage*]: Aunt Nonnie! Hey, Aunt Nonnie!

BOSS: What's he shouting?

TOM JUNIOR: He's shouting at Aunt Nonnie.

BOSS: Where is she?

TOM JUNIOR: Runnin' up the drive like a dog-track rabbit.

BOSS: He ain't followin', is he?

TOM JUNIOR: Nope. He's drove away.

[AUNT NONNIE *appears before the veranda, terribly flustered, rooting in her purse for something, apparently blind to the men on the veranda.*]

BOSS: Whatcha lookin' for, Nonnie?

NONNIE [*stopping short*]: Oh – I didn't notice you, Tom. I was looking for my *door*-key.

BOSS: Door's open, Nonnie, it's wide open, like a church door.

NONNIE [*laughing*]: Oh, ha, ha . . .

BOSS: Why didn't you answer that good-lookin' boy in the Cadillac car that shouted at you, Nonnie?

NONNIE: Oh. I hoped you hadn't seen him. [*Draws a deep breath and comes on to the terrace, closing her white purse.*] That was Chance Wayne. He's back in St Cloud, he's at the Royal Palms, he's –

BOSS: Why did you snub him like that? After all these years of devotion?

NONNIE: I went to the Royal Palms to warn him not to stay here but –

BOSS: He was out showing off in that big white Cadillac with the trumpet horns on it.

NONNIE: I left a message for him, I –

TOM JUNIOR: What was the message, Aunt Nonnie? Love and kisses?

NONNIE: Just get out of St Cloud right away, Chance.

TOM JUNIOR: He's gonna git out, but not in that fish-tail Caddy.

NONNIE [*to* TOM JUNIOR]: I hope you don't mean violence – [*turning to* BOSS] does he, Tom? Violence don't solve problems. It never solves young people's problems. If you will leave it to me, I'll get him out of St Cloud. I can, I will, I promise. I don't think Heavenly knows he's back in St Cloud. Tom, you know, Heavenly says it wasn't Chance that – She says it wasn't Chance.

BOSS: You're like your dead sister, Nonnie, gullible as my wife was. You don't know a lie if you bump into it on a street in the daytime. Now go out there and tell Heavenly I want to see her.

NONNIE: Tom, she's not well enough to –

BOSS: Nonnie, you got a whole lot to answer for.

NONNIE: Have I?

BOSS: Yes, you sure have, Nonnie. You favoured Chance Wayne, encouraged, aided, and abetted him in his corruption of Heavenly over a long, long time. You go get her. You sure do have a lot to answer for. You got a helluva lot to answer for.

NONNIE: I remember when Chance was the finest, nicest, sweetest boy in St Cloud, and he stayed that way till you, till you –

BOSS: Go get her, go get her!

[*She leaves by the far side of the terrace. After a moment her voice is heard calling, 'Heavenly? Heavenly?'*]

It's a curious thing, a mighty peculiar thing, how often a man that rises to high public office is drug back down by every soul he harbours under his roof. He harbours them under his roof, and they pull the roof down on him. Every last living one of them.

TOM JUNIOR: Does that include me, Papa?

BOSS: If the shoe fits, put it on you.

TOM JUNIOR: How does that shoe fit me?

BOSS: If it pinches your foot, just slit it down the sides a little – it'll feel comfortable on you.

TOM JUNIOR: Papa, you are *UNJUST*.

BOSS: What do you want credit for?

TOM JUNIOR: I have devoted the past year to organizin' the 'Youth for Tom Finley' clubs.

BOSS: I'm carryin' Tom Finley Junior on my ticket.

TOM JUNIOR: You're lucky to have me on it.

BOSS: How do you figure I'm lucky to have you on it?

TOM JUNIOR: I got more newspaper coverage in the last six months than . . .

BOSS: Once for drunk drivin', once for a stag party you thrown in Capitol City that cost me five thousand dollars to hush it up!

TOM JUNIOR: You are so unjust, it . . .

BOSS: And everyone knows you had to be drove through school like a blazeface mule pullin' a plough uphill: flunked out of college with grades that only a moron would have an excuse for.

TOM JUNIOR: I got re-admitted to college.

BOSS: At my insistence. By fake examinations, answers provided beforehand, stuck in your fancy pockets. And your promiscuity. Why, these 'Youth for Tom Finley' clubs are practically nothin' but gangs of juvenile delinquents, wearin' badges with my name and my photograph on them.

TOM JUNIOR: How about your well-known promiscuity, Papa? How about your Miss Lucy?

BOSS: Who is Miss Lucy?

TOM JUNIOR [*laughing so hard he staggers*]: Who is Miss Lucy? You don't even know who she is, this woman you keep in a fifty-dollar-a-day hotel suite at the Royal Palms, Papa?

BOSS: What're you talkin' about?

TOM JUNIOR: That rides down the Gulf Stream Highway with a motor-cycle escort blowin' their sirens like the Queen of Sheba was going into New Orleans for the day. To use her charge accounts there. And you ask who's Miss Lucy? She don't even talk good of you. She says you're too old for a lover.

BOSS: That is a goddam lie. Who says Miss Lucy says that?

TOM JUNIOR: She wrote it with lipstick on the ladies' room mirror at the Royal Palms.

BOSS: Wrote what?

TOM JUNIOR: I'll quote it to you exactly. 'Boss Finley,' she wrote, 'is too old to cut the mustard.'

[*Pause: the two stags, the old and the young one, face each other, panting.* SCUDDER *has discreetly withdrawn to a far end of porch.*]

BOSS: I don't believe this story!

TOM JUNIOR: Don't believe it.

BOSS: I will check on it, however.

TOM JUNIOR: I already checked on it. Papa, why don't you get rid of her, huh, Papa?

[BOSS FINLEY *turns away, wounded, baffled: stares out at the audience with his old, bloodshot eyes as if he thought that someone out there had shouted a question at him which he didn't quite hear.*]

BOSS: Mind your own goddam business. A man with a mission, which he holds sacred, and on the strength of which he rises to high public office – crucified in this way, publicly, by his own off-spring. [HEAVENLY *has entered on the gallery.*] Ah, here she is, here's my little girl. [*Stopping* HEAVENLY] You stay here, honey. I think you all had better leave me alone with Heavenly now, huh – yeah ... [TOM JUNIOR *and* SCUDDER *exit.*] Now, honey, you stay here. I want to have a talk with you.

HEAVENLY: Papa, I can't talk now.

BOSS: It's necessary.

HEAVENLY: I can't, I can't talk now.

BOSS: All right, don't talk, just listen.

[*But she doesn't want to listen, starts away. He would have restrained her forcibly if an old coloured manservant,* CHARLES, *had not, at that moment, come out on the porch, He carries a stick, a hat, a package, wrapped as a present. Puts them on a table.*]

CHARLES: It's five o'clock, Mister Finley.

BOSS: Huh? Oh – thanks ...

[CHARLES *turns on a coach lamp by the door. This marks a formal division in the scene. The light change is not realistic; the light doesn't seem to come from the coach lamp but from a spectral radiance in the sky, flooding the terrace.*

The sea wind sings. HEAVENLY *lifts her face to it. Later that night may be stormy, but now there is just a quickness and freshness coming in from the Gulf.* HEAVENLY *is always looking that way, towards the Gulf, so that the light from Point Lookout catches her face with its repeated soft stroke of clarity.*

In her father, a sudden dignity is revived. Looking at his very beautiful daughter, he becomes almost stately. He approaches her, as soon as the coloured man returns inside, like an aged courtier comes deferentially up to a Crown Princess or Infanta. It's important not to think of his attitude towards her in the terms of crudely conscious incestuous feeling, but just in the natural terms of almost any ageing father's feeling for a beautiful young daughter who reminds him of a

39

dead wife that he desired intensely when she was the age of his daughter.

At this point there might be a phrase of stately, Mozartian music, suggesting a court dance. The flagged terrace may suggest the parquet floor of a ballroom and the two players' movements may suggest the stately, formal movements of a court dance of that time; but if this effect is used, it should be just a suggestion. The change towards 'stylization' ought to be held in check.]

BOSS: You're still a beautiful girl.

HEAVENLY: Am I, Papa?

BOSS: Of course you are. Lookin' at you nobody could guess that –

HEAVENLY [*laughs*]: The embalmers must have done a good job on me, Papa . . .

BOSS: You got to quit talkin' like that. [*Then, seeing* CHARLES] Will you get back in the house! [*Phone rings.*]

CHARLES: Yes, sir, I was just –

BOSS: Go on in! If that phone-call is for me, I'm in only to the governor of the state and the president of the Tidewater Oil Corporation.

CHARLES [*offstage*]: It's for Miss Heavenly again.

BOSS: Say she ain't in.

CHARLES: Sorry, she ain't in.

[HEAVENLY *has moved upstage to the low parapet or sea wall that separates the courtyard and lawn from the beach. It is early dusk. The coach lamp has cast a strange light on the setting which is neo-romantic;* HEAVENLY *stops by an ornamental urn containing a tall fern that the salty Gulf wind has stripped nearly bare. The* BOSS *follows her, baffled.]*

BOSS: Honey, you say and do things in the presence of people as if you had no regard of the fact that people have ears to hear you and tongues to repeat what they hear. And so you become a issue.

HEAVENLY: Become what, Papa?

BOSS: A issue, a issue, subject of talk, of scandal – which can defeat the mission that –

HEAVENLY: Don't give me your 'Voice of God' speech. Papa, there was a time when you could have saved me, by letting me marry a boy that was still young and clean, but instead you drove him away, drove him out of St Cloud. And when he came back, you took me out of St Cloud, and tried to force me to marry a fifty-year-old money bag that you wanted something out of –

BOSS: Now, honey –

HEAVENLY: – and then another, another, all of them ones that you wanted something out of. I'd gone, so Chance went away. Tried to compete, make himself big as these big-shots you wanted to use me for a bond with. He went. He tried. The right doors wouldn't open, and so he went in the wrong ones, and – Papa, you married for love, why wouldn't you let me do it, while I was alive, inside, and the boy still clean, still decent?

BOSS: Are you reproaching me for –?

HEAVENLY [shouting]: Yes, I am, Papa, I am. You married for love, but you wouldn't let me do it, and even though you'd done it, you broke Mama's heart, Miss Lucy had been your mistress –

BOSS: Who is Miss Lucy?

HEAVENLY: Oh, Papa, she was your mistress long before Mama died. And Mama was just a front for you. Can I go in now, Papa? Can I go in now?

BOSS: No, no, not till I'm through with you. What a terrible, terrible thing for my baby to say . . . [He takes her in his arms.] Tomorrow, tomorrow morning, when the big after-Easter sales commence in the stores – I'm gonna send you in town with a motor-cycle escort, straight to the Maison Blanche. When you arrive at the store, I want you to go directly up to the office of Mr Harvey C. Petrie and tell him to give you unlimited credit there. Then go down and out-fit yourself as if you was – buyin' a trousseau to marry the Prince of Monaco . . . Purchase a full wardrobe, includin' furs. Keep 'em in storage until winter. Gown? Three, four, five, the most lavish. Slippers? Hell, pairs and pairs of 'em. Not one hat – but a dozen. I made a pile of dough on a deal involvin' the sale of rights to oil under water here lately, and, baby, I want you to buy a piece of jewellery. Now about that, you better tell Harvey to call me. Or better still, maybe Miss Lucy had better help you select it. She's wise as a backhouse rat when it comes to a stone – that's for sure ... Now where'd I buy that clip that I give your mama? D'you remember the clip I bought your mama? Last thing I give your mama before she died ... I knowed she was dyin' when I bought her that clip, and I bought that clip for fifteen thousand dollars mainly to make her think she was going to get well ... When I pinned it on her on the nightgown she was wearing, that poor thing started crying. She said, for God's sake, Boss, what does a dying woman want with such a big diamond? I said to her, honey, look at the price tag on it. What does the price tag say? See them five figures, that one and that five and them three oughts on there? Now, honey, make sense, I told her. If you was dying, if there was any chance of it, would I invest fifteen grand in a diamond clip to pin on the neck of a shroud? Ha, haha. That made the old lady laugh. And she sat up as bright as a little bird in that bed with the diamond clip on, receiving callers all day, and laughing and chatting with them, with that diamond clip on inside and she died before midnight, with that diamond clip on her. And not till the very last minute did she believe that the diamonds wasn't a proof that she wasn't dying.

[*He moves to terrace, takes off robe, and starts to put on tuxedo coat.*]

HEAVENLY: Did you bury her with it?

BOSS: Bury her with it? Hell, no. I took it back to the jewellery store in the morning.

HEAVENLY: Then it didn't cost you fifteen grand after all.

BOSS: Hell, did I care what it cost me? I'm not a small man. I wouldn't have cared one hoot if it cost me a million ... if at that time I had that kind of loot in my pockets. It would have been worth that money to see that one little smile your mama bird give me at noon of the day she was dying.

HEAVENLY: I guess that shows, demonstrates very clearly, that you have got a pretty big heart after all.

BOSS: Who doubts it then? Who? Who ever? [*He laughs.*]

[HEAVENLY *starts to laugh and then screams hysterically. She starts going towards the house.*
BOSS *throws down his cane and grabs her.*]

Just a minute, Missy. Stop it. Stop it. Listen to me, I'm gonna tell you something. Last week in New Bethesda, when I was speaking on the threat of desegregation to white women's chastity in the South, some heckler in the crowd shouted out, 'Hey, Boss Finley, how about your daughter? How about that operation you had done on your daughter at the Thomas J. Finley hospital in St Cloud? Did she put on black in mourning for her appendix?' Same heckler, same question when I spoke in the Coliseum at the state capital.

HEAVENLY: What was your answer to him?

BOSS: He was removed from the hall at both places and roughed up a little outside it.

HEAVENLY: Papa, you have got an illusion of power.

BOSS: I have power, which is not an illusion.

HEAVENLY: Papa, I'm sorry my operation has brought this embarrassment on you, but can you imagine it, Papa? I felt worse than embarrassed when I found out that Dr George Scudder's knife had cut the youth out of my body, made me an old childless woman. Dry, cold, empty, like an old woman. I feel as if I ought to rattle like a dead dried-up vine when the Gulf Wind blows, but, Papa – I won't embarrass you any more. I've made up my mind about something. If they'll let me, accept me, I'm going into a convent.

BOSS [*shouting*]: You ain't going into no convent. This state is a Protestant region and a daughter in a convent would politically ruin me. Oh, I know, you took your mama's religion because in your heart you always wished to defy me. Now, tonight, I'm addressing the 'Youth for Tom Finley' clubs in the ballroom of the Royal Palms Hotel. My speech is going out over a national TV network, and Missy, you're going to march in the ballroom on my arm. You're going to be wearing the stainless white of a virgin, with a 'Youth for Tom Finley' button on one shoulder and a corsage of lilies on the other. You're going to be on the speaker's platform with me, you on one side of me and Tom Junior on the other, to scotch these rumours about your corruption. And you're gonna wear a proud happy smile on your face, you're gonna stare straight out at the crowd in the ballroom with pride and joy in your eyes. Lookin' at you, all in white like a virgin, nobody would dare to speak or believe the ugly stories about you. I'm relying a great deal on this campaign to bring in young voters for the crusade I'm leading. I'm all that stands between the South and the black days of Reconstruction. And you and Tom Junior are going to stand there beside me in the grand crystal ballroom, as shining examples of white Southern youth – in danger.

HEAVENLY [*defiant*]: Papa, I'm not going to do it.

BOSS: I didn't say would you, I said you would, and you will.

HEAVENLY: Suppose I still say I won't.

BOSS: Then you won't, that's all. If you won't, you won't. But there would be consequences you might not like. [*Phone rings.*] Chance Wayne is back in St Cloud.

CHARLES [*offstage*]: Mr Finley's residence. Miss Heavenly? Sorry, she's not in.

BOSS: I'm going to remove him, he's going to be removed from St Cloud. How do you want him to leave, in that white Cadillac he's riding around in, or in the scow that totes the garbage out to the dumping place in the Gulf?

HEAVENLY: You wouldn't dare.

BOSS: You want to take a chance on it!

CHARLES [*enters*]: That call was for you again, Miss Heavenly.

BOSS: A lot of people approve of taking violent action against corrupters. And on all of them that want to adulterate the pure white blood of the South. Hell, when I was fifteen, I come down barefoot out of the red clay hills as if the Voice of God called me. Which it did, I believe. I firmly believe He called me. And nothing, nobody, nowhere is gonna stop me, never . . . [*He motions to* CHARLES *for gift.* CHARLES *hands it to him.*] Thank you, Charles. I'm gonna pay me an early call on Miss Lucy.

[*A sad, uncertain note has come into his voice on this final line. He turns and plods wearily, doggedly off at left.*

THE CURTAIN FALLS

House remains dark for short intermission.]

Scene Two

A corner of cocktail lounge and of outside gallery of the Royal Palms Hotel. This corresponds in style to the bedroom set: Victorian with Moorish influence. Royal palms are projected on the cyclorama which is deep violet with dusk. There are Moorish arches between gallery and interior: over the single table, inside, is suspended the same lamp, stained glass, and ornately wrought metal, that hung in the bedroom. Perhaps on the gallery there is a low stone balustrade that supports, where steps descend into the garden, an electric-light standard with five branches and pear-shaped globes of a dim pearly lustre. Somewhere out of the sightlines an entertainer plays a piano or novachord.

[*The interior table is occupied by two couples that represent society in St Cloud. They are contemporaries of* CHANCE'S. *Behind the bar is* STUFF *who feels the dignity of his recent advancement from drugstore soda-fountain to the Royal Palms cocktail lounge: he has on a white mess-jacket, a scarlet cummerbund, and light-blue trousers, flatteringly close-fitted.* CHANCE WAYNE *was once barman here;* STUFF *moves with an indolent male grace that he may have unconsciously remembered admiring in* CHANCE.

Boss Finley's mistress, MISS LUCY, *enters the cocktail lounge dressed in a ball gown elaborately ruffled and very bouffant like an antebellum Southern belle's. A single blonde curl is arranged to switch girlishly at one side of her sharp little terrier face. She is outraged over something and her glare is concentrated on* STUFF *who 'plays it cool' behind the bar.*]

STUFF: Ev'nin', Miss Lucy.
MISS LUCY: I wasn't allowed to sit at the banquet table. No. I was put at a little side-table, with a couple of state legislators an' wives.

[*She sweeps behind the bar in a proprietary fashion.*] Where's your Grant's twelve-year-old? Hey! Do you have a big mouth? I used to remember a kid that jerked sodas at Walgreen's that had a big mouth . . . Put some ice in this . . . Is yours big, huh? I want to tell you something.

STUFF: What's the matter with your finger?

[*She catches him by his scarlet cummerbund.*]

MISS LUCY: I'm going to tell you just now. The boss came over to me with a big candy Easter egg for me. The top of the egg unscrewed. He told me to unscrew it. So I unscrewed it. Inside was a little blue velvet jewel box, no not little, a big one, as big as somebody's mouth, too.

STUFF: Whose mouth?

MISS LUCY: The mouth of somebody who's not a hundred miles from here.

STUFF [*going off at the left*]: I got to set my chairs. [STUFF *re-enters at once carrying two chairs. Sets them at tables while* MISS LUCY *talks.*]

MISS LUCY: I open the jewel box an' start to remove the great big diamond clip in it. I just got my fingers on it, and start to remove it and the old son-of-a-bitch slams the lid of the box on my fingers. One fingernail is still blue. And the boss says to me, 'Now go downstairs to the cocktail lounge and go in the ladies' room and describe this diamond clip with lipstick on the ladies'-room mirror down there. Hanh?' – and he put the jewel box in his pocket and slammed the door so hard goin' out of my suite that a picture fell off the wall.

STUFF [*setting the chairs at the table*]: Miss Lucy, you are the one that said, 'I wish you would see what's written with lipstick on the ladies'-room mirror' las' Saturday night.

MISS LUCY: To you! Because I thought I could trust you.

STUFF: Other people were here an' all of them heard it.

MISS LUCY: Nobody but you at the bar belonged to the 'Youth for Boss Finley' Club.

[*Both stop short. They've noticed a tall man who has entered the cocktail lounge. He has the length and leanness and luminous pallor*] *of face that El Greco gave to his saints. He has a small bandage near the hairline. His clothes are country.*]

Hey, you.

HECKLER: Evenin', ma'am.

MISS LUCY: You with the Hillbilly Ramblers? You with the band?

HECKLER: I'm a hillbilly, but I'm not with no band.

[*He notices* MISS LUCY'S *steady, interested stare.* STUFF *leaves with a tray of drinks.*]

MISS LUCY: What do you want here?

HECKLER: I come to hear Boss Finley talk. [*His voice is clear but strained. He rubs his large Adam's apple as he speaks.*]

MISS LUCY: You can't get in the ballroom without a jacket and a tie on . . . I know who you are. You're the heckler, aren't you?

HECKLER: I don't heckle. I just ask questions, one question or two or three questions, depending on how much time it takes them to grab me and throw me out of the hall.

MISS LUCY: Those questions are loaded questions. You gonna repeat them tonight?

HECKLER: Yes, ma'am, if I can get in the ballroom, and make myself heard.

MISS LUCY: What's wrong with your voice?

HECKLER: When I shouted my questions in New Bethesda last week I got hit in the Adam's apple with the butt of a pistol, and that affected my voice. It still ain't good, but it's better. [*Starts to go.*]

MISS LUCY [*goes to back of bar, where she gets jacket, the kind kept in places with dress regulations, and throws it to* HECKLER]: Wait. Here, put this on. The Boss's talking on a national TV hookup tonight. There's a tie in the pocket. You sit perfectly still at the bar till the Boss starts speaking. Keep your face back of this *Evening Banner.* Okay?

HECKLER [*opening the paper in front of his face*]: I thank you.

MISS LUCY: I thank you, too, and I wish you more luck than you're likely to have.

[STUFF *re-enters and goes to back of the bar.*]

FLY [*entering on the gallery*]: Paging Chance Wayne. [*Auto horn offstage*] Mr Chance Wayne, please. Paging Chance Wayne. [*He leaves.*]

MISS LUCY [*to* STUFF, *who has re-entered*]: Is Chance Wayne back in St Cloud?

STUFF: You remember Alexandra Del Lago?

MISS LUCY: I guess I do. I was president of her local fan club. Why?

CHANCE [*offstage*]: Hey, Boy, park that car up front and don't wrinkle them fenders.

STUFF: She and Chance Wayne checked in here last night.

MISS LUCY: Well I'll be a dawg's mother. I'm going to look into that. [LUCY *exits.*]

CHANCE [*entering and crossing to the bar*]: Hey, Stuff! [*He takes a cocktail off the bar and sips it.*]

STUFF: Put that down. This ain't no cocktail party.

CHANCE: Man, don't you know . . . phew . . . nobody drinks gin martinis with olives. Everybody drinks vodka martinis with lemon twist nowadays, except the squares in St Cloud. When I had your job, when I was the barman here at the Royal Palms, I created that uniform you've got on . . . I copied it from an outfit Vic Mature wore in a Foreign Legion picture, and I looked better in it than he did, and almost as good in it as you do, ha, ha . . .

AUNT NONNIE [*who has entered at the right*]: Chance. Chance . . .

CHANCE: Aunt Nonnie! [*to* STUFF] Hey, I want a tablecloth on that table, and a bucket of champagne . . . Mumm's Cordon Rouge . . .

AUNT NONNIE: You come out here.

CHANCE: But I just ordered champagne in here. [*Suddenly his effusive manner collapses, as she stares at him gravely.*]

AUNT NONNIE: I can't be seen talking to you . . .

[*She leads him to one side of the stage. A light change has occurred which has made it a royal palm grove with a bench. They cross to it solemnly.* STUFF *busies himself at the bar, which is barely lit. After a moment he exits with a few drinks to main body of the cocktail lounge off left. Bar music: 'Quiereme Mucho'.*]

CHANCE [*following her*]: Why?

48

AUNT NONNIE: I've got just one thing to tell you, Chance, get out of St Cloud.

CHANCE: Why does everybody treat me like a low criminal in the town I was born in?

AUNT NONNIE: Ask yourself that question, ask your conscience that question.

CHANCE: What question?

AUNT NONNIE: You know, and I know you know . . .

CHANCE: Know what?

AUNT NONNIE: I'm not going to talk about it. I just can't talk about it. Your head and your tongue run wild. You can't be trusted. We have to live in St Cloud . . . Oh, Chance, why have you changed like you've changed? Why do you live on nothing but wild dreams now, and have no address where anybody can reach you in time to – reach you?

CHANCE: Wild dreams! Yes. Isn't life a wild dream? I never heard a better description of it . . . [*He takes a pill and a swallow from a flask.*]

AUNT NONNIE: What did you just take, Chance? You took something out of your pocket and washed it down with liquor.

CHANCE: Yes, I took a wild dream and – washed it down with another wild dream, Aunt Nonnie, that's my life now . . .

AUNT NONNIE: Why, son?

CHANCE: Oh, Aunt Nonnie, for God's sake, have you forgotten what was expected of me?

AUNT NONNIE: People that loved you expected just one thing of you – sweetness and honesty and . . .

[STUFF *leaves with tray.*]

CHANCE [*kneeling at her side*]: No, not after the brilliant beginning I made. Why, at seventeen, I put on, directed, and played the leading role in *The Valiant*, that one-act play that won the state drama contest. Heavenly played in it with me, and have you forgotten? You went with us as the girls' chaperon to the national contest held in . . .

AUNT NONNIE: Son, of course I remember.

49

CHANCE: In the parlour car? How we sang together?

AUNT NONNIE: You were in love even then.

CHANCE: God, yes, we were in love!

[*He sings softly*]

'If you like-a me, like I like-a you,
And we like-a both the same'

TOGETHER:

'I'd like-a say, this very day,
I'd like-a change your name.'

[CHANCE *laughs softly, wildly, in the cool light of the palm grove.*
AUNT NONNIE *rises abruptly.* CHANCE *catches her hands.*]

AUNT NONNIE: You – *Do* – Take unfair advantage . . .

CHANCE: Aunt Nonnie, we didn't win that lousy national contest, we just placed second.

AUNT NONNIE: Chance, you didn't place second. You got honourable mention. Fourth place, except it was just called honourable mention.

CHANCE: Just honourable mention. But in a national contest, honourable mention means something . . . We would have won it, but I blew my lines. Yes, I that put on and produced the damn thing, couldn't even hear the damn lines being hissed at me by that fat girl with the book in the wings. [*He buries his face in his hands.*]

AUNT NONNIE: I loved you for that, son, and so did Heavenly, too.

CHANCE: It was on the way home in the train that she and I –

AUNT NONNIE [*with a flurry of feeling*]: I know, I – I –

CHANCE [*rising*]: I bribed the Pullman Conductor to let us use for an hour a vacant compartment on that sad, homegoing train –

AUNT NONNIE: I know, I – I –

CHANCE: Gave him five dollars, but that wasn't enough, and so I gave him my wrist-watch, and my collar pin and tie clip and signet ring and my suit, that I'd bought on credit to go to the contest. First suit I'd ever put on that cost more than thirty dollars.

AUNT NONNIE: Don't go back over that.

CHANCE: – To buy the first hour of love that we had together. When she undressed, I saw that her body was just then, barely, beginning to be a woman's and . . .

AUNT NONNIE: Stop, Chance.

CHANCE: I said, oh, Heavenly, no, but she said yes, and I cried in her arms that night, and didn't know that what I was crying for was – youth, that would go.

AUNT NONNIE: It was from that time on, you've changed.

CHANCE: I swore in my heart that I'd never again come in second in any contest, especially not now that Heavenly was my – Aunt Nonnie, look at this contract.

[*He snatches out papers and lights lighter.*]

AUNT NONNIE: I don't want to see false papers.

CHANCE: These are genuine papers. Look at the notary's seal and the signatures of the three witnesses on them. Aunt Nonnie, do you know who I'm with? I'm with Alexandra Del Lago, the Princess Kosmonopolis is my –

AUNT NONNIE: Is your what?

CHANCE: Patroness! Agent! Producer! She hasn't been seen much lately, but still has influence, power, and money – money that can open all doors. That I've knocked at all these years till my knuckles are bloody.

AUNT NONNIE: Chance, even now, if you came back here simply saying, 'I couldn't remember the lines, I lost the contest, I – failed,' but you've come back here again with –

CHANCE: Will you just listen one minute more? Aunt Nonnie, here is the plan. A local-contest-of-Beauty.

AUNT NONNIE: Oh, Chance.

CHANCE: A local contest of talent that she will win.

AUNT NONNIE: Who?

CHANCE: Heavenly.

AUNT NONNIE: No, Chance. She's not young now, she's faded, she's . . .

CHANCE: Nothing goes that quick, not even youth.

AUNT NONNIE: Yes, it does.

CHANCE: It will come back like magic. Soon as I . . .

AUNT NONNIE: For what? For a fake contest?

CHANCE: For love. The moment I hold her.

AUNT NONNIE: Chance.

CHANCE: It's not going to be a local thing, Aunt Nonnie. It's going to get national coverage. The Princess Kosmonopolis's best friend is that sob sister, Sally Powers. Even you know Sally Powers. Most powerful movie columnist in the world. Whose name is law in the motion . . .

AUNT NONNIE: Chance, lower your voice.

CHANCE: I want people to hear me.

AUNT NONNIE: No, you don't, no you don't. Because if your voice gets to Boss Finley, you'll be in great danger, Chance.

CHANCE: I go back to Heavenly, or I don't. I live or die. There's nothing in between for me.

AUNT NONNIE: What you want to go back to is your clean, unashamed youth. And you can't.

CHANCE: You still don't believe me, Aunt Nonnie?

AUNT NONNIE: No, I don't. Please go. Go away from here, Chance.

CHANCE: Please.

AUNT NONNIE: No, no, go away!

CHANCE: Where to? Where can I go? This is the home of my heart. Don't make me homeless.

AUNT NONNIE: Oh, Chance.

CHANCE: Aunt Nonnie. Please.

AUNT NONNIE [*rises and starts to go*]: I'll write to you. Send me an address. I'll write to you.

[*She exits through bar.* STUFF *enters and moves to bar.*]

CHANCE: Aunt Nonnie . . .

[*She's gone.*

CHANCE *removes a pint bottle of vodka from his pocket and something else which he washes down with the vodka. He stands back as two couples come up the steps and cross the gallery into the bar: they sit at a table.* CHANCE *takes a deep breath.* FLY *enters* lighted area inside, singing out 'Paging Mr Chance Wayne, Mr Chance Wayne, pagin' Mr Chance Wayne.' – Turns about smartly and goes back out through lobby. The name has stirred a commotion at the bar and table visible inside.]

EDNA: Did you hear that? Is *Chance Wayne* back in St Cloud?

[CHANCE *draws a deep breath. Then, he stalks back into the main part of the cocktail lounge like a matador entering a bull ring.*]

VIOLET: My God, yes – there he is.

[CHANCE *reads* FLY's *message.*]

CHANCE [*to* FLY]: Not now, later, later.

[*The entertainer off left begins to play a piano . . . The 'evening' in the cocktail lounge is just beginning.*
FLY *leaves through the gallery.*]

Well! Same old place, same old gang. Time doesn't pass in St Cloud. [*To* BUD *and* SCOTTY] Hi!

BUD: How are you . . . ?

CHANCE [*shouting offstage as* FLY *enters and stands on terrace*]: Hey, Jackie . . . [*Piano stops.* CHANCE *crosses over to the table that holds the foursome.*] . . . remember my song? Do you – remember my song? . . . You see, he remembers my song. [*The entertainer swings into 'It's a Big Wide Wonderful World'.*] Now I feel at home. In my home town . . . Come on, everybody – sing!

[*This token of apparent acceptance reassures him. The foursome at the table on stage studiously ignore him. He sings.*]

'When you're in love you're a master
Of all you survey, you're a gay Santa Claus.
There's a great big star-spangled sky up above you,
When you're in love you're a hero . . .'
Come on! Sing, ev'rybody!

[*In the old days they did; now they don't. He goes on, singing a bit; then his voice dies out on a note of embarrassment. Somebody at*

53

the bar whispers something and another laughs. CHANCE *chuckles uneasily and speaks.*]

What's wrong here? The place is dead.

STUFF: You been away too long, Chance.

CHANCE: Is that the trouble?

STUFF: That's all . . .

[JACKIE, *off, finishes with an arpeggio. The piano lid slams. There is a curious hush in the bar.* CHANCE *looks at the table.* VIOLET *whispers something to* BUD. *Both girls rise abruptly and cross out of the bar.*]

BUD [*yelling at* STUFF]: Check, Stuff.

CHANCE [*with exaggerated surprise*]: Well, *Bud and Scotty.* I didn't see you at all. Wasn't that Violet and Edna at your table? [*He sits at the table between* BUD *and* SCOTTY.]

SCOTTY: I guess they didn't recognize you, Chance.

BUD: Violet did.

SCOTTY: Did Violet?

BUD: She said, 'My God, Chance Wayne.'

SCOTTY: That's recognition and profanity, too.

CHANCE: I don't mind. I've been snubbed by experts, and I've done some snubbing myself . . . Hey! [MISS LUCY *has entered at left.* CHANCE *sees her and goes towards her.*] – Is that Miss Lucy or is that Scarlett O'Hara?

MISS LUCY: Hello there, Chance Wayne. Somebody said that you were back in St Cloud, but I didn't believe them. I said I'd have to see it with my own eyes before . . . Usually there's an item in the paper, in Gwen Phillips's column saying 'St Cloud youth home on visit is slated to play featured role in important new picture,' and me being a movie fan I'm always thrilled by it . . . [*She ruffles his hair.*]

CHANCE: Never do that to a man with thinning hair.

[CHANCE'S *smile is unflinching; it gets harder and brighter.*]

MISS LUCY: Is your hair thinning, baby? Maybe that's the difference I noticed in your appearance. Don't go 'way till I get back with my drink . . .

[*She goes to back of bar to mix herself a drink. Meanwhile* CHANCE *combs his hair.*]

SCOTTY [*to* CHANCE]: Don't throw away those golden hairs you combed out, Chance. Save 'em and send 'em each in letters to your fan clubs.

BUD: Does Chance Wayne have a fan club?

SCOTTY: The most patient one in the world. They've been waiting years for him to show up on the screen for more than five seconds in a crowd scene.

MISS LUCY [*returning to the table*]: Y'know, this boy Chance Wayne used to be so attractive I couldn't stand it. But now I can, almost stand it. Every Sunday in summer I used to drive out to the municipal beach and watch him dive off the high tower. I'd take binoculars with me when he put on those free divin' exhibitions. You still dive, Chance? Or have you given that up?

CHANCE [*uneasily*]: I did some diving last Sunday.

MISS LUCY: Good, as ever?

CHANCE: I was a little off form, but the crowd didn't notice. I can still get away with a double back somersault and a –

MISS LUCY: Where was this, in Palm Beach, Florida, Chance?

[HATCHER *enters.*]

CHANCE [*stiffening*]: Why Palm Beach? Why there?

MISS LUCY: Who was it said they seen you last month in Palm Beach? Oh yes, Hatcher – that you had a job as a beach-boy at some big hotel there?

HATCHER [*stopping at steps of the terrace, then leaving across the gallery*]: Yeah, that's what I heard.

CHANCE: Had a job – as a beach-boy?

STUFF: Rubbing oil into big fat millionaires.

CHANCE: What joker thought up that one? [*His laugh is a little too loud.*]

SCOTTY: You ought to get their names and sue them for slander.

CHANCE: I long ago gave up tracking down sources of rumours about me. Of course, it's flattering, it's gratifying to know that you're still being talked about in your old home town, even if what they say is completely fantastic. Hahaha.

[*Entertainer returns, sweeps into 'Quiereme Mucho'.*]

MISS LUCY: Baby, you've changed in some way, but I can't put my finger on it. You all see a change in him, or has he just gotten older? [*She sits down next to* CHANCE.]

CHANCE [*quickly*]: To change is to live, Miss Lucy, to live is to change, and not to change is to die. You know that, don't you? It used to scare me sometimes. I'm not scared of it now. Are you scared of it, Miss Lucy? Does it scare you?

[*Behind* CHANCE's *back one of the girls has appeared and signalled the boys to join them outside.* SCOTTY *nods and holds up two fingers to mean they'll come in a couple of minutes. The girl goes back out with an angry head-toss.*]

SCOTTY: Chance, did you know Boss Finley was holding a 'Youth for Tom Finley' rally upstairs tonight?

CHANCE: I saw the announcements of it all over town.

BUD: He's going to state his position on that emasculation business that's stirred up such a mess in the state. Had you heard about that?

CHANCE: No.

SCOTTY: He must have been up in some earth satellite if he hasn't heard about that.

CHANCE: No, just out of St Cloud.

SCOTTY: Well, they picked out a nigger at random and castrated the bastard to show they mean business about white women's protection in this state.

BUD: Some people think they went too far about it. There's been a whole lot of Northern agitation all over the country.

SCOTTY: The Boss is going to state his own position about that thing before the 'Youth for Boss Finley' rally upstairs in the Crystal Ballroom.

CHANCE: Aw. Tonight?

STUFF: Yeah, t'night.

BUD: They say that Heavenly Finley and Tom Junior are going to be standing on the platform with him.

PAGEBOY [*entering*]: Paging Chance Wayne. Paging . . .

[*He is stopped short by* EDNA.]

CHANCE: I *doubt* that story, somehow I *doubt* that story.

SCOTTY: You doubt they cut that nigger?

CHANCE: Oh, no, that I don't doubt. You know what that is, don't you? Sex-envy is what that is, and the revenge for sex-envy which is a widespread disease that I have run into personally too often for me to doubt its existence or any manifestation. [*The group push back their chairs, snubbing him.* CHANCE *takes the message from the* PAGEBOY, *reads it, and throws it on the floor.*] Hey, Stuff – What d'ya have to do, stand on your head to get a drink around here? – Later, tell her. – Miss Lucy, can you get that Walgreen's soda jerk to give me a shot of vodka on the rocks? [*She snaps her fingers at* STUFF. *He shrugs and sloshes some vodka on to ice.*]

MISS LUCY: Chance? You're too loud, baby.

CHANCE: Not loud enough, Miss Lucy. No. What I meant that I doubt is that Heavenly Finley, that only I know in St Cloud, would stoop to stand on a platform next to her father while he explains and excuses on TV this random emasculation of a young Nigra caught on a street after midnight. [CHANCE *is speaking with an almost incoherent excitement, one knee resting on the seat of his chair, swaying the chair back and forth. The* HECKLER *lowers his newspaper from his face; a slow fierce smile spreads over his face as he leans forward with tensed throat muscles to catch* CHANCE'S *burst of oratory.*] No! That's what I do not believe. If I believed it, oh, I'd give you a diving exhibition. I'd dive off municipal pier and swim straight out to Diamond Key and past it, and keep on swimming till sharks and barracuda took me for live bait, brother. [*His chair topples over backwards, and he sprawls to the floor. The* HECKLER *springs up to catch him.* MISS LUCY *springs up too, and sweeps between* CHANCE *and the* HECKLER, *pushing the* HECKLER *back with a quick, warning look or gesture. Nobody notices the* HECKLER. CHANCE *scrambles back to his feet, flushed, laughing.* BUD *and* SCOTTY *outlaugh him.* CHANCE *picks up his chair and continues. The laughter stops.*] Because I have come back to St Cloud to take her out of St Cloud. Where I'll take her is not to a place anywhere except to her place in my heart. [*He has removed a pink capsule from his pocket, quickly and furtively, and drunk it down with his vodka.*]

BUD: Chance, what did you swallow just now?

CHANCE: Some hundred-proof vodka.

BUD: You washed something down with it that you took out of your pocket.

SCOTTY: It looked like a little pink pill.

CHANCE: Oh, ha, ha. Yes, I washed down a goof-ball. You want one? I got a bunch of them. I always carry them with me. When you're not having fun, it makes you have it. When you're having fun, it makes you have more of it. Have one and see.

SCOTTY: Don't that damage the brain?

CHANCE: No, the contrary. It stimulates the brain cells.

SCOTTY: Don't it make your eyes look different, Chance?

MISS LUCY: Maybe that's what I noticed. [*As if wishing to change the subject*] Chance, I wish you'd settle an argument for me.

CHANCE: What argument, Miss Lucy?

MISS LUCY: About who you're travelling with. I heard you checked in here with a famous old movie star.

[*They all stare at him . . . In a way he now has what he wants. He's the centre of attraction; everybody is looking at him, even though with hostility, suspicion, and a cruel sense of sport.*]

CHANCE: Miss Lucy, I'm travelling with the vice-president and major-stockholder of the film studio which just signed me.

MISS LUCY: Wasn't she once in the movies and very well known?

CHANCE: She was and still is and never will cease to be an important, a legendary figure in the picture industry, here and all over the world, and I am now under personal contract to her.

MISS LUCY: What's her name, Chance?

CHANCE: She doesn't want her name known. Like all great figures, world-known, she doesn't want or need and refuses to have the wrong type of attention. Privacy is a luxury to great stars. Don't ask me her name. I respect her too much to speak her name at this table. I'm obligated to her because she has shown faith in me. It took a long hard time to find that sort of faith in my talent that this woman has shown me. And I refuse to betray it at this table. [*His voice rises; he is already 'high'.*]

MISS LUCY: Baby, why are you sweating and your hands shaking so? You're not sick, are you?

CHANCE: Sick? Who's sick? I'm the least sick one you know.

MISS LUCY: Well, baby, you know you oughtn't to stay in St Cloud. Y'know that, don't you? I couldn't believe my ears when I heard you were back here. [*To the two boys*] Could you all believe he was back here?

SCOTTY: What did you come back for?

CHANCE: I wish you would give me one reason why I shouldn't come back to visit the grave of my mother and pick out a monument for her, and share my happiness with a girl that I've loved many years. It's her, Heavenly Finley, that I've fought my way up for, and now that I've made it, the glory will be hers, too. And I've just about persuaded the powers to be to let her appear with me in a picture I'm signed for. Because I . . .

BUD: What is the name of this picture?

CHANCE: . . . Name of it? *Youth*!

BUD: Just *Youth*?

CHANCE: Isn't that a great title for a picture introducing young talent? You all look doubtful. If you don't believe me, well, look. Look at this contract. [*Removes it from his pocket.*]

SCOTTY: You carry the contract with you?

CHANCE: I happen to have it in this jacket pocket.

MISS LUCY: Leaving, Scotty? [SCOTTY *has risen from the table.*]

SCOTTY: It's getting too deep at this table.

BUD: The girls are waiting.

CHANCE [*quickly*]: Gee, Bud, that's a clean set of rags you're wearing, but let me give you a tip for your tailor. A guy of medium stature looks better with natural shoulders, the padding cuts down your height, it broadens your figure, and gives you a sort of squat look.

BUD: Thanks, Chance.

SCOTTY: You got any helpful hints for my tailor, Chance?

CHANCE: Scotty, there's no tailor on earth that can disguise a sedentary occupation.

MISS LUCY: Chance, Baby . . .

CHANCE: You still work down at the bank? You sit on your can all day countin' century notes and once every week they let you slip one in your pockets? That's a fine set-up, Scotty, if you're satisfied with it but it's starting to give you a little pot and a can.

VIOLET [*appearing in the door, angry*]: Bud! Scotty! Come on.

SCOTTY: I don't get by on my looks, but I drive my own car. It isn't a Caddy, but it's my own car. And if my own mother died, I'd bury her myself; I wouldn't let a church take up a collection to do it.

VIOLET [*impatiently*]: Scotty, if you all don't come now I'm going home in a taxi.

[*The two boys follow her into the Palm Garden. There they can be seen giving their wives cab money, and indicating they are staying.*]

CHANCE: The squares have left us, Miss Lucy.

MISS LUCY: Yeah.

CHANCE: Well . . . I didn't come back here to fight with old friends of mine . . . Well, it's quarter past seven.

MISS LUCY: Is it?

[*There are a number of men, now, sitting around in the darker corners of the bar, looking at him. They are not ominous in their attitudes. They are simply waiting for something, for the meeting to start upstairs, for something . . . MISS LUCY stares at CHANCE and the men, then again at CHANCE, nearsightedly, her head cocked like a puzzled terrier's. CHANCE is discomfited.*]

CHANCE: Yep . . . How is that Hickory Hollow for steaks? Is it still the best place in town for a steak?

STUFF [*answering the phone at the bar*]: Yeah, it's him. He's here. [*Looks at CHANCE ever so briefly, hangs up.*]

MISS LUCY: Baby, I'll go to the checkroom and pick up my wrap and call for my car and I'll drive you out to the airport. They've got an air-taxi out there, a whirly-bird taxi, a helicopter, you know, that'll hop you to New Orleans in fifteen minutes.

CHANCE: I'm not leaving St Cloud. What did I say to make you think I was?

MISS LUCY: I thought you had sense enough to know that you'd better.

CHANCE: Miss Lucy, you've been drinking, it's gone to your sweet little head.

MISS LUCY: Think it over while I'm getting my wrap. You still got a friend in St Cloud.

CHANCE: I still have a girl in St Cloud, and I'm not leaving without her.

PAGEBOY [*offstage*]: Paging Chance Wayne, Mr Chance Wayne, please.

PRINCESS [*entering with* PAGEBOY]: Louder, young man, louder . . . Oh, never mind, here he is!

[*But* CHANCE *has already rushed out on to the gallery. The* PRINCESS *looks as if she had thrown on her clothes to escape a building on fire. Her blue-sequined gown is unzipped, or partially zipped, her hair is dishevelled, her eyes have a dazed, drugged brightness; she is holding up the eyeglasses with the broken lens, shakily, hanging on to her mink stole with the other hand; her movements are unsteady.*]

MISS LUCY: I know who you are. Alexandra Del Lago.

[*Loud whispering. A pause.*]

PRINCESS [*on the step to the gallery*]: What? Chance!

MISS LUCY: Honey, let me fix that zipper for you. Hold still just a second. Honey, let me take you upstairs. You mustn't be seen down here in this condition . . .

[CHANCE *suddenly rushes in from the gallery: he conducts the* PRINCESS *outside: she is on the verge of panic. The* PRINCESS *rushes half-down the steps to the palm garden: leans panting on the stone balustrade under the ornamental light standard with its five great pearls of light. The interior is dimmed as* CHANCE *comes out behind her.*]

PRINCESS: Chance! Chance! Chance! Chance!

CHANCE [*softly*]: If you'd stayed upstairs that wouldn't have happened to you.

PRINCESS: I did, I stayed.

CHANCE: I told you to wait.

PRINCESS: I waited.

CHANCE: Didn't I tell you to wait till I got back?

PRINCESS: I did, I waited forever, I waited forever for you. Then finally I heard those long sad silver trumpets blowing through the palm garden and then – Chance, the most wonderful thing has happened to me. Will you listen to me? Will you let me tell you?

MISS LUCY [*to the group at the bar*]: Shhh!

PRINCESS: Chance, when I saw you driving under the window with your head held high, with that terrible stiff-necked pride of the defeated which I know so well; I knew that your come-back had been a failure like mine. And I felt something in my heart for you. That's a miracle, Chance. That's the wonderful thing that happened to me. I felt something for someone besides myself. That means my heart's still alive, at least some part of it is, not all of my heart is dead yet. Part's alive still . . . Chance, please listen to me. I'm ashamed of this morning. I'll never degrade you again, I'll never degrade myself, you and me, again by – I wasn't always this monster. Once I wasn't this monster. And what I felt in my heart when I saw you returning, defeated, to this palm garden, Chance, gave me hope that I could stop being a monster. Chance, you've got to help me stop being the monster that I was this morning, and you can do it, can help me. I won't be ungrateful for it. I almost died this morning, suffocated in a panic. But even through my panic, I saw your kindness. I saw a true kindness in you that you have almost destroyed, but that's still there, a little . . .

CHANCE: What kind thing did I do?

PRINCESS: You gave my oxygen to me.

CHANCE: Anyone would do that.

PRINCESS: It could have taken you longer to give it to me.

CHANCE: I'm not that kind of monster.

PRINCESS: You're no kind of monster. You're just –

CHANCE: What?

PRINCESS: Lost in the beanstalk country, the ogre's country at the top of the beanstalk, the country of the flesh-hungry, blood-thirsty ogre –

[*Suddenly a voice is heard from off.*]

VOICE: Wayne?

[*The call is distinct but not loud.* CHANCE *hears it, but doesn't turn towards it; he freezes momentarily, like a stag scenting hunters. Among the people gathered inside in the cocktail lounge we see the speaker,* DAN HATCHER. *In appearance, dress, and manner he is the apotheosis of the assistant hotel manager, about Chance's age, thin, blond-haired, trim blond moustache, suave, boyish, betraying an instinct for murder only by the ruby-glass studs in his matching cufflinks and tie-clip.*]

HATCHER: Wayne!

[*He steps forward a little and at the same instant* TOM JUNIOR *and* SCOTTY *appear behind him, just in view.* SCOTTY *strikes a match for* TOM JUNIOR'S *cigarette as they wait there.* CHANCE *suddenly gives the* PRINCESS *his complete and tender attention, putting an arm around her and turning her towards the Moorish arch to the bar entrance.*]

CHANCE [*loudly*]: I'll get you a drink, and then I'll take you upstairs. You're not well enough to stay down here.

HATCHER [*crossing quickly to the foot of the stairs*]: Wayne!

[*The call is too loud to ignore:* CHANCE *half-turns and calls back.*]

CHANCE: Who's that?

HATCHER: Step down here a minute!

CHANCE: Oh, *Hatcher*! I'll be right with you.

PRINCESS: Chance, don't leave me alone.

[*At this moment the arrival of* BOSS FINLEY *is heralded by the sirens of several squad cars. The forestage is suddenly brightened from off left, presumably the floodlights of the cars arriving at the entrance to the hotel. This is the signal the men at the bar have been waiting for. Everybody rushes off left. In the hot light all alone on stage is* CHANCE; *behind him is the* PRINCESS. *And the* HECKLER *is at the bar. The entertainer plays a feverish tango. Now, off left,* BOSS FINLEY *can be heard, his public personality very much 'on'. Amid the flash of flash bulbs we hear off:*]

BOSS [*off*]: Hahaha! Little Bit, smile! Go on, smile for the birdie! Ain't she Heavenly, ain't that the right name for her!

HEAVENLY [*off*]: Papa, I want to go in!

[*At this instant she runs in – to face* CHANCE ... *The* HECKLER *rises. For a long instant,* CHANCE *and* HEAVENLY *stand there: he on the steps leading to the Palm Garden and gallery; she in the cocktail lounge. They simply look at each other ... the* HECKLER *between them. Then the* BOSS *comes in and seizes her by the arm ... And there he is facing the* HECKLER *and* CHANCE *both ... For a split second he faces them, half-lifts his cane to strike at them, but doesn't strike ... then pulls* HEAVENLY *back off left stage ... where the photographing and interviews proceed during what follows.* CHANCE *has seen that* HEAVENLY *is going to go on the platform with her father ... He stands there stunned ...*]

PRINCESS: Chance! Chance? [*He turns to her blindly.*] Call the car and let's go. Everything's packed, even the ... tape recorder with my shameless voice on it ...

[*The* HECKLER *has returned to his position at the bar. Now* HATCHER *and* SCOTTY *and a couple of other of the boys have come out ... The* PRINCESS *sees them and is silent ... She's never been in anything like this before ...*]

HATCHER: Wayne, step down here, will you.

CHANCE: What for, what do you want?

HATCHER: Come down here, I'll tell you.

CHANCE: You come up here and tell me.

TOM JUNIOR: Come on, you chicken-gut bastard.

CHANCE: Why, hello, Tom Junior. Why are you hiding down there?

TOM JUNIOR: You're hiding, not me, chicken-gut.

CHANCE: You're in the dark, not me.

HATCHER: Tom Junior wants to talk to you privately down here.

CHANCE: He can talk to me privately up here.

TOM JUNIOR: Hatcher, tell him I'll talk to him in the washroom on the mezzanine floor.

CHANCE: I don't hold conversations with people in washrooms . . .

[TOM JUNIOR, *infuriated, starts to rush forward. Men restrain him.*]

What is all this anyhow? It's fantastic. You all having a little conference there? I used to leave places when I was told to. Not now. That time's over. Now I leave when I'm ready. Hear that, Tom Junior? Give your father that message. This is my town. I was born in St Cloud, not him. He was just called here. He was just called down from the hills to preach hate. I was born here to make love. Tell him about that difference between him and me, and ask him which he thinks has more right to stay here . . . [*He gets no answer from the huddled little group which is restraining* TOM JUNIOR *from perpetrating murder right there in the cocktail lounge. After all, that would be a bad incident to precede the* BOSS's *all-South-wide TV appearance . . . and they all know it.* CHANCE, *at the same time, continues to taunt them.*] Tom, Tom Junior! What do you want me for? To pay me back for the ball game and picture-show money I gave you when you were cutting your father's yard grass for a dollar on Saturday? Thank me for the times I gave you my motor-cycle and got you a girl to ride the buddy seat with you? Come here! I'll give you the keys to my Caddy. I'll give you the price of any whore in St Cloud. You still got credit with me because you're Heavenly's brother.

TOM JUNIOR [*almost bursting free*]: Don't say the name of my sister!

CHANCE: I said the name of my girl!

TOM JUNIOR [*breaking away from the group*]: I'm all right, I'm all right. Leave us alone, will you. I don't want Chance to feel that he's outnumbered. [*He herds them out.*] Okay? Come on down here.

PRINCESS [*trying to restrain* CHANCE]: No, Chance, don't.

TOM JUNIOR: Excuse yourself from the lady and come on down here. Don't be scared to. I just want to talk to you quietly. Just talk. Quiet talk.

CHANCE: Tom Junior, I know that since the last time I was here something has happened to Heavenly and I –

TOM JUNIOR: Don't – speak the name of my sister. Just leave her name off your tongue –

CHANCE: Just tell me what happened to her.

TOM JUNIOR: Just keep your ruttin' voice down.

CHANCE: I know I've done many wrong things in my life, many more than I can name or number, but I swear I never hurt Heavenly in my life.

TOM JUNIOR: You mean to say my sister was had by somebody else – diseased by somebody else the last time you were in St Cloud? . . . I know, it's possible, it's barely possible that you didn't know what you done to my little sister the last time you come to St Cloud. You remember that time when you came home broke? My sister had to pick up your tabs in restaurants and bars, and had to cover bad cheques you wrote on banks where you had no accounts. Until you met this rich bitch, Minnie, the Texas one with the yacht, and started spending weekends on her yacht, and coming back Mondays with money from Minnie to go on with my sister. I mean, you'd sleep with Minnie, that slept with any goddam gigolo bastard she could pick up on Bourbon Street or the docks, and then you would go on sleeping again with my sister. And sometime, during that time, you got something besides your gigolo fee from Minnie and passed it on to my sister, my little sister that had hardly even heard of a thing like that, and didn't know what it was till it had gone on too long and –

CHANCE: I left town before I found out I –

[*The lamentation music is heard.*]

TOM JUNIOR: You found out! Did you tell my little sister?

CHANCE: I thought if something was wrong she'd write me or call me –

TOM JUNIOR: How could she write you or call you, there're no addresses, no phone numbers in gutters. I'm itching to kill you – here, on this spot! . . . My little sister, Heavenly, didn't know about the diseases and operations of whores, till she had to be cleaned and cured – I mean spayed like a dawg by Dr George Scudder's knife. That's right – by the knife! . . . And tonight – if you stay here tonight, if you're here after this rally, you're gonna get the knife, too. You know? The knife? That's all. Now go on back to the lady, I'm going back to my father. [TOM JUNIOR *exits.*]

PRINCESS [*as* CHANCE *returns to her*]: Chance, for God's sake, let's go now . . .

> [*The 'Lament' is in the air. It blends with the wind-blown sound of the palms.*]

All day I've kept hearing a sort of lament that drifts through the air of this place. It says, 'Lost, lost, never to be found again.' Palm gardens by the sea and olive groves on Mediterranean islands all have that lament drifting through them. 'Lost, lost' . . . The isle of Cyprus, Monte Carlo, San Remo, Torremolinos, Tangiers. They're all places of exile from whatever we loved. Dark glasses, wide-brimmed hats, and whispers, 'Is that her?' Shocked whispers . . . Oh, Chance, believe me, after failure comes flight. Nothing ever comes after failure but flight. Face it. Call the car, have them bring down the luggage, and let's go on along the Old Spanish Trail. [*She tries to hold him.*]

CHANCE: Keep your grabbing hands off me.

> [*Marchers offstage start to sing 'Bonnie Blue Flag'.*]

PRINCESS: There's no one but me to hold you back from destruction in this place.

CHANCE: I don't want to be held.

PRINCESS: Don't leave me. If you do I'll turn into the monster again. I'll be the first lady of the Beanstalk Country.

CHANCE: Go back to the room.

PRINCESS: I'm going nowhere alone. I can't.

CHANCE [*in desperation*]: Wheel chair! [*Marchers enter from the left,*

TOM JUNIOR and BOSS *with them.*] Wheel chair! Stuff, get the lady a wheel chair! She's having another attack!

[STUFF *and a* BELLBOY *catch at her ... but she pushes* CHANCE *away and stares at him reproachfully ... The* BELLBOY *takes her by the arm. She accepts this anonymous arm and exits.* CHANCE *and the* HECKLER *are alone on stage.*]

CHANCE [*as if reassuring, comforting somebody besides himself*]: It's all right, I'm alone now, nobody's hanging on to me.

[*He is panting. Loosens his tie and collar. Band in the Crystal Ballroom, muted, strikes up a lively but lyrically distorted variation of some such popular tune as the 'Liechtensteiner Polka'.* CHANCE *turns towards the sound. Then, from left stage, comes a drum majorette, bearing a gold and purple silk banner inscribed, 'Youth for Tom Finley', prancing and followed by* BOSS FINLEY, HEAVENLY, *and* TOM JUNIOR, *with a tight grip on her arm, as if he were conducting her to a death chamber.*]

TOM JUNIOR: Papa? Papa! Will you tell Sister to march?

BOSS: Little Bit, you hold you haid up *high* when we march into that ballroom. [*Music up high ... They march up the steps and on to the gallery in the rear ... then start across it. The* BOSS *calling out.*] Now march! [*And they disappear up the stairs.*]

VOICE [*offstage*]: Now let us pray. [*There is a prayer mumbled by many voices.*]

MISS LUCY [*who has remained behind*]: You still want to try it?

HECKLER: I'm going to take a shot at it. How's my voice?

MISS LUCY: Better.

HECKLER: I better wait here till he starts talkin', huh?

MISS LUCY: Wait till they turn down the chandeliers in the ballroom ... Why don't you switch to a question that won't hurt his daughter?

HECKLER: I don't want to hurt his daughter. But he's going to hold her up as the fair white virgin exposed to black lust in the South, and that's his build-up, his lead into his Voice of God speech.

MISS LUCY: He honestly believes it.

HECKLER: I don't believe it. I believe that the silence of God, the absolute speechlessness of Him is a long, long and awful thing that the whole world is lost because of. I think it's yet to be broken to any man, living or any yet lived on earth – no exceptions, and least of all Boss Finley.

[STUFF *enters, goes to table, starts to wipe it. The chandelier lights go down.*]

MISS LUCY [*with admiration*]: It takes a hillbilly to cut down a hillbilly . . . [*to* STUFF] Turn on the television, baby.

VOICE [*offstage*]: I give you the beloved Thomas J. Finley.

[STUFF *makes a gesture as if to turn on the* TV, *which we play in the fourth wall. A wavering beam of light, flickering, narrow, intense, comes from the balcony rail.* STUFF *moves his head so that he's in it, looking into it* . . . CHANCE *walks slowly downstage, his head also in the narrow flickering beam of light. As he walks downstage, there suddenly appears on the big TV screen, which is the whole back wall of the stage, the image of* BOSS FINLEY. *His arm is around* HEAVENLY *and he is speaking . . . When* CHANCE *sees the* BOSS'S *arm around Heavenly, he makes a noise in his throat like a hard fist hit him low . . . Now the sound, which always follows the picture by an instant, comes on . . . loud.*]

BOSS [*on* TV *screen*]: Thank you, my friends, neighbours, kinfolk, fellow Americans . . . I have told you before, but I will tell you again. I got a mission that I hold sacred to perform in the Southland . . . When I was fifteen I came down barefooted out of the red clay hills . . . Why? Because the Voice of God called me to execute this mission.

MISS LUCY [*to* STUFF]: He's too loud.

HECKLER: Listen!

BOSS: And what is this mission? I have told you before but I will tell you again. To shield from pollution a blood that I think is not only sacred to me, but sacred to Him.

[*Upstage we see the* HECKLER *step up the last steps and make a gesture as if he were throwing doors open . . . He advances into the hall, out of our sight.*]

MISS LUCY: Turn it down, Stuff.

69

STUFF [*motioning to her*]: Shh!

BOSS: Who is the coloured man's best friend in the South? That's right . . .

MISS LUCY: Stuff, turn down the volume.

BOSS: It's me, Tom Finley. So recognized by both races.

STUFF [*shouting*]: He's speaking the word. Pour it on!

BOSS: However – I can't and will not accept, tolerate, condone this threat of a blood pollution.

[MISS LUCY *turns down the volume of the* TV *set.*]

BOSS: As you all know I had no part in a certain operation on a young black gentleman. I call that incident a deplorable thing. That is the one thing about which I am in total agreement with the Northern radical Press. It was a deplorable thing. However . . . I understand the emotions that lay behind it. The passion to protect by this violent emotion something that we hold sacred: our purity of our own blood. But I had no part in, and I did not condone the operation performed on the unfortunate coloured gentleman caught prowling the midnight streets of our Capital City . . .

CHANCE: Christ! What lies. What a liar!

MISS LUCY: Wait! . . . Chance, you can still go. I can still help you, baby.

CHANCE [*putting hands on* MISS LUCY'*s shoulders*]: Thanks, but no thank you, Miss Lucy. Tonight, God help me, somehow, I don't know how, but somehow I'll take her out of St Cloud. I'll wake her up in my arms, and I'll give her life back to her. Yes, somehow, God help me, somehow!

[STUFF *turns up volume of* TV *set.*]

HECKLER [*as voice on the* TV]: Hey, Boss Finley! [*The* TV *camera swings to show him at the back of the hall.*] How about your daughter's operation? How about that operation your daughter had done on her at the Thomas J. Finley hospital here in St Cloud? Did she put on black in mourning for her appendix? . . .

[*We hear a gasp, as if the* HECKLER *had been hit.*

Picture: HEAVENLY *horrified. Sounds of a disturbance. Then the doors at the top of stairs up left burst open and the* HECKLER *tumbles down . . . The picture changes to* BOSS FINLEY. *He is trying to dominate the disturbance in the hall.*]

BOSS: Will you repeat that question? Have that man step forward. I will answer his question. Where is he? Have that man step forward, I will answer his question . . . Last Friday . . . Last Friday, Good Friday. I said last Friday, Good Friday . . . Quiet, may I have your attention please . . . Last Friday, Good Friday, I seen a horrible thing on the campus of our great State University, which I built for the State. A hideous straw-stuffed effigy of myself, Tom Finley, was hung and set fire to in the main quadrangle of the college. This outrage was inspired . . . inspired by the Northern radical Press. However, that was Good Friday. Today is Easter. I say that was Good Friday. Today is Easter Sunday and I am in St Cloud.

[*During this a gruesome, not-lighted, silent struggle has been going on. The* HECKLER *defended himself, but finally has been overwhelmed and rather systematically beaten . . . The tight intense follow-spot beam stayed on* CHANCE. *If he had any impulse to go to the* HECK-LER'S *aid, he'd be discouraged by* STUFF *and another man who stand behind him, watching him . . . At the height of the beating, there are bursts of great applause . . . At a point during it,* HEAVENLY *is suddenly escorted down the stairs, sobbing, and collapses . . .*]

CURTAIN

Act Three

[*A while later that night: the hotel bedroom. The shutters in the Moorish Corner are thrown open on the Palm Garden: scattered sounds of disturbance are still heard: something burns in the Palm Garden: an effigy, an emblem? Flickering light from it falls on the* PRINCESS. *Over the interior scene, the constant serene projection of royal palms, branched among stars.*]

PRINCESS [*pacing with the phone*]: Operator! What's happened to my driver?

[CHANCE *enters on the gallery, sees someone approaching on other side – quickly pulls back and stands in shadows on the gallery.*]

You told me you'd get me a driver . . . Why can't you get me a driver when you said that you would? Somebody in this hotel can surely get me somebody to drive me at any price asked! – out of this infernal . . .

[*She turns suddenly as* DAN HATCHER *knocks at the corridor door. Behind him appear* TOM JUNIOR, BUD, *and* SCOTTY, *sweaty, dishevelled from the riot in the Palm Garden.*]

Who's that?

SCOTTY: She ain't gonna open, break it in.

PRINCESS [*dropping phone*]: What do you want?

HATCHER: Miss Del Lago . . .

BUD: Don't answer till she opens.

PRINCESS: Who's out there! What do you want?

72

SCOTTY [*to shaky* HATCHER]: Tell her you want her out of the god-
    dam room.

HATCHER [*with forced note of authority*]: Shut up. Let me handle this
    . . . Miss Del Lago, your check-out time was three-thirty P.M., and
    it's now after midnight . . . I'm sorry but you can't hold this room
    any longer.

PRINCESS [*throwing open the door*]: What did you say? Will you repeat
    what you said! [*Her imperious voice, jewels, furs, and commanding
    presence abash them for a moment.*]

HATCHER: Miss Del Lago . . .

TOM JUNIOR [*recovering quickest*]: This is Mr Hatcher, assistant man-
    ager here. You checked in last night with a character not wanted
    here, and we been informed he's stayin' in your room with you.
    We brought Mr Hatcher up here to remind you that the check-
    out time is long past and –

PRINCESS [*powerfully*]: My check-out time at any hotel in the world is
    when I want to check out . . .

TOM JUNIOR: This ain't any hotel in the world.

PRINCESS [*making no room for entrance*]: Also, I don't talk to assistant
    managers of hotels when I have complaints to make about dis-
    courtesies to me, which I do most certainly have to make about
    my experiences here. I don't even talk to managers of hotels, I
    talk to owners of them. Directly to hotel owners about discour-
    tesies to me. [*Picks up satin sheets on bed.*] These sheets are mine,
    they go with me. And I have never suffered such dreadful discour-
    tesies to me at any hotel at any time or place anywhere in the
    world. Now I have found out the name of this hotel owner. This
    is a chain hotel under the ownership of a personal friend of mine
    whose guest I have been in foreign capitals such as . . . [TOM JUN-
    IOR *has pushed past her into the room.*] What in hell is he doing in
    my room?

TOM JUNIOR: Where is Chance Wayne?

PRINCESS: Is that what you've come here for? You can go away then.
    He hasn't been in this room since he left this morning.

TOM JUNIOR: Scotty, check the bathroom . . . [*He checks a closet, stoops to peer under the bed.* SCOTTY *goes off at right.*] Like I told you before, we know you're Alexandra. Del Lago travelling with a degenerate that I'm sure you don't know. That's why you can't stay in St Cloud, especially after this ruckus that we – [SCOTTY *re-enters from the bathroom and indicates to* TOM JUNIOR *that Chance is not there.*] – Now if you need any help in getting out of St Cloud, I'll be –

PRINCESS [*cutting in*]: Yes. I want a driver. Someone to drive my car. I want to leave here. I'm desperate to leave here. I'm not able to drive. I have to be driven away!

TOM JUNIOR: Scotty, you and Hatcher wait outside while I explain something to her . . . [*They go and wait outside the door, on the left end of the gallery.*] I'm gonna git you a driver, Miss Del Lago. I'll get you a state trooper, half a dozen state troopers if I can't get you no driver. Okay? Some time come back to our town 'n' see us, hear? We'll lay out a red carpet for you. Okay? G'night, Miss Del Lago.

[*They disappear down the hall, which is then dimmed out.* CHANCE *now turns from where he's been waiting at the other end of the corridor and slowly, cautiously, approaches the entrance to the room. Wind sweeps the Palm Garden; it seems to dissolve the walls; the rest of the play is acted against the night sky. The shuttered doors on the veranda open and* CHANCE *enters the room. He has gone a good deal farther across the border of reason since we last saw him. The* PRINCESS *isn't aware of his entrance until he slams the shuttered doors. She turns, startled, to face him.*]

PRINCESS: Chance!

CHANCE: You had some company here.

PRINCESS: Some men were here looking for you. They told me I wasn't welcome in this hotel and this town because I had come here with 'a criminal degenerate'. I asked them to get me a driver so I can go.

CHANCE: I'm your driver. I'm still your driver, Princess.

PRINCESS: You couldn't drive through the palm garden.

CHANCE: I'll be all right in a minute.

PRINCESS: It takes more than a minute. Chance, will you listen to me? Can you listen to me? I listened to you this morning, with understanding and pity, I did, I listened with pity to your story this morning. I felt something in my heart for you which I thought I couldn't feel. I remembered young men who were what you are or what you're hoping to be. I saw them all clearly, all clearly, eyes, voices, smiles, bodies clearly. But their names wouldn't come back to me. I couldn't get their names back without digging into old programmes of plays that I starred in at twenty in which they said, 'Madam, the Count's waiting for you,' or – Chance? They almost made it. Oh, oh, Franz! Yes, Franz . . . what? Albertzart. Franz Albertzart, oh God, God, Franz Albertzart . . . I had to fire him. He held me too tight in the waltz scene, his anxious fingers left bruises once so violent, they, they dislocated a disc in my spine, and –

CHANCE: I'm waiting for you to shut up.

PRINCESS: I saw him in Monte Carlo not too long ago. He was with a woman of seventy, and his eyes looked older than hers. She held him, she led him by an invisible chain through Grand Hotel . . . lobbies and casinos and bars like a blind, dying lap dog; he wasn't much older than you are now. Not long after that he drove his Alfa-Romeo or Ferrari off the Grand Corniche – accidentally? – Broke his skull like an eggshell. I wonder what they found in it? Old, despaired-of ambitions, little treacheries, possibly even little attempts at blackmail that didn't quite come off, and whatever traces are left of really great charm and sweetness. Chance, Franz Albertzart is Chance Wayne. Will you please try to face it so we can go on together?

CHANCE [*pulls away from her*]: Are you through? Have you finished?

PRINCESS: You didn't listen, did you?

CHANCE [*picking up the phone*]: I didn't have to. I told you that story this morning – I'm not going to drive off nothing and crack my head like an eggshell.

PRINCESS: No, because you can't drive.

CHANCE: Operator? Long distance.

PRINCESS: You would drive into a palm tree. Franz Albertzart . . .

CHANCE: Where's your address book, your book of telephone numbers?

PRINCESS: I don't know what you think that you are up to, but it's no good. The only hope for you now is to let me lead you by that invisible loving steel chain through Carltons and Ritzes and Grand Hotels and –

CHANCE: Don't you know, I'd die first? I would rather die first . . . [*into phone*] Operator? This is an urgent person-to-person call from Miss Alexandra Del Lago to Miss Sally Powers in Beverly Hills, California . . .

PRINCESS: Oh, no! . . . Chance!

CHANCE: Miss Sally Powers, the Hollywood columnist, yes, Sally Powers. Yes, well get information. I'll wait, I'll wait . . .

PRINCESS: Her number is Coldwater five-nine thousand . . . [*Her hand goes to her mouth – but too late.*]

CHANCE: In Beverly Hills, California, Coldwater five-nine thousand.

[*The* PRINCESS *moves out on to forestage; surrounding areas dim till nothing is clear behind her but the palm garden.*]

PRINCESS: Why did I give him the number? Well, why not, after all, I'd have to know sooner or later . . . I started to call several times, picked up the phone, put it down again. Well, let him do it for me. Something's happened. I'm breathing freely and deeply as if the panic was over. Maybe it's over. He's doing the dreadful thing for me, asking the answer for me. He doesn't exist for me now except as somebody making this awful call for me, asking the answer for me. The light's on me. He's almost invisible now. What does that mean? Does it mean that I still wasn't ready to be washed up, counted out?

CHANCE: All right, call Chasen's. Try to reach her at Chasen's.

PRINCESS: Well, one thing's sure. It's only this call I care for. I seem to be standing in light with everything else dimmed out. He's in the dimmed-out background as if he'd never left the obscurity he was born in. I've taken the light again as a crown on my head to which I am suited by something in the cells of my blood and body from the time of my birth. It's mine, I was born to own it, as he was born to make this phone call for me to Sally Powers, dear faithful custodian of my outlived legend. [*Phone rings in distance.*] The legend that I've outlived . . . Monsters don't die early;

they hang on long. Awfully long. Their vanity's infinite, almost as infinite as their disgust with themselves . . . [*Phone rings louder: it brings the stage light back up on the hotel bedroom. She turns to* CHANCE *and the play returns to a more realistic level.*] The phone's still ringing.

CHANCE: They gave me another number . . .

PRINCESS: If she isn't there, give my name and ask them where I can reach her.

CHANCE: Princess?

PRINCESS: What?

CHANCE: I have a personal reason for making this phone call.

PRINCESS: I'm quite certain of that.

CHANCE [*into phone*]: I'm calling for Alexandra Del Lago. She wants to speak to Miss Sally Powers – Oh, is there any number where the Princess could reach her?

PRINCESS: It will be a good sign if they give you a number.

CHANCE: Oh? – Good, I'll call that number . . . Operator? Try another number for Miss Sally Powers. It's Canyon seven-five thousand . . . Say it's urgent, it's Princess Kosmonopolis . . .

PRINCESS: Alexandra Del Lago.

CHANCE: Alexandra Del Lago is calling Miss Powers.

PRINCESS [*to herself*]: Oxygen, please, a little . . .

CHANCE: Is that you, Miss Powers? This is Chance Wayne talking . . . I'm calling for the Princess Kosmonopolis, she wants to speak to you. She'll come to the phone in a minute.

PRINCESS: I can't . . . Say I've . . .

CHANCE [*stretching phone cord*]: This is as far as I can stretch the cord, Princess, you've got to meet it halfway.

[PRINCESS *hesitates; then advances to the extended phone.*]

PRINCESS [*in a low, strident whisper*]: Sally? Sally? Is it really you, Sally? Yes, it's me, Alexandra. It's what's left of me, Sally. Oh, yes, I was there, but I only stayed a few minutes. Soon as they started laughing in the wrong places, I fled up the aisle and into the street screaming 'Taxi' – and never stopped running till now. No, I've talked to nobody, heard nothing, read nothing . . . just wanted –

dark . . . What? You're just being kind.

CHANCE [*as if to himself*]: Tell her that you've discovered a pair of new stars. Two of them.

PRINCESS: One moment, Sally, I'm – breathless!

CHANCE [*gripping her arm*]: And lay it on thick. Tell her to break it tomorrow in her column, in all of her columns, and in her radio talks . . . that you've discovered a pair of young people who are the stars of tomorrow!

PRINCESS [*to* CHANCE]: Go into the bathroom. Stick your head under cold water . . . Sally . . . Do you really think so? You're not just being nice, Sally, because of old times – Grown, did you say? My talent? In what way, Sally? More depth? More what, did you say? More power! well, Sally, God bless you, dear Sally.

CHANCE: Cut the chatter. Talk about me and *HEAVENLY*!

PRINCESS: No, of course I didn't read the reviews. I told you I flew, I flew. I flew as far and fast as I could. Oh. Oh? Oh . . . How very sweet of you, Sally. I don't even care if you're not altogether sincere in that statement, Sally. I think you know what the past fifteen years have been like, because I do have the – 'out-crying heart of an – artist'. Excuse me, Sally, I'm crying, and I don't have any Kleenex. Excuse me, Sally, I'm crying . . .

CHANCE [*hissing behind her*]: Hey. Talk about me! [*She kicks* CHANCE'S *leg.*]

PRINCESS: What's that, Sally? Do you really believe so? Who? For what part? Oh, my God! . . . Oxygen, oxygen, quick!

CHANCE [*seizing her by the hair and hissing*]: Me! Me! – You bitch!

PRINCESS: Sally? I'm too overwhelmed. Can I call you back later? Sally, I'll call back later . . . [*She drops phone in a daze of rapture.*] My picture has broken box-office records. In New York and L.A.!

CHANCE: Call her back, get her on the phone.

PRINCESS: Broken box-office records. The greatest comeback in the history of the industry, that's what she calls it . . .

CHANCE: You didn't mention me to her.

PRINCESS [*to herself*]: I can't appear, not yet. I'll need a week in a clinic, then a week or ten days at the Morning Star Ranch at Vegas. I'd better get Ackermann down there for a series of shots before I go on to the Coast . . .

CHANCE [*at phone*]: Come back here, call her again.

PRINCESS: I'll leave the car in New Orleans and go on by plane to, to, to – Tucson. I'd better get Strauss working on publicity for me. I'd better be sure my tracks are covered up well these last few weeks in – hell! –

CHANCE: Here. Here, get her back on this phone.

PRINCESS: Do what?

CHANCE: Talk about me and talk about Heavenly to her.

PRINCESS: Talk about a beach-boy I picked up for pleasure, distraction from panic? Now? When the nightmare is over? Involve my name, which is Alexandra Del Lago, with the record of a – You've just been using me. Using me. When I needed you downstairs I shouted, 'Get her a wheel chair!' Well, I didn't need a wheel chair, I came up alone, as always. I climbed back alone up the beanstalk to the ogre's country where I live, now, alone. Chance, you've gone past something you couldn't afford to go past; your time, your youth, you've passed it. It's all you had, and you've had it.

CHANCE: Who in hell's talking! Look. [*He turns her forcibly to the mirror.*] Look in that mirror. What do you see in that mirror?

PRINCESS: I see – Alexandra Del Lago, artist and star! Now it's your turn, you look and what do you see?

CHANCE: I see – Chance Wayne . . .

PRINCESS: The face of a Franz Albertzart, a face that tomorrow's sun will touch without mercy. Of course, you were crowned with laurel in the beginning, your gold hair was wreathed with laurel, but the gold is thinning and the laurel has withered. Face it – pitiful monster. [*She touches the crown of his head.*] . . . Of course, I know I'm one too. But one with a difference. Do you know what that difference is? No, you don't know. I'll tell you. We are two monsters, but with this difference between us. Out of the passion and torment of my existence I have created a thing that I can unveil, a sculpture, almost heroic, that I can unveil, which is true. But you? You've come back to the town you were born in, to a girl that won't see you because you put such rot in her body she had to be gutted and hung on a butcher's hook, like a chicken dressed for

Sunday . . . [*He wheels about to strike at her but his raised fist changes its course and strikes down at his own belly and he bends double with a sick cry. Palm Garden wind: whisper of the 'Lament'.*] Yes, and her brother who was one of my callers, threatens the same thing for you: castration, if you stay here.

CHANCE: That can't be done to me twice. You did that to me this morning, here on this bed, where I had the honour, where I had the great honour . . .

[*Windy sound rises: they move away from each other, he to the bed, she close to her portable dressing table.*]

PRINCESS: Age does the same thing to a woman . . . [*Scrapes pearls and pillboxes off table top into handbag.*] Well . . .

[*All at once her power is exhausted, her fury gone. Something uncertain appears in her face and voice betraying the fact which she probably suddenly knows, that her future course is not a progression of triumphs. She still maintains a grand air as she snatches up her platinum mink stole and tosses it about her: it slides immediately off her shoulders; she doesn't seem to notice. He picks the stole up for her, puts it about her shoulders. She grunts disdainfully, her back to him; then resolution falters; she turns to face him with great, dark eyes that are fearful, lonely, and tender.*]

I am going, now, on my way. [*He nods slightly, loosening the Windsor-knot of his knitted black silk tie. Her eyes stay on him.*] Well, are you leaving or staying?

CHANCE: Staying.

PRINCESS: You can't stay here. I'll take you to the next town.

CHANCE: Thanks but no, thank you, Princess.

PRINCESS [*seizing his arm*]: Come on, you've got to leave with me. My name is connected with you, we checked in here to-gether. Whatever happens to you, my name will be dragged in with it.

CHANCE: Whatever happens to me's already happened.

PRINCESS: What are you trying to prove?

CHANCE: Something's got to mean something, don't it, Princess? I mean like your life means nothing, except that you never could make it, always almost, never quite? Well, something's still got to mean something.

PRINCESS: I'll send a boy up for my luggage. You'd better come down with my luggage.

CHANCE: I'm not part of your luggage.

PRINCESS: What else can you be?

CHANCE: Nothing . . . but not part of your luggage.

[NOTE: *in this area it is very important that Chance's attitude should be self-recognition but not self-pity – a sort of deathbed dignity and honesty apparent in it. In both Chance and the Princess, we should return to the huddling-together of the lost, but not with sentiment, which is false, but with whatever is truthful in the moments when people share doom, face firing squads together. Because the Princess is really equally doomed. She can't turn back the clock any more than can Chance, and the clock is equally relentless to them both. For the Princess: a little, very temporary, return to, recapture of, the spurious glory. The report from Sally Powers may be and probably is a factually accurate report: but to indicate she is going on to further triumph would be to falsify her future. The* PRINCESS *makes this instinctive admission to herself when she sits down by* CHANCE *on the bed, facing the audience. Both are faced with castration, and in her heart she knows it. They sit side by side on the bed like two passengers on a train sharing a bench.*]

PRINCESS: Chance, we've got to go on.

CHANCE: Go on to where? I couldn't go past my youth, but I've gone past it.

[*The 'Lament' fades in, continues through the scene to the last curtain.*]

PRINCESS: You're still young, Chance.

CHANCE: Princess, the age of some people can only be calculated by the level of – level of – rot in them. And by that measure I'm ancient.

PRINCESS: What am I? – I know, I'm dead, as old Egypt . . . Isn't it funny? We're still sitting here together, side by side in this room, like we were occupying the same bench on a train – going on together . . . Look. That little donkey's marching around and around to draw water out of a well . . . [*She points off at something as if outside a train window.*] Look, a shepherd boy's leading a flock. – What an old country, timeless. – Look –

[*The sound of a clock ticking is heard, louder and louder.*]

CHANCE: No, listen. I didn't know there was a clock in this room.

PRINCESS: I guess there's a clock in every room people live in . . .

CHANCE: It goes tick-tick, it's quieter than your heart-beat, but it's slow dynamite, a gradual explosion, blasting the world we lived in to burnt-out pieces . . . Time – who could beat it, who could defeat it ever? Maybe some saints and heroes, but not Chance Wayne. I lived on something, that – time?

PRINCESS: Yes, time.

CHANCE: . . . Gnaws away, like a rat gnaws off its own foot caught in a trap, and then, with its foot gnawed off and the rat set free, couldn't run, couldn't go, bled and died . . .

[*The clock ticking fades away.*]

TOM JUNIOR [*offstage left*]: Miss Del Lago . . .

PRINCESS: I think they're calling our – station . . .

TOM JUNIOR [*still offstage*]: Miss Del Lago, I have got a driver for you.

[*A trooper enters and waits on gallery.*
  With a sort of tired grace, she rises from the bed, one hand lingering on her seat-companion's shoulder as she moves a little unsteadily to the door. When she opens it, she is confronted by TOM JUNIOR.]

PRINCESS: Come on, Chance, we're going to change trains at this station . . . So, come on, we've got to go on . . . Chance, please . . .

[CHANCE *shakes his head and the* PRINCESS *gives up. She weaves out of sight with the trooper down the corridor.*
  TOM JUNIOR *enters from steps, pauses, and then gives a low whis-*

tle to SCOTTY, BUD, *and third man, who enter and stand waiting.* TOM JUNIOR *comes down bedroom steps and stands on bottom step.*]

CHANCE [*rising and advancing to the forestage*]: I don't ask for your pity, but just for your understanding – not even that – no. Just for your recognition of me in you, and the enemy, time, in us all.

CURTAIN

Period of Adjustment

To the director and the cast

The Cast

The first English production of this play was at the Theatre Royal, Bristol, on Monday, 4 September 1961, with the following cast:

RALPH BATES	*Harry H. Corbett*
ISABEL HAVERSTICK	*Elizabeth Shepherd*
GEORGE HAVERSTICK	*John Franklyn Robbins*
SUSIE	*Hazel Prance*
MRS MCGILLICUDDY	*Elizabeth Spriggs*
MR MCGILLICUDDY	*Derek Smith*
POLICE OFFICER	*Pierre Aumonier*
DOROTHEA BATES	*Rhoda Lewis*

Directed by VAL MAY
Designed by GRAHAM BARLOW

Act One

The Scene
The action of the play takes place in Ralph Bates's home,
Memphis, Tennessee. The time is Christmas Eve.

The set is the interior and entrance of a 'cute' little Spanish-type suburban
bungalow. Two rooms are visible onstage, the living-room with its small
dining alcove and the bedroom. There are doors to the kitchen and bath. A
bit of the stucco exterior surrounds the entrance, downstage right or left. A
Christmas wreath is on the door, while above the door is an ornamental
porch light, or coach lantern, with amber glass or possibly glass in several
colours. The fireplace in the fourth wall of the set is represented by a flicker-
ing red light. Of course, the living-room contains a TV set with its back to
the audience, its face to a big sofa that opens into a bed. The dog is a cocker
spaniel. There's a rather large Christmas tree, decorated with a child's toys
under it and a woman's fur coat in an open box, but no child and no woman.
RALPH BATES, *a boyish-looking man in his middle thirties, is approaching*
the TV set, facing upstage, with a can of beer and opener.

TV COMMERCIAL: Millions of Americans each day are discovering the
difference between this new miracle product and the old horse-
and-buggy type of cleanser which made wash-day a torture to
Mom and left her too tired at sundown to light up the house with
the sunshine of her smile.

RALPH: *No snow!*

[*He hoists himself on to a very high bar stool facing the TV.*]

TV COMMERCIAL: So don't let unnecessary fatigue cast a shadow over
your household, especially not at this –

[*He leaps off the stool and crouches to change the channel. He gets snatches of several dramatic and musical offerings, settles for a chorus of 'White Christmas', sighs, picks up a poker and stabs at the flickering ruddy light in the fourth wall. It comes up brighter. He crouches to fan the fire with an antique bellows: the fire brightens. He sighs again, hoists himself back on to the brass-studded red-leather-topped stool, which has evidently been removed from the 'cute' little bar, which is upstage. For theatrical purpose, this stool is about half a foot higher than any other sitting-surface on the stage. Whenever* RALPH *assumes a seat on this stool he is like a judge mounting his judicial bench, except he's not pompous or bewigged about it. He is detached, considering, thinking, and over his face comes that characteristic look of a gentle gravity which is the heart of* RALPH. *Perhaps his pose should suggest Rodin's 'Thinker'.* RALPH *is one of those rare people that have the capacity of heart to truly care, and care deeply, about other people.*

A car horn, urgent, is heard out front, offstage. RALPH *slides off the stool and rushes out of the front door; he stands under the amber coach lantern. It's snowing, the snowflakes are projected on his figure, tiny, obliquely falling particles of shadow. There's a muffled shout from the car that's stopped below the terrace of the bungalow.*]

RALPH [*shouting back*]: Hey, there, drive her up under th' carport!

GEORGE [*Texas voice*]: Whacha say, boy?

RALPH: PUT 'ER UNDER THE CARPORT!

GEORGE: Wheels won't catch, too steep!

RALPH: Back her all the way out and then shoot 'er up in first!

ISABEL'S VOICE [*high-pitched with strain*]: Will you please let me out first, George!

[*There is the sound of a car door.* RALPH *ducks in, grinning, and seizes a carton of rice.*]

RALPH: Yeah, come on in, little lady.

[ISABEL *appears before the house, small and white-faced with fatigue, eyes dark-circled, manner dazed and uncertain. She wears a cheap navy-blue cloth coat, carries a shiny new patent-leather purse, has on red wool mittens.* RALPH *pelts her with rice. She ducks the bombardment with a laugh that's more like a sob.*]

ISABEL: Oh, no, please! I never want to see rice again in my life, not uncooked anyhow . . . That fire looks wonderful to me. I'm Isabel Crane, Mr Bates.

[*She removes a red mitten and extends her hand.*]

RALPH: I thought you'd married that boy.

[*Both speak in deep Southern voices; hers is distinctly Texan.*]

ISABEL: I mean Mrs George Haverstick.

[*She says her new name with a hint of grimness.*]

RALPH [*still in the door*]: Wait'll I put m'shoes on, I'll come out!

[*This shout is unheard.*]

ISABEL: You have a sweet little house.

RALPH [*with a touch of amiable grimness*]: Yeah, we sure do! Wheels cain't git any traction, 'stoo damn steep.

[*He shouts down.*]

LOCK IT UP, LEAVE IT OUT FRONT! – I guess he's gonna do that, yep, that's what he's doin', uh-huh, that's what he's doin' . . .

ISABEL: Does it snow often in Memphis?

RALPH: No, no, rarely, rarely.

[*He gives her a glance.* RALPH *has a sometimes disconcerting way of seeming either oblivious to a person he's with or regarding the person with a sudden intense concentration, as if he'd just noticed something startling or puzzling about them. But this is a mannerism that the actor should use with restraint.*]

ISABEL: It was snowing all the way down here; it's my first acquaintance with snow except for one little flurry of snow in Saint Louis the day befo' Thanksgivin' day, this is my first real acquaintance with, with – with a real *snow* . . . What *is* he doing down there?

RALPH: He's unloadin' th' car.

ISABEL: I just want my small zipper bag. Will you please call down to him that's all I want of my things?

RALPH [*shouting*]: Leave all that stuff till later. Ha ha! I didn't know you could get all that in a car.

ISABEL: Surely he isn't removing our wedding presents! Is he *insane*, Mr Bates?

[*She goes to the door.*]

George! Just my small zipper bag, not everything in the car! Oh, Lord!

[*She retreats into the room.*]

He must think we're going to *live* here for the rest of our *lives*! He didn' even warn you all we were coming.

RALPH: He called me up from West Memphis.

ISABEL: Yes, just across the river.

RALPH: What is that car, a Caddy?

ISABEL: It's a fifty-two Cadillac with a mileage close to a hundred and twenty thousand. It ought to be retired with an old-age pension, Mr Bates.

RALPH [*at the door*]: It looks like one of them funeral limousines.

ISABEL [*wryly*]: Mr Bates, you have hit the nail on the head with the head of the hammer. That is just what it was. It's piled up a hundred and twenty thousand miles between Burkemeyer's Mortuary and various graveyards serving Greater Saint Louis. JAWGE, CAN YOU HEAR ME, JAWGE? Excuse me, Mr Bates.

[*She slips past him on to the terrace again.*]

JAWGE, JUST MY SMALL ZIPPER BAG.

[*Indistinct shout from below. She turns back in.*]

I give up, Mr Bates.

[*She ducks under his arm to enter the house again and stands behind Ralph in the doorway.*]

RALPH [*still chuckling at the door*]: What's he want with a funeral limousine? On a honeymoon trip?

ISABEL: I asked him that same question and got a very odd answer.
He said there's no better credit card in the world than driving up
at a bank door in a Cadillac limousine.

[*She tries to laugh.*]

Oh, I don't know, I – love Spanish-type architecture, Spanish
mission-type houses, I – don't think you ought to stand in that door
with just that light shirt on you, this is a – such a – *sweet* house . . .

[*She seems close to tears. Something in her tone catches his attention
and he comes in, closing the door.*]

RALPH: Ha, ha, well, how's it going? Is the marriage in orbit?

ISABEL [*tries to laugh at this, too*]: Oh! Will you please do me a favour?
Don't encourage him, please don't invite him to spend the night
here, Mr Bates! I'm thinking of your wife, because last night – in
Cape Girardeau, Missouri? – he thought it would be very nice to
look up an old war buddy he had there, too. He sincerely thought
so, and possibly the war buddy thought so, too, but NOT the
wife! Oh, no, not *that* lady, no! They'd hardly got through their
first beer cans with – remembrances of Korea, when that bright
little woman began to direct us to a highway motel which she said
was only a hop, skip and jump from their house but turned out to
be almost across the state line into – Arkansas? Yaias, Arkansas. I
think I can take this off, now!

[*She removes a red woollen muffler. He takes it from her and she murmurs 'Thanks.'*]

What is holding him up? Why is he –? Mr Bates, I did tell him that
this is one night of the year when you just don't intrude on
another young married couple.

RALPH: Aw, come off that, little lady! Why, I been beggin' that boy
ever since we got out of the service to come to Memphis. He had
to git married to make it. Why, every time I'd git drunk, I'd call
that boy on the phone to say 'Git to hell down here, you old Texas

jack rabbit!' And I'd just about given up hope he'd ever show!

ISABEL: Is he still fooling with luggage?

[*There is a noise outside.* RALPH *goes to the open door.*]

RALPH: *Hey!*

ISABEL: *What?*

RALPH: Ha ha ha! He put these bags at the door and run back down to the car.

ISABEL: *What* did he –?

RALPH: Gone back down for more luggage. I'll take these in.

ISABEL [*as the bags are brought in*]: Those are *my* pieces of luggage! All but the small zipper which is all that I wanted!

RALPH [*calling out the open door*]: *Hey!*

ISABEL: *What?*

RALPH: *Hey, boy!* He's gotten back in the car an' driven off, ha ha!

ISABEL [*rushing to the door*]: *Driven? Off?* Did you say? My heavens. You're right, he's *gone!* Mr Bates, he's *deposited me on your hands and driven away.*

[*She is stunned.*]

Oh, *how funny!* Isn't this *funny!*

[*Laughs wildly, close to sobbing.*]

It's no *surprise* to me, though! All the way down here from Cape Girardeau, where we stopped for our wedding night, Mr Bates, I had a feeling that the first chance he got to, he would abandon me somewhere!

RALPH: Aw, now, take it easy!

ISABEL: That's what he's done! Put me and my bags in your hands and run away.

RALPH: Aw, now, no! The old boy wouldn't do that, ha ha, for Chrissakes. He just remembered something he had to, had to – go and get at a – drugstore.

ISABEL: If that was the case wouldn't he mention it to me?

RALPH: Aw now, I known that boy a long time and he's always been sort of way out, but never way out that far!

ISABEL: Where is your wife? Where's Mrs Bates, Mr Bates?

RALPH: Oh, she's not here, right now.

ISABEL: I'm SUCH A FOOL!

[*She giggles a little hysterically.*]

Oh, I'm such a *fool!* ... Why didn't I know better, can you answer me that? ... I hope the news of our approach didn't drive your wife away on Christmas Eve, Mr Bates ...

RALPH: No, honey.

ISABEL: He brought up everything but the little blue zipper bag which is all I asked faw! ... It had my, all my, it had my – *night* things in it ...

RALPH: Just let me get you a drink. I'm sorry I don't have any egg nog. But I can make a wonderful hot buttered rum. How about a little hot buttered rum?

ISABEL: Thank you, no, I don't drink ...

RALPH: It's never too late to begin to.

ISABEL: No, I don't want liquor.

RALPH: Coffee? Want some hot coffee?

ISABEL: Where is your wife, Mr Bates?

RALPH: Oh, she's – not here now, I'll tell you about that later.

ISABEL: She will be outraged. This is one night of the year when you don't want outside disturbances – on your hands ...

RALPH: I think I know what to give you.

ISABEL: I did expect it but yet I didn't expect it! – I mean it occurred to me, the possibility of it, but I thought I was just being morbid.

RALPH: Aw, now, I know that boy. We been through two wars together, took basic training together and officer's training together. He wouldn't ditch you like that unless he's gone crazy.

ISABEL: George Haverstick is a very sick man, Mr Bates. He was a patient in neurological at Barnes Hospital in Saint Louis, that's how I met him. I was a student nurse there.

[*She is talking quickly, shrilly. She has a prim, severe manner that disguises her prettiness.*]

RALPH: Yeah? What was wrong with him in the hospital, honey?

ISABEL: If we see him again, if he ever comes back to this house, you will *see* what's wrong. *He shakes!* Sometimes it's just barely noticeable, just a constant, slight tremor, you know, a sort of – vibration, like a – like an electric vibration in his muscles or nerves?

RALPH: Aw. That old tremor has come back on him, huh? He had that thing in Korea.

ISABEL: How bad did he have it in Korea, Mr Bates?

RALPH: You know – like a heavy drinker – except he didn't drink heavy.

ISABEL: It's like he had Parkinson's disease but he doesn't have it.

[*She speaks like an outraged spinster, which is quite incongruous to her pretty, child-like appearance.*]

RALPH: What in hell is it then?

ISABEL: THAT is a MYSTERY! He shakes, that's all. He just shakes. Sometimes you'd think that he was shaking to pieces . . . Was that a car out front?

[*She goes to the window.*]

No! I've caught a head cold, darn it.

[*Blows her nose.*]

When I met Mr George Haverstick – Excuse me, you're watching TV!

RALPH [*turning off set*]: Naw, I'm not watchin' TV.

ISABEL: I'm so wound up, sitting in silence all day beside my – silent bridegroom, I can't seem to stop talking now, although I – hardly know you. Yes. I met him at Barnes Hospital, the biggest one in Saint Louis, where I was taking my training as a nurse, he had gone in Barnes instead of the Veterans Hospital because in the Veterans Hospital they couldn't discover any physical cause of this tremor and he thought they just said there wasn't any physical cause in order to avoid having to pay him a physical disability – compensation! I had him as a patient at Barnes Hospital, on the night shift. My, did he keep me running! The little buzzer was never out of his hand. Couldn't sleep under any kind of sedation less than enough to knock an elephant out! – Well, that's where I met George, I was very touched by him, honestly, very, very touched by the boy! I thought he sincerely loved me . . . Yes, I *have* caught a head cold, or am I crying? I guess it's fatigue – exhaustion.

RALPH: You're just going through a period of adjustment.

ISABEL: Of course at Barnes he got the same diagnosis, or lack of diagnosis, that he'd gotten at the Vets Hospital in Korea and Texas and elsewhere, no physical basis for the tremor, perfect physical health, suggested – psychiatry to him! He blew the roof off! You'd think they'd accused him of beating up his grandmother, at least, if not worse! I swear! Mr Bates, I still have sympathy for him, but it wasn't fair of him not to let me know he'd quit his job at the airfield till after our marriage. He gave me that information after the wedding, right after the wedding he told me, right on the bridge, Eads Bridge between Saint Louis and East Saint Louis, he said, 'Little Bit? Take a good look at Saint Louie because it may be your last one!' I'm quoting him exactly, those were his words. I don't know why I didn't say drive me right back . . . Isn't it strange that I didn't say turn around on the other side of this bridge and drive me right back? I gave up student nursing at a great hospital to marry a man not honest enough to let me know he'd given up his job till an hour after the wedding!

RALPH: George is a high-strung boy. But they don't make them any better.

ISABEL: A man's opinion of a man! If they don't make them any better than George Haverstick they ought to stop production!

[RALPH *throws back his head, laughing heartily.*]

No, I mean it, if they don't make them better than a man that would abandon his bride in less than – how many hours? – on the doorstep of a war buddy and drive on without her or any apology to her, if that's the best they make them, I say *don't make them!*

[*There is a pause. She has crouched before the fire again, holding her hands out to the flickering glow.*]

Did George tell you on the phone that he's quit his job?

RALPH [*pouring brandy*]: What job did he quit, honey?

ISABEL: He was a ground mechanic at Lambert's airfield in Saint Louis. I had lost my job too, I hadn't quit, no, I was politely dismissed. My first day in surgery? – I *fainted!* – when the doctor made the incision and I saw the blood, I keeled over . . .

RALPH: That's understandable, honey.

ISABEL: Not in a nurse, not in a girl that had set her heart on nursing, that – how long has he been gone?

RALPH: Just a few minutes, honey. Christmas Eve traffic is heavy and George being George, he may have stopped at a bar on his way back here . . . You'd been going steady how long?

ISABEL: Ever since his discharge from Barnes Hospital. Isn't this suburb called High Point?

RALPH: Yes. High Point over a cavern.

ISABEL: His place was in High Point, too. Another suburb called High Point, spelled Hi dash Point – hyphenated.

RALPH: I guess all fair-sized American cities have got a suburb called High Point, hyphenated or not, but this is the only one I know of that's built on a cavern.

ISABEL [*without really listening to him*]: Cavern?

[*She laughs faintly as if it were a weak joke.*]

Well, I said, George, on the bridge, we're not driving down to Florida in that case. We're going to find you a job; we're going from city to city until you find a new job and I don't care if we cross the Rio Grande, we're not going to stop until you find one! Did I or didn't I make the right decision? In your opinion, Mr Bates.

RALPH: Well. How did he react to it?

ISABEL: Stopped talking and started shaking! So violently I was scared he would drive that funeral car off the road! Ever since then it's been hell! And I am –

[*She springs up from the fireplace chair.*]

– not exactly the spirit of Christmas, am I?

[*She goes to the window to look out; sees nothing but windy snow. There is a low rumble. A picture falls off the wall.*]

What was that?

RALPH: Oh, nothing. The ground just settled a little. We get that all the time here because this suburb, High Point, is built over a great big underground cavern and is sinking into it gradually, an inch or two inches a year. It would cost three thousand dollars to stabilize the foundation of this house even temporarily! But it's not publicly known and we homeowners and the promoters of the project have got together to keep it a secret till we have sold out, in alphabetical order, at a loss but not a complete sacrifice. Collusion, connivance. Disgusting but necessary.

[*She doesn't hear this, murmurs 'What?' as she crosses back to the window at the sound of a car going by.*]

ISABEL: It's funny, I had a hunch he was going to leave me somewhere.

[*She laughs sadly, forlornly, and lets the white window curtains fall together.*]

RALPH: Why don't you take off your coat and sit back down by the fire? That coat keeps the heat off you, honey. That boy's comin' back.

ISABEL: Thank you.

[*She removes her coat.*]

RALPH [*observing with solemn appreciation the perfect neatness of her small body*]: I'm *sure* that boy's coming back. I am now *positive* of it! That's a cute little suit you're wearing. Were you married in that?

ISABEL: Yes, I was married in this travelling suit. Appropriately.

RALPH: You couldn't have looked any prettier in white satin.

[RALPH *is at the bar preparing a snifter of brandy for her. Now he puts a match to it and as it flares up blue, she cries out a little.*]

ISABEL: What is, what are you –?

RALPH: Something to warm up your insides, little lady.

ISABEL: Well, isn't that sweet of you? Will it burn if I touch it?

RALPH: Naw, naw, naw, take it, take it.

ISABEL: Beautiful. Let me hold it to warm my hands first, before I –

[*He puts the snifter glass of blue-flaming brandy in her hands and they return to the fireplace.*]

I'm not a drinker, I don't think doctors or nurses have any right to be, but I guess *now* – I'm *out* of the nursing profession! *So* . . . What a sweet little bar. What a sweet little house. And such a sweet Christmas tree.

RALPH: Yeah. Everything's sweet here. I married a homely girl, honey, but I tried to love her.

[ISABEL *doesn't really hear this remark.*]

ISABEL: I hope your wife didn't take your little boy out because we were coming.

RALPH: I sure did make an effort to love that woman. I almost stopped realizing that she was homely.

ISABEL: So he didn't actually tell you he was going to a drugstore, Mr Bates?

RALPH [*uncomfortably*]: He didn't say so. I just figured he was.

ISABEL: I – well, he's abandoned me here.

RALPH: How long've you known George?

ISABEL: I'm afraid I married a stranger.

RALPH: Everybody does that.

ISABEL: Where did you say your wife was?

RALPH: My wife has quit me.

ISABEL: No! You're joking, aren't you?

RALPH: She walked out on me this evening when I let her know I'd quit my job.

ISABEL [*beginning to listen to him*]: Surely it's just temporary, Mr Bates.

RALPH: Nope. Don't think so. I quit my job and so my wife quit me.

ISABEL: I don't think a woman leaves a man as nice as you, Mr Bates, for such a reason as that.

RALPH: Marriage is an economic arrangement in many ways, let's face it, honey. Also, the situation between us was complicated by the fact that I worked for her father. But that's another story. That's a long other story and you got your mind on George.

ISABEL: I think my pride has been hurt.

RALPH: I told you he's coming back and I'm just as sure of it as I'm sure Dorothea isn't. Or if she does, that she'll find me waiting for her. Ohhhhh, nooooo! I'm cutting out of this High Point over a Cavern on the first military transport I can catch out of Memphis.

ISABEL [*vaguely*]: You don't mean that, Mr Bates, you're talking through your hat, out of hurt feelings, hurt pride.

[*She opens the front door and stands looking out as forlornly as a lost child. She really does have a remarkably cute little figure and RALPH takes slow, continual and rather wistful stock of it with his eyes.*]

RALPH: I got what I had comin' to me, that I admit, for marryin' a girl that didn't attract me.

[*He comes up behind her at the door.*]

ISABEL: Did you say didn't attract you?

RALPH: Naw, she didn't attract me in the beginning. She's one year older'n me and I'm no chicken. But I guess I'm not the only man that would marry the only daughter of an old millionaire with diabetes and gallstones and one kidney. Am I?

ISABEL: It's nice out here.

RALPH: But I'm telling you I'm convinced there is no greater assurance of longevity in this world than one kidney, gallstones an' diabetes! That old man has been cheating the undertaker for yea many years. Seems to thrive on one kidney and . . .

[*He tosses the beer can down the terrace.*]

Oh, they live on anything – nothing!

ISABEL: Do you always throw beer cans on your front lawn, Mr Bates?

RALPH: Never before in my life. I sure enjoyed it. George is gonna be shocked when he sees me. I sacrificed my youth to –

ISABEL: What?

RALPH: Yep, it's nice out here. I mean, nicer than in there.

ISABEL: You sacrificed your youth?

RALPH: Oh, that. Yeah! I'll tell you more about that unless it bores you.

ISABEL: No.

RALPH: She had fallen into the hands of a psychiatrist when I married this girl. This psychiatrist was charging her father fifty dollars a session to treat her for a condition that he diagnosed as 'psychological frigidity'. She would shiver violently every time she came within touching distance of a possible boy friend. Well – I think the psychiatrist misunderstood her shivers.

ISABEL: She might have shivered because of –

RALPH: That's what I *mean*! Why, the night I met her, I heard a noise like castanets at a distance. I thought some Spanish dancers were about to come on! Ha ha! Then I noticed her teeth – she had buck teeth at that time which were later extracted – were chattering together and her whole body was uncontrollably shaking!

ISABEL: We both married into the shakes! But Mr Bates, I don't think it's very nice of you to ridicule the appearance of your wife.

RALPH: Oh, I'm not!

ISABEL: You WERE!

RALPH: At my suggestion she had the buck teeth extracted. It was like kissing a rock pile before the extractions! I swear!

ISABEL: Now, Mr Bates.

RALPH: This snow almost feels as warm as white ashes out of a – chimney.

ISABEL: Excuse me. I'll get my – sweater.

[*She goes in. He remains on the little paved terrace. When she comes out again in her cardigan, he goes on talking as if there'd been no interruption.*]

RALPH: Yep, her old man was payin' this head-shrinker fifty dollars per session for this condition he diagnosed as 'psychological frigidity'. I cured her of that completely almost overnight. But at thirty-seven, my age, you ain't middle-aged but you're in the shadow of it and it's a spooky shadow. I mean, when you look at *late* middle-aged couples like the McGillicuddys, my absent wife's parents . . .

ISABEL: Mr Bates, don't you think I should go downtown and take a hotel room? Even if George comes back, he ought not to find me here like a checked package waiting for him to return with the claim check. Because if you give up your pride, what are you left with, really?

[*She turns and goes back inside. He follows her in. Immediately after they enter, a* NEGRO GIRL *appears on the terrace.*]

Don't you agree, Mr Bates?

[*The* GIRL *rings the doorbell.*]

RALPH: Here he is now. You see?

[ISABEL, *who had sunk on to a hassock before the fireplace, now rises tensely as* RALPH *calls out:*]

COME ON IN, LOVER BOY! THAT DOOR AIN'T LOCKED!

[RALPH *opens the door.*]

Oh . . . What can I do fo' you, Susie?

[SUSIE *comes into the room with a sheepish grin.*]

SUSIE: 'Scuse me for comin' to the front door, Mr Bates, but that snow's wet and I got a hole in muh shoe!

RALPH: You alone?

SUSIE: Yes, suh.

RALPH: They sent you for somethin'?

SUSIE: Yes, suh, they sent me faw th' chile's Santie Claus.

RALPH: Aw, they did, huh? Well, you go right back an' tell the McGillicuddys that 'the chile's Santie Claus' is stayin' right here till the chile comes over for it, because I bought it, not them, and I am at least *half* responsible for the 'chile's' existence, *also*. Tell them the chile did not come into the world without a father and it's about time for the chile to acknowledge that fact and for them to acknowledge that fact and – How did you git here, Susie?

SUSIE: Charlie brought me.

RALPH: Who's Charlie?

SUSIE: Charlie's they new *showfer*, Mr Bates.

RALPH: Aw. Well, tell my wife and her folks, the McGillicuddys, that I won't be here tomorrow but 'the chile's Santie Claus' will be here under the tree and say that I said Merry Christmas. Can you remember all that?

SUSIE: Yes, suh.

[*She turns and shouts through the door.*]

Charlie! Don't come up, I'm comin' right down, Charlie!

[*The sound of a Cadillac motor starting is heard below the terrace as* SUSIE *leaves.* RALPH *looks out of the open door till the car is gone, then slams it shut.*]

RALPH: Dig that, will yuh! Sent a coloured girl over to collect the kid's Christmas! This is typical of the Stuart McGillicuddys. I'd like to have seen Mr Stuart McGillicuddy, the look on his face, when the Western Union messenger give him my message of resignation this afternoon and he was at last exposed to my true opinions of him!

ISABEL: You should have let her take the child's Christmas to it.

RALPH: They'll be over. Don't worry. And – I will be waiting for them with both barrels, man – will I blast 'em! Think of the psychiatrist fees that I saved her fat-head father! I even made her think that she was attractive, and over a five-year period got one pay rise when she give birth to my son which she has turned to a sissy.

[ISABEL *hasn't listened to his speech.*]

ISABEL: I thought that was George at the door . . .

RALPH: That's life for you.

ISABEL: What?

RALPH: I said isn't that life for you!

ISABEL: *What* is life for us *all*?

[*She sighs.*]

My philosophy professor at the Baptist college I went to, he said one day, 'We are all of us born, live and die in the shadow of a giant question mark that refers to three questions: Where do we *come* from? *Why? And where, oh where, are we going!*'

RALPH: When did you say you got married?

ISABEL: Yesterday. Yesterday morning.

RALPH: That lately? Well, he'll be back before you can say – Joe Blow.

[*He appreciates her neat figure again.*]

ISABEL: What?

RALPH: Nothing.

ISABEL: Well!

RALPH: D'you like Christmas music?

ISABEL: Everything but 'White Christmas'.

[*As she extends her palms to the imaginary fireplace, RALPH is standing a little behind her, still looking her up and down with solemn appreciation.*]

RALPH: Aw, y' don't like 'White Christmas'?

ISABEL: The radio in that car is practically the only thing in it that *works*! We had it on all the time.

[*She gives a little tired laugh.*]

Conversation was impossible, even if there had been a desire to talk! It kept playing 'White Christmas' because it was snowing I guess all the way down here, yesterday and – today . . .

RALPH: A radio in a funeral limousine?

ISABEL: I guess they just played it on the way back from the grave-yard. Anyway, once I reached over and turned the volume down. He didn't say anything, he just reached over and turned the volume back up. Isn't it funny how a little thing like that can be so insulting to you? Then I started crying and still haven't stopped! I pretended to be looking out the car window till it got dark.

RALPH: You're just going through a little period of adjustment to each other.

ISABEL: What do you do with a bride left on your doorstep, Mr Bates?

RALPH: Well, I, *ha ha!* – never *had* that experience!

ISABEL: Before? Well, now you're faced with it, I hope you know how to handle it. You know why I know he's left me? He only took in my bags, he left his own in the car, he brought in all of mine except my little blue zipper overnight bag, *that* he kept for some reason. Perhaps he intends to pick up another female companion who could use its contents.

RALPH: Little lady, you're in a bad state of nerves.

ISABEL: Have you ever been so tired that you don't know what you're doing or saying?

RALPH: Yes. Often.

ISABEL: That's my condition, so make allowances for it. Yes, indeed, that *sure* is a mighty *far* drugstore . . .

[*She wanders back to the window, and parts the curtain to peer out.*]

RALPH: He seems gone twice as long because you're thinking about it.

ISABEL: I don't know why I should care except for my overnight bag with my toilet articles in it.

RALPH [*obliquely investigating*]: Where did you spend last night?

ISABEL [*vaguely*]: Where did we spend last night?

RALPH: Yeah. Where did you stop for the night?

ISABEL [*rubbing her forehead and sighing with perplexity*]: In a, in a – oh, a tourist camp called the – Old Man River Motel? Yes, the Old Man River Motel.

RALPH: That's a mistake. The first night ought to be spent in a real fine place regardless of what it cost you. It's so important to get off on the right foot.

[*He has freshened his drink and come around to the front of the bar. She has gone back to the window at the sound of a car.*]

If you get off on the wrong foot, it can take a long time to correct it.

[*She nods in slow confirmation of this opinion.*]

Un-hmmm. Walls are built up between people a hell of a damn sight faster than – broken down . . . Y'want me to give you my word that he's coming back? I will, I'll give you my word. Hey.

[*He snaps his fingers.*]

Had he brought me a Christmas present? If not, *that's* what he's doing. *That* explains where he went to.

[*There is a pause. She sits sadly by the fireplace.*]

What went wrong last night?

ISABEL: Let's not talk about that.

RALPH: I don't mean to pry into such a private, intimate thing, but –

ISABEL: No, let's don't! I'll just put it this way and perhaps you will understand me. In spite of my being a student nurse, till discharged – my experience has been limited, Mr Bates. Perhaps it's because I grew up in a small town, an only child, too protected. I wasn't allowed to date till my last year at High and then my father insisted on meeting the boys I went out with and laid down pretty strict rules, such as when to bring me home from parties and so forth. If he smelled liquor on the breath of a boy? At the door? That boy would not enter the door! And that little rule ruled out a goodly number.

RALPH: I bet it did. They should've ate peanuts befo' they called for you, honey.

[*He chuckles, reflectively poking at the fire.*]

That's what we done at the Sisters of Mercy Orphans' Home in Mobile.

ISABEL [*touched*]: Oh. Were you an *orphan*, Mr Bates?

RALPH: Yes, I had that advantage.

[*He slides off the high stool again to poke at the fire. She picks up the antique bellows and fans the flames, crouching beside him.*]

ISABEL: So you were an orphan! People that grow up orphans, don't they value love more?

RALPH: Well, let's put it this way. They get it less easy. To get it, they have to give it: so, yeah, they do value it more.

[*He slides back on to the bar stool. She crouches at the fireplace to fan the fire with the bellows; the flickering light brightens their shy, tender faces.*]

ISABEL: But it's also an advantage to have a parent like my daddy.

[*She's again close to tears.*]

Very strict but devoted. Opposed me going into the nursing profession but I had my heart set on it, I thought I had a vocation, I saw myself as a Florence Nightingale nurse. A lamp in her hand? Establishin' clinics in the – upper Amazon country . . .

[*She laughs a little ruefully.*]

Yais, I had heroic daydreams about myself as a dedicated young nurse working side by side with a –

[*She pauses shyly.*]

RALPH: With a dedicated young doctor?

ISABEL: No, the doctor would be older, well, not too old, but – older. I saw myself passing among the pallets, you know, the straw mats, administering to the plague victims in the jungle, exposing myself to contagion . . .

[*She exhibits a bit of humour here.*]

RALPH: *Catchin'* it?

ISABEL: Yais, contractin' it eventually *m'self* . . .

RALPH: What were the symptoms of it?

ISABEL: A slight blemish appearing on the – hands?

[*She gives him a darting smile.*]

RALPH [*joining in the fantasy with her*]: Which you'd wear gloves to conceal?

ISABEL: Yais, rubber gloves all the time.

RALPH: A crusty-lookin' blemish or more like a fungus?

[*They laugh together.*]

ISABEL: I don't think I – yais, I did, I imagined it being like *scaa-ales*! Like silver fish scales appearing on my hainds and then progressing gradually to the wrists and *fo'*-arms . . .

RALPH: And the young doctor discovering you were concealing this condition?

ISABEL: The *youngish middle-aged* doctor, Mr Bates! Yais, discovering I had contracted the plague myself and then a big scene in which she says, Oh, no, you mustn't touch me but he seizes her passionately in his arms, of course, and – exposes himself to contagion.

[RALPH *chuckles heartily, getting off the stool to poke at the fire again. She joins him on the floor to fan the flames with the bellows.*]

And love is stronger than death. You get the picture?

RALPH: Yep, I've seen the picture.

ISABEL: We've had a good laugh together. You're a magician, Ralph, to make me laugh tonight in my present situation. George and I never laugh, we never laugh together. Oh, he makes JOKES, YAIS! But we never have a really genuine laugh together and that's a bad sign, I think, because I don't think a married couple can go through life without laughs together any more than they can without tears.

RALPH: Nope.

[*He removes his shoes.*]

Take your slippers off, honey.

ISABEL: I have the funniest sensation in the back of my head, like –

RALPH: Like a tight rope was coming unknotted?

ISABEL: Exactly! Like a tight rope was being unknotted!

[*He removes her slippers and puts them on the hearth, crosses into the bedroom and comes out with a pair of fluffy pink bedroom slippers. He crouches beside her and feels the sole of her stocking.*]

RALPH: Yep, damp. Take those damp stockings off.

ISABEL [*unconsciously following the suggestion*]: Does George have a sense of humour? In your opinion? Has he got the ability to laugh at himself and at life and at – human sitations? Outside of off-colour jokes? In your opinion, Mr Bates?

RALPH [*taking the damp stockings from her and hanging them over the footlights*]: Yes. We had some good laughs together, me an' – 'Gawge', ha ha! . . .

ISABEL: We never had any together.

RALPH: That's the solemnity of romantic love, little lady, I mean like Romeo and Juliet was not exactly a joke book, ha ha ha!

ISABEL: 'The solemnity of romantic love'! – I wouldn't expect an old war buddy of George's to use an expression like that.

RALPH: Lemme put these on your feet, little lady.

[*She sighs and extends her feet and he slips the soft fleecy pink slippers on them.*]

But you know something? I'm gonna tell you something which isn't out of the joke books either. You got a wonderful boy in your hands, on your hands, they don't make them any better than him and I mean it.

[*He does.*]

ISABEL: I appreciate your loyalty to an old war buddy.

RALPH: Naw, naw, it's not just that.

ISABEL: But if they don't make them any better than George Haverstick, they ought to stop making them, they ought to *cease producing*!

[*She utters a sort of wild, sad laugh which stops as abruptly as it started. Suddenly she observes the bedroom slippers on her feet.*]

What's these, where did they come from?

RALPH: Honey, I just put them on you. Didn't you know?

ISABEL: No! – How strange! – I didn't, I wasn't at all aware of it . . .

[*They are both a little embarrassed.*]

Where is your wife, Mr Bates?

RALPH: Honey, I told you she quit me and went home to her folks.

ISABEL: Oh, excuse me, I remember. You told me . . .

[*Suddenly the blazing logs make a sharp cracking noise; a spark apparently has spat out of the grate on to ISABEL's skirt. She gasps and springs up, retreating from the fireplace, and RALPH jumps off the bar stool to brush at her skirt. Under the material of the angora wool skirt is the equal and warmer softness of her young body.* RALPH *is abruptly embarrassed, coughs, turns back to the fireplace and picks up copper tongs to shift the position of crackling logs.*

This is a moment between them that must be done just right to avoid misinterpretation. RALPH *would never make a play for the bride of a buddy. What should come out of the moment is not a suggestion that he will or might but that Dotty's body never felt that way. He remembers bodies that did. What comes out of Isabel's reaction is a warm understanding of his warm understanding; just that, nothing more, at all.*]

ISABEL: Thank you. This angora wool is, is – highly inflammable stuff, at least I would – think it – might be . . .

RALPH: Yeah, and I don't want 'Gawge' to come back here and find a toasted marshmallow bride . . . by my fireplace.

[*They sit down rather self-consciously,* RALPH *on the high stool,* ISABEL *on the low hassock.*]

ISABEL: Yais . . .

RALPH: Huh?

ISABEL: Daddy opposed me going into nursing so much that he didn't speak to me, wouldn't even look at me for a whole week before I took off for Saint Louie.

RALPH: Aw? Tch!

ISABEL: However, at the last moment, just before the train pulled out of the depot, he came stalking up the platform to the coach window with a gift package and an envelope. The package contained flannel nighties and the envelope had in it a list of moral instructions in the form of prayers such as: 'O Heavenly Father, give thy weak daughter strength to –

[*She giggles.*]

– resist the –'

[*She covers her mouth with a hand to suppress a spasm of laughter.*]

Oh, my Lord! Well, you would have to know Daddy to appreciate
the –

RALPH: Honey, I reckon I know your daddy. That's what I meant
about the orphan's advantage, honey.

[*They laugh together.*]

ISABEL: We sure do have some good laughs together, Mr Bates.
Where did I get *these*?

[*She means the bedroom slippers.*]

These aren't mine, where did, how did – ? *Oh* – *yes*, you –

[*They resume their grave contemplation of the fire.*]

'Heavenly Father, give thy weak daughter the strength of will to
resist the lusts of men. Amen.'

[RALPH *chuckles sadly.*]

And I was never tempted to, *not* to, resist them, till – George . . .

RALPH: Did George arouse a –?

ISABEL: I don't suppose another man could see George the way I
see him: SAW him. So *handsome*? And so *afflicted*? So afflicted
and – *handsome*? With that mysterious *tremor*? With those
SHAKES?

RALPH: How did 'Gawge' come on?

ISABEL: Huh? Oh. No. I don't mean he came on like a –

RALPH: Bull? Exactly?

ISABEL: No, no, no, no. It was very strange, very – strange . . .

RALPH: What?

ISABEL: He always wanted us to go out on double dates or with a
whole bunch of – others. And when we were alone? Together?
There was a – funny, oh, a very *odd* – sort of – *timidity!* – between
us . . . And that, of course, is what touched me; oh, that – *touched*
me . . .

[*There is a pause in the talk.* RALPH *descends from his high perch
and passes behind her low hassock with a smile behind her back*

which is a recognition of the truth of her romantic commitment to George. This is also in the slight, tender pat that he gives to the honey-coloured crown of her head.]

An' so although I had many strong opportunities to give in to my 'weakness' on, on – week-end dates with young interns and doctors at Barnes? – I was never tempted to do so. But with George –

RALPH: You did? Give in?

ISABEL: Mr Bates, George Haverstick married a virgin, and I can't say for sure that it was my strength of will and not *his* that – deserves the credit . . .

[RALPH *returns to fireplace with beer.*]

RALPH: Yeah, well. Now I'm going to tell you something about that boy that might surprise you after your experience last night at the Old Man River Motel.

[*He opens a beer can.*]

He always bluffs about his ferocious treatment of women, believe me! To hear him talk you'd think he spared them no pity! However, I happen to know he didn't come on as strong with those dolls in Tokyo and Hong Kong and Korea as he liked to pretend to. Because I heard from those dolls . . . He'd just sit up there on a pillow and drink that rice wine with them and teach them *English*! Then come downstairs from there, hitching his belt and shouting, '*Oh, man! Oh, brother!*' – like he'd laid 'em to waste.

ISABEL: That was not his behaviour in the Old Man River Motel. Last night.

RALPH: What went wrong in the Old Man River Motel?

ISABEL: Too many men think that girls in the nursing profession must be – *shock*proof. I'm not, I wasn't – last night . . .

RALPH: Oh. Was he drunk?

ISABEL: He'd been drinking all day in that heaterless retired funeral hack in a snowstorm to keep himself warm. Since I don't drink, I just had to endure it. Then we stopped at the Old Man River Motel, as dreary a place as you could find on this earth! The electric heater in our cabin lit up but gave off no heat! Oh, *George* was comfortable there! Threw off his clothes and sat down in front of the heater as if I were not even present.

RALPH: Aw.

ISABEL: Continuing drinking!

RALPH: Aw.

ISABEL: Then began the courtship, and, oh, what a courtship it was, such tenderness, romance! I finally screamed. I locked myself in the bathroom and didn't come out till he had gotten to bed and then I – slept in a chair . . .

RALPH: You wouldn't –

ISABEL: Mr Bates, I just couldn't! The atmosphere just wasn't right. And he –

[*She covers her face.*]

– I can't tell you more about it just now except that it was a nightmare, him in the bed, pretending to be asleep, and me in the chair pretending to be asleep too and both of us knowing the other one *wasn't* asleep and, and – I can't tell you more about it right now, I just can't tell more than I've told you about it, I –

[*Her sobs become violent and there is a pause.*]

RALPH: Hey! Let me kiss the bride! Huh? Can I kiss the bride?

ISABEL: You're very kind, Mr Bates. I'm sure you were more understanding with your wife when you were going through this –

RALPH: – period of adjustment? Yeah. That's all it is, it's just a little – period of adjustment.

[*He bestows a kiss on her tear-stained cheek and a pat on her head. She squeezes his hand and sinks down again before the fireplace.*]

ISABEL: It isn't as if I'd given him to believe that I was *experienced*! I made it clear that I wasn't. He knows my background and we'd talked at great *length* about my – inhibitions which I know are – *inhibitions*, but – which an understanding husband wouldn't expect his bride to overcome at *once*, in a tourist cabin, after a *long – silent – ride*! – in a *funeral hack* in a *snowstorm* with the *heater not*

working in a *shocked condition*! – having just been told that – we
were *both* unemployed, and –

RALPH: Little Bit, Little Bit – you had a sleepless night in that motel
– why don't you put in a little sack time now. You need it, honey.
Take Dotty's bed in there and think about nothing till morning.

ISABEL: You mean you know, now, that George is not coming back?

RALPH: No. I mean that Dotty's not coming back.

ISABEL: I don't think you ever thought that he would come back for
me any more than I did.

RALPH: Take Dotty's bed, get some sleep on that foam-rubber mattress while I sit here and watch the Late Late Show on TV.

ISABEL: But, Mister Bates, if your wife does come back here I
wouldn't want her to find a stranger in your bedroom.

RALPH: Honey, finding a stranger in a bedroom is far from being the
biggest surprise of a lifetime. So you go on in there and lock the
door.

ISABEL: Thank you, Mister Bates.

[*She enters bedroom.*]

I'm only locking the door because of the slight possibility that
Mister George Haverstick the Fourth might come back drunk and
try to repeat the comedy and tragedy of last night. I hope you
realize that.

RALPH: Oh, sure. Good night, sleep tight, honey.

[*She locks the bedroom door as* RALPH *returns to the fireplace.*]

[*to himself and the audience*]: What a bitch of a Christmas!

CURTAIN

Act Two

No time lapse.

> [ISABEL *jumps up as a car is heard stopping out front. She looks wildly at* RALPH, *who gives her a nod and a smile as he crosses to the front door. Snow blows into the living-room as he goes out and shouts:*]

RALPH: HEY!

> [ISABEL *catches her breath, waiting.*]

Ha ha!

> [ISABEL *expels her breath and sits down.* RALPH, *shouting through snow:*]

Your wife thought she was deserted!

GEORGE [*from a distance*]: Hey!

> [ISABEL *springs up and rushes to a mirror to wipe away tears.*
> *A car door is heard slamming in front of the house.* ISABEL *sits down.*
> *She immediately rises, rubbing her hands together, and then sits down again. Then she springs up and starts towards the bedroom. Stops short as* GEORGE *enters.*]

I'm the son of a camel, ha ha! My mother was a camel with two humps, a double hump – dromedary! Ha ha ha!

> [GEORGE *and* RALPH *catch each other in a big, rocking hug.* ISABEL *stares, ignored, as the male greetings continue.*]

RALPH: *You ole son of a tail gun!*

GEORGE: *How'sa young squirrel? Ha ha!*
RALPH: *How'sa Texas jack rabbit?*

[*There is a sudden, incongruous stillness. They stare, all three of them,* ISABEL *at* GEORGE, GEORGE *and* RALPH *at each other.* GEORGE *is suddenly embarrassed and says:*]

GEORGE: Well, I see yuh still got yuh dawg.
RALPH: Yeah, m'wife's folks are cat lovers.
GEORGE: You'll get your wife back tomorrow.
RALPH: Hell, I don't want her back.
GEORGE: Y'don't want 'er back?
RALPH: That's right.
GEORGE: Hell, in that case, you won't be able to beat 'er off with a stick, ha ha!

[*His laugh expires as he catches* ISABEL'*s outraged look.*]

Won't be able to beat her away from the door with a stick t'morrow . . .

[*They stare at each other brightly, with little chuckles, a constant series of little chuckles.* ISABEL *feels ignored.*]

ISABEL: I doubt that Mr Bates means it.
GEORGE: Didn't you all have a kid of some kind? I don't remember if it was a boy or a girl.
ISABEL: The toys under the tree might give you a clue as to that.
RALPH: Yeah, it's a boy, I guess. Drink?
GEORGE: You bet.

[GEORGE *goes to the bar and starts mixing drinks.*]

ISABEL: How old is your little boy?
RALPH: Three years old and she's awready made him a sissy.
GEORGE: They'll do it ev'ry time, man.

[*He keeps chuckling, as does* RALPH.]

RALPH: I didn't want this kind of a dawg, either. I wanted a Dobermann pinscher, a dawg with some guts, not a whiner! But she wanted a poodle and this flop-eared sad sack of a spaniel was a compromise which turned out to be worse'n a poodle, ha, ha! . . .

GEORGE: I'll bet yuh dollars to doughnuts your wife and kid'll be back here tomorrow.

RALPH [*in his slow drawl*]: They won't find me here if they do. I'm all packed to go. I would of been gone when you called but I'm waitin' t' git a call from a boy about t' git married. I want him to come over here an' make a cash offer on all this household stuff since I spent too much on Christmas and won't be around to collect my unemployment.

GEORGE: Come along with us. We got a big car out there an' we're as free as a breeze. Ain't that right, Little Bit?

ISABEL: Don't ask me what's right. I don't know! I *do* know, though, that couples with children don't separate at Christmas, and, George, let your friend work out his problems himself. You don't know the situation and don't have any right to interfere in it. And now will you please go get my little blue zipper bag for me? *Please?*

RALPH [*to* GEORGE, *as if she hadn't spoken*]: Naw, I'm just going out to the army airfield a couple miles down the highway and catch the first plane going west.

GEORGE: We'll talk about that.

ISABEL: *George!*

GEORGE: AW, HERE! I forgot to give you your present! After drivin' almost back into Memphis to find a liquor store open.

[*He extends a gift-wrapped magnum of champagne.*]

RALPH: Lover Jesus! Champagne?

GEORGE: Imported and already cold.

RALPH [*glancing briefly at* ISABEL]: Didn't I tell you that he was buyin' me something? She thought you'd deserted her, boy.

ISABEL: *All right, I'll get it myself! I'll go out and get it out of the car myself!*

[*She rushes out into snow, leaving the door open.*
GEORGE *closes the door without apparently noticing her exit.*]

GEORGE: Boy, you an' me have got a lot to talk over.

RALPH: We sure got lots of territory to cover.

GEORGE: So your goddam marriage has cracked up on yuh, has it?

RALPH: How's yours goin'? So far?

GEORGE: We'll talk about it *later*. Discuss it *thoroughly*! *Later*!

RALPH: Y' got married yestiddy mawnin'?

GEORGE: Yeah.

RALPH: How was last night?

GEORGE: We'll talk about *that* later, too.

[ISABEL *rushes into the room in outrage, panting.*]

ISABEL: *I* can't break the lock on that *car*!

GEORGE: Little Bit, I didn't know that you wuh bawn in a barn.

[*He means she left the door open again.*]

ISABEL: I didn't know a lot about you, either!

[GEORGE *closes door.*]

Mr Bates! Mr Bates!

[*He turns towards her with a vague smile.*]

The gentleman I married refuses to get my zipper bag out of the car or unlock the car so I can get it myself.

[*The phone rings.* RALPH *picks it up.*]

RALPH [*in a slow, hoarse drawl, at the phone*]: Aw, hi, Smokey. I'm glad you got my message. Look. I quit Regal Dairy Products and I'm flyin' out of here late tonight or early tomorrow morning and I thought maybe you might like to look over some of my stuff here, the household equipment, and make me a cash offer for it. I'll take less in cash than a cheque since I'm not gonna stop at the Coast, I'm flying straight through to Hong Kong so it would be difficult for me to cash yuh cheque an' of course I expect to make a sacrifice on the stuff here. Hey! Would you like a beaver-skin coat, sheared beaver-skin coat for Gertrude? Aw. I'd let you have if for a, for a – third off! Aw. Well, anyhow, come over right away, Smokey, and make me an offer in cash on as much of this household stuff as you figure that you could use when you git married. O.K.?

[*He hangs up.*]

GEORGE: Hong Kong?

RALPH: Yeah.

GEORGE: Well, how about that! Back to Miss Lotus Blossom in the Pavilion of Joys?

RALPH: I never had it so good. At least not *since*.

ISABEL [*acidly*]: Mr Bates, your character has changed since my gypsy husband appeared! He seems to have had an immediate influence on you, and not a good one. May I wash up in your bathroom?

[*They both look at her with slight, enigmatic smiles.*]

RALPH: What's that, honey?

ISABEL: Will you let me use your bathroom?

RALPH: Aw, sure, honey. I'm sorry you –

GEORGE: Now what's the matter with her?

[*He turns to* ISABEL.]

Now what's the matter with you?

ISABEL: May I talk to you alone? In another room?

RALPH: You all go in the bedroom and straighten things out.

[RALPH *goes out into the snow flurry.* GEORGE *leads* ISABEL *into next room.*]

GEORGE: Now what's the matter with you?

ISABEL: Is this a sample of how I'm going to be treated?

GEORGE: What do you mean? How have I treated you, huh?

ISABEL: I might as well not be present! For all the attention I have been paid since you and your buddy had this tender reunion!

GEORGE: Aren't you being a little unreasonable, honey?

ISABEL: I don't think so. George? If you are unhappy, our marriage can still be annulled. Y'know that, don't you?

GEORGE: You want to get *out* of it, do you?

[RALPH *comes back in with her travelling case. He sets it down and goes to the kitchenette.*]

ISABEL: I don't think it's really very unreasonable of me to want to be treated as if I LIVED! EXISTED!

GEORGE: Will you quit actin' like a spoiled little bitch? I want to tell you something. You're the first woman that ever put me down! Sleepin' las' night in a chair? What kind of basis is that for a happy marriage?

ISABEL: You had to get drunk on a highway! In a heaterless funeral car, after informing me you had just quit your job! Blasting my eardrums, afterwards, with a car radio you wouldn't let me turn down. How was I supposed to react to such kindness? Women are human beings and I am not an exception to that rule, I assure you! I HATED YOU LAST NIGHT AFTER YOU HAD BEEN HATING ME AND TORTURING ME ALL DAY LONG!

[RALPH *comes back into the front room.*]

GEORGE: Torturing you, did you say? WHY DON'T YOU SIMMER DOWN! We ain't ALONE here, y'know!

RALPH [*quietly, from the living room*]: You all are just goin' through a perfectly usual little period of adjustment. That's all it is, I told her –

GEORGE: Aw! You all have been talking?

ISABEL: What did you think we'd been doing while you were gone in that instrument of torture you have for a car?

GEORGE: You've got to simmer down to a lower boiling point, baby.

RALPH [*entering the bedroom*]: Just goin' through a period of adjustment . . .

ISABEL: Adjustment to what, Mr Bates? Humiliation? For the rest of my life? Well, I won't have it! I don't want such an 'adjustment'. I want to – May I –

[*She sobs.*]

– freshen up a little bit in your bathroom before we drive downtown? To check in at a hotel?

RALPH: Sure you can.

GEORGE: I ain't goin' downtown – or checkin' in no hotel.

[*He goes back into the living-room.*]

ISABEL: YOU may do as you *please*! *I'm* checking in a hotel.

RALPH [*offering her a glass*]: You never finished your drink.

ISABEL: I don't care to, thanks. Too many people think that liquor solves problems, all problems. I think all it does is *confuse* them!

RALPH: I would say that it – *obfuscates* them a little, but –

ISABEL: Does *what* to them, Mr Bates?

RALPH: I work crossword puzzles. I – ha ha! – pick up a lot of long words. Obfuscates means obscures. And problems need obfuscation now and then, honey. I don't mean total or permanent obfuscation, I just mean *temporary* obfuscation, that's all.

[*He is touched by the girl and he is standing close to her, still holding the glass out towards her. He has a fine, simple sweetness and gentleness when he's not 'bugged' by people.*]

D'ya always say *Mister* to men?

ISABEL: Yes, I do till I know them. I had an old-fashioned upbringing and I can't say I regret it. Yes.

[*She is still peering out of the door at her new husband.*]

RALPH: I wish you would say Ralph to me like you *know* me, honey. You got a tension between you, and tensions obfuscate love. Why don't you get that cross look off your face and give him a loving expression? Obfuscate his problems with a sweet smile on your face and –

ISABEL: YOU do that! I'm not in a mood to 'obfuscate' his problems. Mr Bates, I think he'd do better to face them like I'm facing mine, such as the problem of having married a man that seems to dislike me after one day of marriage.

RALPH: Finish this drink and obfuscate that problem because it doesn't exist.

[*He closes the bedroom door. As he comes back to* ISABEL *with the glass,* GEORGE *reopens the door between the two rooms, glares in for a moment and switches the overhead light on, then goes back into the parlour.* RALPH *smiles tolerantly at this show of distrust which is not justified.*]

ISABEL: You have a sweet little bedroom, Mr Bates.

RALPH: I married a *sweet, homely* woman. Almost started to *like* her. I can like *anybody*, but –

ISABEL: Mr Bates? Ralph? This house has a *sweetness* about it!

RALPH: You don't think it's 'tacky'?

ISABEL: No. I think it's – sweet!

RALPH: We got it cheap because this section of town is built right over a cavern.

ISABEL [*without listening*]: What?

RALPH: This High Point suburb is built over an underground cavern and is gradually sinking down in it. You see those cracks in the walls?

ISABEL: Oh . . .

[*She hasn't listened to him or looked.*]

Oh! My little blue bag. May I have it?

RALPH [*through the door*]: She wants a little blue bag.

GEORGE: *Here, give it to her, goddam it!*

[*He tosses the bag into the bedroom.* ISABEL *screams.* RALPH *catches the bag.*]

Now whatcha screamin' faw?

ISABEL: Thank heaven Mr Bates is such a good catch. All my colognes and perfumes are in that bag, including a twenty-five-dollar bottle of Vol-de-nuit. Mr Bates, will it be necessary for me to phone the hotel?

GEORGE: Didn't you hear what I said?

ISABEL: Mr Bates! Would you mind phoning some clean, inexpensive hotel to hold a room for us tonight?

GEORGE: I said I'm not gonna check in a hotel tonight!

ISABEL: Reserve a *single* room, please!

RALPH: Sure, sure, honey, I'll do that. Now you just rest an' fresh up an' – Come on, George, let her alone here now, so she can rest an' calm down.

[*He leads* GEORGE *back into the parlour.*]

GEORGE: Look at my hands! Willya look at my hands?

RALPH: What about your hands?

GEORGE: Remember that tremor? Which I had in Korea? Those shakes? Which started in Korea?

RALPH: Aw, is it come back on yuh?

GEORGE: Are you blind, man?

RALPH: Yeah. How's your drink?

GEORGE: She in the bathroom yet?

RALPH: Naw, she's still in the bedroom.

GEORGE: Wait'll she gits in the bathroom so we can talk.

RALPH: What's your drink, ole son?

GEORGE: Beer's fine. Jesus!

RALPH [*at the bar*]: Rough?

GEORGE: Just wait'll she gits in the bathroom so I can tell you about last night.

RALPH: Here.

[*He hands him a beer.*]

GEORGE [*at the bedroom door*]: She's still sittin' there bawling on that bed. Step outside a minute.

[*He goes to the front door and out on to the tiny paved porch. The interior dims as* RALPH *follows him out. For a while they just stand drinking beer with the snow shadows swarming about them.*]

RALPH: Chilly.

GEORGE: I don't feel chilly.

RALPH: *I* do.

[*He pauses.*]

You're not for that little lady in that damn silly little sissy mess of a bedroom!

GEORGE: What's wrong with the bedroom, it looked like a nice little bedroom.

RALPH: A bedroom is just as nice as whoever sleeps in it with you.

GEORGE: I missed that. What was that, now?

[*He rests an arm on Ralph's shoulders.*]

RALPH: How would you like ev'ry time you wint t'bed with your wife, you had to imagine on the bed in the dark that it wasn't her on it with you, in the dark with you, but any one of a list of a thousand or so lovely lays? I done a despicable thing. I married a girl that had no attraction for me excepting I felt sorry for her and her old man's money! I got what I should have gotten: nothing! Just a goddam desk job at Regal Dairy Products, one of her daddy's business operations in Memphis, at eight-five lousy rutten dollars a week! With my background? In the Air Force?

GEORGE: Man, an air record will cut you no ice on the ground. All it leaves you is a – mysterious tremor. Come on back in. I'm freezing to death out here. I'll git her into that bathroom so we can talk.

[*He tosses the beer cans into yard.*]

RALPH: Don't y'know better'n to throw beer cans in a man's front yard?

[*He says this vaguely, glumly, as he follows* GEORGE *back into the cottage and shuts the door behind them.* GEORGE *goes to bedroom.*]

GEORGE [*entering*]: Little Bit, you told me you couldn't wait to get under a good hot shower. There's a good shower in that bathroom. Why don't you go and get under that good hot shower?

ISABEL: I have a lot to think over, George.

GEORGE: Think it over under a good shower in that bathroom, will you? I want to take a bath, too.

ISABEL [*suddenly turning to face him from the bed*]: George, I feel so lonely!

GEORGE: Yeah, and whose fault is that?

ISABEL: I don't know why I suddenly felt so lonely!

[*She sobs again. He regards her coolly from the door.*]

GEORGE: Little Bit, go in the bathroom and take your shower, so I can go take mine, or do you want us to go in and take one together?

[*She rises with a sigh and goes to bathroom door.*]

Naw, I didn't think so.

[*She enters the bathroom. He waits till the shower starts, then returns to the front room.*]

There now, she's in!

[*He shakes both fists in the air with a grimace of torment.*]

Look! I got to get rid of that girl. I got to get rid of her quick. Jesus! You got to help me. I can't stay with that girl.

RALPH: Man, you're married to her.

GEORGE: You're married to one! Where's yours? You son of a tail gun! Don't tell me I'm married to her when we ain't exchanged five remarks with each other since we drove out of Cape Girardeau where she refused to – has she come out of the bathroom? No! – Even *undress*! But huddled up in a chair all night in a blanket, crying? Because she had the misfortune to be my wife?

RALPH: I wouldn't count on it.

GEORGE: On what?

RALPH: Her thinking it's such a misfortune.

GEORGE: I described to you how we passed the night, last night!

RALPH: Is this girl a virgin?

GEORGE: She is a *cast-iron* virgin! And's going to stay one! Determined!

RALPH: I wouldn't count on that.

GEORGE: I would. I count on it. First thing I do tomorrow is pack her on to a plane back to Saint Louie.

RALPH: You must have done something to shock her.

GEORGE: That's the truth, I tried to sleep with her.

RALPH: Maybe you handled the little lady too rough.

GEORGE: Now don't talk to me like a wise old man of the mountain about how to deal with a woman. Who was it had to make dates for who at Big Springs and who was it even had to make arrangements for you with those Tokyo dolls?

RALPH: That's not women, that's gash.

GEORGE: Gash are women.

RALPH: They are used women. You've got a unused woman and got to approach her as one.

GEORGE: She's gonna stay unused as far as I am concerned.

[*He stoops by the Christmas tree.*]

Now what the hell is this thing?

[*He has crouched among the toys under the tree.*]

RALPH: Rocket launcher. Miniature of the rocket-launchin' pad at Cape Canaveral.

GEORGE: No snow! How's it work?

RALPH: Gimme the countdown. I'll show you.

GEORGE: Ten. Nine. Eight. Seven. Six. Five. Four. Three. Two. Oww!

[*The rocket has fired in his face.*]

RALPH: Ain't you got sense enough to stand clear of a rocket launcher? Ha ha! Last week, just last week, I caught the little bugger playin' with a rag doll. Well, I snatched that doll away from him an' pitched it into the fireplace. He tried to pull it out an' burned his hand! Dotty called me a monster! The child screamed 'I hate you!' an' kicked my shins black an' blue! But I'll be damned if any son of Ralph Bates will grow up playin' with dolls. Why, I'll bet you he rides this hawss side-saddle! Naw, a sissy tendency in a boy's got to be nipped in the bud, otherwise the bud will blossom.

GEORGE: I would prefer to have a little girl.

[*He says this wistfully, still rubbing his bruised forehead.*]

Little girls prefer Daddy. Female instinct comes out early in them.

RALPH: I wanted a boy but I'm not sure I got one. However, I got him a real red-blooded boy's Christmas, at no small expense for a man in my income bracket!

[ISABEL *comes out of the bathroom.*]

I like the kid, I mean I – sure would suffer worse than he would if the neighbourhood gang called him 'Sissy!' I'm tolerant. By nature. But if I git partial custody of the kid, even one month in summer, I will correct the sissy tendency in him. Because in this world you got to be what your physical sex is or correct it in Denmark. I mean we got a *man's* world coming up, man! Technical! Terrific! And it's gotta be *fearless! Terrific!*

ISABEL: Mr Bates.

GEORGE [*on his way to the door*]: Whadaya want?

ISABEL: I called for Mistuh Bates.

GEORGE: Mistuh Bates, Mrs Haverstick is anxious to talk to you, suh.

ISABEL: I just want to know if you have called the hotel.

RALPH [*entering*]: Sure, sure, honey. Don't worry about a thing. Everything's gonna be fine.

ISABEL [*she is in a silk robe*]: Thanks, Ralph. You've been awf'ly kind to me. Oh! I helped myself to a little Pepto-Bismol I found in your sweet little bathroom.

RALPH: Aw, that pink stuff? Take it all. I never touch it. It's Dorothea's. She used to get acid stomach.

ISABEL: It's very soothing.

[GEORGE *crosses to the bedroom door, head cocked, somewhat suspicious.*]

RALPH: Well, I cured her of that. I doubt that she's hit that Pepto-Bismol bottle once in the last five years.

ISABEL: I rarely suffer from an upset stomach. Rarely as snow in Memphis!

[*She laughs lightly.*]

But the human stomach is an emotional barometer with some people. Some get headaches, others get upset stomachs.

RALPH: Some even git diarrhoea.

ISABEL: The combination of nervous strain and – Oh! What's this?

[*She picks up a gorgeously robed statue of the infant Jesus.*]

RALPH: Aw, that.

[*He moves farther into the bedroom.* GEORGE *moves closer to the door.*]

That's the Infant of Prague. Prague, Czechoslovakia?

ISABEL: Oh?

RALPH: It was discovered there in the ruins of an old monastery. It has miraculous properties.

ISABEL: Does it?

RALPH: They say that it does. Whoever gives you the Infant of Prague gives you a piece of money to put underneath it for luck. Her father presented this infant to Dorothea so the piece of money was *naturally one penny*. It's s'posed to give you prosperity if you're not prosperous and a child if you're childless. It give us a child but the money is yet to come in, the money's just been goin' out. However, I don't blame the Infant of Prague for that, because –

ISABEL: Mr Bates? Ralph? You know, very often people can be absolutely blind, stupid, and helpless about their own problems and still have a keen intuition about the problems of others?

RALPH: Yeah?

ISABEL: There is such a tender atmosphere in this sweet little house, especially this little bedroom, you can almost – touch it, feel it! I mean you can *breathe* the tender atmosphere in it!

RALPH [*in a slow, sad drawl*]: The colour scheme in this bedroom is battleship grey. And will you notice the cute inscriptions on the twin beds? 'His' on this one, 'Hers' on that one? The linen's marked his and hers, too. Well. The space between the two beds was no-man's-land for a while. Her psychological frigidity was like a, like a – artillery barrage! – between his and hers. I didn't try to break through it the first few nights. Nope. I said to myself, 'Let *her* make the first move.'

ISABEL: *Did she?*

RALPH: What do *you* think?

ISABEL: I think she *did*.

RALPH: *Right you are!*

[*He gives her a little congratulatory pat on the shoulder.*]

GEORGE: What's this heart-to-heart talk goin' on in here?

RALPH [*chuckling*]: Come on out of here, boy. I got something to tell you.

[*He leads* GEORGE *out.*]

GEORGE: What were you up to in there?

RALPH [*whispering loudly*]: Go in there, quick, before she gets dressed, you fool!

GEORGE: I'll be damned if I will!

RALPH: I'll turn the TV on loud.

ISABEL [*calling out*]: I'll be dressed in a jiffy!

RALPH: GO ON! You just got a jiffy!

GEORGE: Yeah, and I've got some pride, too. She put me down last night, first woman ever to put me down in –

RALPH: I know, you told me. GO IN! Lock the door and –

GEORGE: YOU go in! That's what you WANT to do! I never had a girl yet that you didn't want to take over. This time you're welcome. GO IN! GO BACK IN AND BREATHE THE TENDER ATMOSPHERE OF THAT –

RALPH: Gawge? Hey – You're *shakin'*, man, you're shakin' to pieces! What kind of a son-of-a-bitch d'you take me faw?

GEORGE: The kind which you are, which you always have been!

RALPH: She is right about you. You are not well, son . . .

GEORGE: Where d'ya git this 'son' stuff! Don't call me 'son'.

RALPH: Then grow up, will yuh! What's your drink? Same?

GEORGE: Same . . .

RALPH: You're shakin' because you want to go in that bedroom. GO IN! Take the bottle in with you! I'll sit here and watch TV till –

[ISABEL *has put on her travelling suit. She comes into the living-room.*]

Too late *now*!

ISABEL [*in a sweet Texas drawl*]: Mr Bates? Ralph? It breaks my heart to see all those lovely child's toys under the tree and the little boy not here to have his Christmas.

RALPH: He's with his mother.

ISABEL: I know, but his Christmas is here.

RALPH: He's a Mama's boy. He's better off with his Mama.

ISABEL: How are *you* feeling, now, George?

> [GEORGE *grunts and turns to the bar..*
> ISABEL *makes a despairing gesture to Ralph.*
> GEORGE *wheels about abruptly, suspecting some dumb-play.*
> ISABEL *laughs lightly and then sighs deeply.*]

GEORGE: I thought you'd set your heart on a single hotel room tonight.

ISABEL: George, you're shaking worse than I've ever seen you.

GEORGE: That's, that's not your problem, that's – *my* problem, not yours!

RALPH [*to Isabel*]: Honey? Come here a minute.

> [*He whispers something to her.*]

ISABEL: Oh, no. No! Mr Bates, you are confusing the function of a wife with that of a – I feel sorry, I feel very sorry for you not-so-young young men who've depended for love, for tenderness in your lives, on the sort of women available near army camps, in occupied territories! Mr Bates? Ralph?

RALPH: Just take his hand and lead him into the –

ISABEL: RALPH! NO! BELIEVE ME!

RALPH: All right . . .

> [*There is a pause.*]

ISABEL: Ralph, why did you quit YOUR job? Did you get the shakes, too?

GEORGE: Don't get bitchy with him.

ISABEL: I WASN'T BEING BITCHY!

RALPH: She wasn't being bitchy. She asked a logical question.

ISABEL: Just a question!

GEORGE: Can't you mind your own business for a change? You got fired too, don't forget! All three of us here is jobless!

ISABEL: I am not forgetting.

> [*Primly, with dignity.*]

I am not forgetting a thing, and I have a lot to remember.

GEORGE: Good. I hope you remember it. *Memorize* it!

[*He is getting tight.*]

ISABEL [*sniffing a little*]: I think I caught cold in that car.

GEORGE: Hell, you were born with a cold –

ISABEL: *Stop that!*

GEORGE: In your damn little –

ISABEL: MR BATES, MAKE HIM STOP

} *Overlapping, barely intelligible*

RALPH: Let him blow off some steam.

GEORGE: Incurable cold! You didn't catch it from me.

ISABEL: I wish you had shown this side of your nature before, just a hint, just a clue, so I'd have known what I was in for.

GEORGE: What hint did you give *me*? What clue did *I* have to *your* nature?

ISABEL: Did I disguise my nature?

GEORGE: You sure in hell did!

ISABEL: In what *way*, tell me, please!

GEORGE: You didn't put the freeze on me at Barnes Hospital!

[*To Ralph.*]

She was nurse at Barnes when I went there for those tests. To find out the cause of my shakes. She was my night nurse at Barnes.

ISABEL: Oh, stop! Don't be so crude! How can you be so crude!

GEORGE: She was my night nurse at Barnes and gave me alcohol rub-downs at bedtime.

ISABEL: That was my job. I had to.

GEORGE: Hell, she stroked and petted me with her hands like she had on a pair of silk gloves.

ISABEL: This is insufferable. I am going downtown.

[*She covers her face, sobbing.*]

Just give me carfare downtown.

GEORGE: You remember those dolls with silk gloves on their hands in Tokyo, Ralph? Hell, she could of given them Jap dolls lessons!

ISABEL: I DID NOT TOUCH YOUR BODY EXCEPT AS A NURSE HIRED TO DO IT! YOU KNOW I DIDN'T! I DID

NOT TOUCH YOUR BIG OLD LECHEROUS BODY.

GEORGE: How'd you give me a rubdown without touching my body? Huh? How could you give me rubdowns without touching my body? Huh?

ISABEL: Please, please, make him be still. Mr Bates? You believe me? He's making out I seduced him while I was his nurse.

GEORGE: I didn't say that. Don't say I said that. I didn't say that. I said you had soft little fingers and you knew what you were doing. She'd say, 'Turn over.' I couldn't turn over. I had to stay on my stomach. I was embarrassed not to.

ISABEL: Ah – I feel nauseated. What filth you have in your mind!

RALPH: Honey? Little lady? Come over and sit here with me. All this will all straighten out. It's going to be all straightened out.

[GEORGE *pours himself a drink. The glass slips out of his shaking fingers.*]

GEORGE: *Worse than ever, worse than ever before!* How could I have kept that job? A ground mechanic with hands that can't hold tools?

ISABEL: Go take your tranquillizers. They're in my zipper bag.

GEORGE: Oh, Jesus!

RALPH [*picking up the dropped glass*]: See, honey? That boy isn't well. Make some allowances for him. You're both nice kids, both of you, wonderful people. And very good-looking people. I'm afraid you're doomed to be happy for a long time together, soon as this little period of adjustment that you're going through right now passes over.

[GEORGE *holds his violently shaking hands in front of him, staring at them fiercely.*
He goes to the bedroom.]

ISABEL: May I call my father, collect?

RALPH: Don't call home, now. Why upset the old people on Christmas Eve?

ISABEL: I'll just say I miss them and want to come home for Christmas.

RALPH: They'll know something's wrong if you go home without your brand-new husband.

ISABEL: Husband! What husband? That man who describes me as a

Tokyo whore? Implies that I seduced him in a hospital because I
was required to give him alcohol rubdowns at night?

RALPH: All he meant was you excited him, honey.

ISABEL: I assure you that was *not* my intention! I am naturally gentle,
I am gentle by nature, and if my touch on his big lecherous body
created – *sexual fantasies* in his *mind*! – that's hardly my fault, is it?

GEORGE [*returning*]: I am sorry that I upset you.

ISABEL: Will you tell him the truth?

GEORGE: Sure I will. What about?

ISABEL: Did I deliberately excite you in Barnes Hospital?

GEORGE: No. I never said that.

ISABEL: Anybody that heard you would get that impression.

GEORGE: You didn't deliberately do it, you just did it because I was
horny for you, that's all, that's all, that's – all . . .

[*He slumps in a chair with a long, despairing sigh.
There is a silent pause.*]

ISABEL: I don't blame you alone, George. I blame myself, too. Not
for deliberate sexual provocation, but for not realizing before our
marriage yesterday that we were – opposite types.

GEORGE [*sadly*]: Yes, opposite types . . .

ISABEL: *I want to talk to my father!*

GEORGE: Talk to him. Call him. I'll pay Ralph the charges.

ISABEL: May I?

RALPH: Sure, honey, call your folks and wish 'em a Merry Christmas.

ISABEL: Thank you. I will if I can stop crying.

RALPH: George? This little girl needs you. Go on, be nice to her, boy.

GEORGE: I need somebody, too. She hasn't got the incurable shakes,
I have, *I* got 'em! Was *she* nice to *me*? *Last night*?

ISABEL [*tearfully*]: Operator? I want to call long distance, Sweetwater,
Texas. Oh-seven-oh-three. No, anybody that answers. It will be
Daddy, Mama can't get out of –

[*She sobs.*]

– bed!

[RALPH *makes a sign to George to go over and sit by her.*
GEORGE *disregards the suggestion.*]

RALPH: You better hang up and let them call you back. Long distance
is very busy on Christmas Eve. Everyone callin' the home folks.

ISABEL: I just hope I stop crying! I don't want Daddy to hear me.

[*She pauses.*]

Poor ole thing. So sweet and faithful to Mama, bedridden with
arthritis for seven years, now . . . Hello? What? Oh. You'll call me
back when you complete the connection, will you, because it's
very important, it's really very urgent . . .

[*She hangs up. There is silence.*]

RALPH [*finally*]: One bad night in a rutten highway motel and you all
are acting like born enemies towards each other!

GEORGE: Don't upset her, she's going to talk to her daddy. And tell
him she's married to a stinker.

ISABEL: No, I'm not. I'm going to tell him that I am blissfully happy,
married to the kindest man in the world, the second kindest man
next to my daddy!

GEORGE: Thanks.

ISABEL: Waits hand and foot on Mama, bedridden with arthritis.

GEORGE: You told Ralph about that.

ISABEL: And has held down a job in a pharmacy all these years . . .

GEORGE: Wonderful. I didn't expect to marry a girl in love with her
father.

ISABEL: George Haverstick, you are truly a monster!

[*The phone rings.*
She snatches it up.]

What? – DAD! OH, PRECIOUS DADDY!

[*She bursts into violent tears.*]

Can't talk, can't talk, can't talk, can't talk, *can't – talk!*

RALPH: Honey, gi' me the phone!

[*She surrenders it to him.*]

Hello? Hi, Pop, Merry Christmas. No, this isn't George, this is a buddy of his. Isabel wants to talk to you to tell you how happy she is, but she just broke up with emotion. You know how it is, don't you, Pop? Newlyweds? They're naturally full of emotion. They got to go through a little period of adjustment between them – Fine, yes, she's fine. She'll talk to you soon as she blows her nose. Hey, honey? Your daddy wants to talk to you.

[*She takes the phone, then bursts into violent sobbing again, covering her mouth and handing the phone back to* RALPH.]

Pop? I'll have to talk for her. She's all shook up.

[*He forces the phone back into* ISABEL'*s hand.*]

ISABEL [*choked*]: Dad?

[*She bawls again, covering the mouthpiece.* RALPH *takes the phone back from her.*]

RALPH: Pop? Just talk to her, Pop. She's too shook up to talk back.

[*He forces the phone into her hands again.*]

ISABEL: Dad? How are you, Daddy? Are you? That's wonderful, Daddy. Oh, I'm fine, too. I got married yesterday. Yesterday . . . How is Mom? Just the same? Daddy? I may be seeing you soon. Yes. You know I gave up my nursing job at Barnes when I married and so I have lots of free time and I might just suddenly pop in on you – *tomorrow!* – I love you and miss you so much! Good-bye, Merry Christmas, Daddy!

[*She hangs up blindly and goes over to the Christmas tree.*]

I think it's awful your little boy's missing his Christmas. Such a wonderful Christmas. A choo-choo train with depot and tunnel, cowboy outfit, chemical set and a set of alphabet blocks . . .

GEORGE: He knows what he got for his kid, you don't have to tell him.

[*There is a pause.*]

ISABEL: Well, now, I feel better, after talking to Daddy.

GEORGE: Does it make you feel uplifted, spiritually?

ISABEL: I feel less lonely. That's all.

GEORGE: I wonder if it would have that effect on me if I called my daddy or mama in Amarillo? That's in Texas, too. Maybe I'd feel less lonely. Huh, Little Bit?

[*She starts out.*]

Just wait a minute. I want to tell you something. In my thirty-four years I've been with a fair share of women and you are the first, you are the first of the lot, that has found me repulsive.

ISABEL: I don't find you 'repulsive', not even your vanity, George, silly but not repulsive.

RALPH: Hey, now, you all quit this.

GEORGE: Can you stand there and tell me you find me attractive?

ISABEL: I'm afraid I can't, at this moment.

GEORGE: Well, goddam it, what in hell did you marry me faw?

ISABEL: Mr Bates, your animal is standing by the door as if it wants out. Shall I let it out for you?

RALPH: You two are just goin' through this adjustment period that all young couples go through.

ISABEL: Such a sweet animal! What is this animal's name?

GEORGE: The animal is a dog.

ISABEL: I know it's a dog.

GEORGE: Then why don't you call it a dog!

RALPH: Better put 'er lead on 'er. Her name is Bess.

ISABEL: Shall we take a walk, Bessie? Huh? A nice little run in the snow. See! She does want out. Oh! My coat . . .

RALPH: Here, put on this one, honey.

[*He takes the beaver coat out of the Christmas box under the tree.*]

ISABEL: Oh, what beautiful sheared beaver! It's your wife's Christmas present?

RALPH: It was but it ain't no more.

ISABEL: How soft! Now I know that you love her. You couldn't feel the softness of this fur and not know it was bought as a present for someone you love.

RALPH: Put it on. It's yours. A wedding present to you.

ISABEL: Oh, no I –

RALPH: WILL YOU PLEASE PUT IT ON YUH?

ISABEL: I guess the snow won't hurt it. Come on, Bessie, that's a good lady, come on . . .

[*She goes out.*]

GEORGE: I know of *two* animals that want out and one of them ain't no dawg!

ISABEL [*returning*]: I heard you say that!

GEORGE: Well, good.

ISABEL: If you want out of our marriage, a divorce isn't necessary. We can just get an annulment! So maybe last night was fortunate after all!

[*She stares at him a moment and then goes back out with the dog. As they leave, the dog is barking at something outside.*
GEORGE comes up beside Ralph and rests an affectionate arm on his shoulders.
The tempo now becomes very fast.]

RALPH: You old Texas jack rabbit!

GEORGE: You tail-gunner son of a – How you feel?

RALPH: I feel fine!

[*They chuckle shyly together. Then:*
They catch each other in an affectionate bear hug.]

GEORGE: How much money you got?

RALPH: Why?

GEORGE: Remember how we talked about going into something together when we got out of the service? Well, we're out of the service. How much money do you think you can raise?

RALPH: What are *your* assets, Buddy?

GEORGE: I've saved five hundred dollars and can get a thousand for that '52 Caddy.

RALPH: You can't go into no business on as little as that.

GEORGE: You're selling out this house and everything in it, ain't you?

RALPH: I'd have to split it with Dorothea, I reckon.

GEORGE: Look. Let's cut out tomorrow. Let's go to Texas together.

We can swing the financing to pick up a piece of ranchland near San Antone and raise us a herd of fine cattle.

RALPH: Why San Antone?

GEORGE: I said near it. It's a beautiful town. A winding river goes through it.

RALPH: Uh-huh. You mentioned 'swing the financing'. How did you – visualize – that?

GEORGE: Noticed my car out there?

RALPH: That funeral limousine?

GEORGE: We cut out of here tomorrow bright and early and drive straight through to West Texas. In West Texas we git us a col-oured boy, put a showfer's cap on him an' set him back of the wheel. He drives us up in front of the biggest San Antone bank and there we demand an immediate interview with the presi-dent of it. My folks staked out West Texas. The name of the first George Haverstick in West Texas is engraved on the memo-rial tablet to the Alamo heroes in San Antone! I'm not snowin' you, man! An' they's no better credit card in West Texas than an ancestor's name on that memorial tablet. We will arrive at lunch time an' – invite this bank executive to lunch at the San Antone country club to which I can git us a guest card an' befo' we're in sight of the golf links the financing deal will be swung!

RALPH: Man, a bank president has rode in a awful lot of funeral pro-cessions. It's almost one of his main professional duties. He's rode in too many funeral limousines not to know when he's in one. And ain't you afraid that he might, well – notice your shakes?

GEORGE: This little tremor would disappear completely the moment I crossed into Texas!

RALPH: I hope so, man, permanently and completely, but –

GEORGE: Go on. Tear down the project!

RALPH: There's no Ralph Bates, first, second, third, fourth or fifth on that memorial tablet to those – Alamo heroes.

GEORGE: Haven't you blazoned your name in the memory of two wars?

RALPH: Who remembers two wars? Or even one, after some years. There's a great public amnesia about a former war hero.

[*He goes reflectively to the front door.*]

GEORGE: Where you goin'?

RALPH: I'm goin' out to think in this cool night air.

[*He exits on to the paved terrace, switching off the interior lights.* GEORGE *follows gravely.* RALPH *stoops to light up a string of coloured bulbs that cover the arched entrance to the carport.*
It casts a dim rainbow glow on the terrace. Shadowy flakes of snow drift through it.]

Why San Antone? Why cattle? Why not electric equipment?

GEORGE: I know San Antone and cattle!

RALPH: And I know electric equipment.

GEORGE: Yes, you can turn on a set of little Christmas tree lights.

RALPH: I don't want to be your ranch hand!

GEORGE: We'd buy in *equal*.

RALPH: How? One minute you say you'll liquidate all your assets that only appear to be an old funeral car, the next you say we'll drive a bank president out in this funeral car, and you want me to put up all that I realize on the sale of this property here? Your sense of equity is very unequal, and shit-fire anyhow, even if I sell this property, by remote control, from Hong Kong, and Dotty's folks would sure in hell block the transaction – well, look at the cracks in this stucco, y'know how they got there? This goddam High Point suburb – *listen!* – happens to be built over a great big underground cavern into which it is *sinking*!

GEORGE: *Sinking?*

RALPH: I'm not snowing you, man, this whole community here is gradually sinking, inch by inch by year, into this subterranean cavern and the property owners and the real-estate promoters are in collusion to keep this secret about it: so we can sell out to the next bunch of suckers: DISGUSTING!

GEORGE: Built over a –

RALPH: *Cavern: yes*! – *a big subterranean cavern*, but so is *your* project, not to mention your *marriage. Cattle! – Cattle?*

GEORGE: The Texas Longhorn isn't just cattle, it's a – dignified beast.

RALPH: Did you say Texas Longhorn? Son, the Texas Longhorn is not only dignified, it is *obsolete*.

GEORGE: Historical, yeah, like the Haversticks of West Texas.

RALPH: The Haversticks of West Texas are not yet obsolete, are they?

GEORGE: I am the last one of 'em an' the prospects of another don't look bright at this moment. But the Texas Longhorn –

[*He exhales.*]

– compared to modern beef cattle such as your Hereford or your Black Angus – it has no carcass value.

RALPH: Well, in that case, why don't you *breed* the Black Angus or the –

GEORGE: I anticipated that question.

RALPH: I hope you're prepared with some answer . . .

GEORGE [*draws on cigarette and flips it away*]: Le' me put it this way. How would you like to breed a herd of noble cattle, a herd that stood for the frontier days of this country! – an' ride to the depot one mawnin' in your station wagon, the name of your ranch stamped on it, to watch these great, dignified beasts being herded on to a string of flatcars, penned in and hauled off to K City packin' houses, Chicago slaughterhouses, the shockin' atrocities which cannot even be thought about without a shudder! – an' wave 'em good-bye as if they was off for a mother-lovin' church picnic?

RALPH: It's a – heart-breakin' pitcher!

[*He chuckles.*]

But I do love a good steak, ha ha! A prime-cut sirloin, however – What would you want to breed this noble herd for? For *kicks*, for –?

GEORGE: *You* got TV in there, ain't you? Turn on your TV any late afternoon or early evenin' and what do you get – beside the commercials, I mean? A goddam Western, on film. Y'know what I see, outside the camera range? A big painted sign that says 'Haverstick-Bates Ranch' – or 'Bates-Haverstick', you can have top billing! – 'The Last Stand of the Texas Longhorn, a Dignified Beast! We breed cattle for TV Westerns.' We breed us some buffalo, too. The buffalo is also a dignified beast, almost extinct, only thirty thousand head of the buffalo left in this land. We'll increase that number by a sizeable fraction. Hell, we could double that number befo' we –

RALPH: Hang up our boots an' saddles under the – dignified sky of West Texas?

GEORGE [*with feeling*]: There *is* dignity in that sky! There's dignity in the agrarian, the pastoral – way of – existence! A dignity too long lost out of the – American dream –

[*He is shaking a good deal with emotion.*]

– as it used to be in the West Texas-Haverstick days . . .

RALPH: But I want to be dignified, too.

GEORGE: Human dignity's what I'm –

RALPH: I don't want to be caught short by a Texas Longhorn while crossing a pasture one mawnin' in West Texas! Ha ha ha! Naw, I don't want to catch me an ass full of Texas Longhorns before I can jump a fence rail out of that West Texas pasture. I –

GEORGE: SHUT UP! WILL YUH? YOU TV WATCHIN', CANNED-BEER DRINKIN', SPANISH-SUBURBAN-STUCCO-TYPE SON OF – Y'KNOW I THINK BEER IS DOPED? I THINK THEY DOPE IT TO CREATE A NATIONAL TOLERANCE OF THE TV COMMERCIAL! No – No – I'm sorry I come through Memphis . . .

[*He moves away, sadly.*]

I cherished a memory of you –

[CAROLLERS *are heard from a distance.*]

– idolized an old picture of which I was suddenly faced with a, with a – *goddam travesty* of it! – When you opened the door and I was confronted with a – DEFEATED! MIDDLE-AGED! NEGATIVE! LOST! – poor bastard . . .

RALPH: What do you think I saw when I opened that door? A ghostly apparition!

GEORGE: ME?

RALPH: A young man I used to know with an old man's affliction: the palsy!

GEORGE: Thanks! – I appreciate that.

[*Next door the* CAROLLERS *sing: 'God Rest Ye Merry, Gentlemen, May Nothing Ye Dismay!'*]

Oh, man, oh brother, I sure do appreciate that!

[*He sits down quickly, shaking fiercely, in a metal porch chair, turning it away from Ralph to face the audience.* RALPH *is immediately and truly contrite.*]

Yeah. In addition to those other changes I mentioned in you, you've now exposed another which is the worst of the bunch. You've turned *vicious!*

RALPH: Aw, now –

GEORGE: Yeah, yeah, bitter and vicious! To ridicule an affliction like mine, like *this*, is vicious, *vicious!*

[*He holds up his shaky hand.* RALPH *reaches his hand out to take it but doesn't. Instead he drops his hand on George's shoulder.*]

Take that mother-grabbin' hand off my shoulder or I'll break it off you!

RALPH: You ridiculed *my* afflictions.

GEORGE: What afflictions?

RALPH: My life has been an affliction.

[*He says this without self-pity, simply as a matter of fact.*]

GEORGE: Now don't make me cry into this can of Budweiser with that sad story of your childhood in that home for illegitimate orphans.

RALPH: *Foundlings!* Home. I was not illegitimate.

GEORGE: Foundlings are illegitimate.

RALPH: Not – *necessarily* – *always* . . .

> [*He says this with a humility that might be touching to anyone less absorbed in his own problems than George.* RALPH *looks up at the drift of snow from the dark.*]

No, I meant to live a life in a Spanish-type stucco cottage in a – high point over a cavern, that is an affliction for someone that wanted and dreamed of – *oh, I wish I could be the first man in a moon rocket!* No, not the moon, but Mars, Venus! Hell, I'd like to be transported and transplanted to colonize and fertilize, to be the Adam on a – star in a different *galaxy*, yeah, that far away even! – It's wonderful knowing that such a thing is no longer inconceivable, huh?

GEORGE: You're talking out of character. You're a dedicated conformist, the most earthbound earth man on earth.

RALPH: If you think that about me, you never known me.

GEORGE [*starts off the terrace*]: I'm going walking, alone!

> [*He stops abruptly.*]

Naw, if she sees me walking, she'll think I'm out looking for her.

RALPH: Goddam it, why don't you? Intercept her and don't say a word, just stick your hand inside that beaver-skin coat I give her and apply a little soft pressure to her – solar plexus – putting your other arm around her waist, and bring her back here, gently . . .

GEORGE: That's what *you* want to do. Go on, *you* intercept her! And bring her back here gently!

RALPH: O.K., I *would* like to do it. But do you think I'd *do* it?

GEORGE: Can you honestly say you wouldn't put the make on her if you thought she'd give in?

RALPH: Nope! I wouldn't do it. And if you don't believe me, git back in that funeral hack and drive to West Texas in it, you – *legitimate* bastard.

GEORGE: Nope, I don't think you would. You're too much of a square.

RALPH: *There's her! There she is!*

GEORGE: Where?

RALPH: Corner. Why's she turning around? She must be lost, go get her. Look. She's joining the carollers!

GEORGE: Good, let her stay with them, and sing! Carols!

RALPH: Naw, I better go get her.

GEORGE: Go and get your *own* wife: leave mine alone!

[RALPH *puts his arm around George's shoulder.*]

And I told you to keep your rutten hand off my shoulder.

RALPH: Break it off me.

GEORGE: What I mean is, the point is – you *chose* your afflictions! Married into them. Mine I didn't choose! It just come on me, mysteriously: my shakes. You wouldn't even be interested in the awful implications of an affliction like mine.

[*He holds up his shaking hand.*]

RALPH: Sure, I'm interested in it, but –

GEORGE: S'pose it never lets up? This thing they can't treat or even find the cause of! S'pose I shake all my life like, like – dice in a crap shooter's fist? – Huh? – I mean at all moments of tension, all times of crisis, I shake! . . . Huh? And there's other aspects to it beside the career side. It could affect my love life. Huh? I could start shaking so hard when I started to make out with a girl that I couldn't do it. You know? Couldn't make the scene with her . . .

[*There is a slight pause.*]

RALPH: Aw. Was that it?

GEORGE: Was what what?

RALPH: Was that the trouble at the Old Man River Motel, last night, you were scared of impotence with her? Was that the problem?

GEORGE: I don't have that problem. I *never* had that problem.

RALPH: No?

GEORGE: *No!*

[*Tense pause.*]

WHY? Do *you* have that problem?

145

RALPH: Sometimes. I wasn't excited enough by Dotty to satisfy her, sometimes . . .

GEORGE: The thought of her old man's money couldn't always excite you?

RALPH: Nope, it couldn't always, that's the truth.

[*He switches off the lights, senselessly, and switches them back on again.*]

Poor ole Dotty. She's got so she always wants it and when I can't give it to her I feel guilty, guilty . . .

[*He turns the Christmas lights off again, turns them back on again.*]

GEORGE: Well, you know *me*. An Eveready battery, built-in in me.

RALPH [*turning to him with a slow, gentle smile*]: Yeah, I understand, son.

GEORGE: *Don't be so damned understanding!*

RALPH: Well, there she goes – Mrs George Haverstick the Fifth. Look. She's going up to the wrong Spanish-type stucco cottage, there's five almost identical ones in this block.

GEORGE: Don't your dawg know where it lives?

RALPH: Aw, it's a dignified beast. A constant Frigidaire pointer. Points at the Westinghouse Frij an' whines for a handout whenever you enter the kitchen. Knows everyone on the block an' pays calls like a new preacher wherever he thinks –

[*Whistles at dog.*]

– he might be offered a –

[*Whistles.*]

– handout.

[VOICES *down the block, hearty, drunken.*]

You better go git your wife. That Spanish-type stucco cottage is occupied by a bachelor decorator and you know how they destroy wimmen . . . He is running a sort of a unofficial USO at his house. Service men congregate there.

GEORGE: HAH!

[*He is amused by the picture.*]

RALPH: I got to climb back in a back window because you shut this door and I had put the catch on it.

[*He crosses out the door to the carport as* GEORGE *gazes gravely off.*

The CAROLLERS *are closer. They go into 'God Rest Ye Merry, Gentlemen' again.*

GEORGE *is not inclined to be merry. He glares into the starless air. In the bedroom, a windowpane is smashed and* RALPH's *arm reaches through, his fingers groping for the window latch. He finds it, gets the window up and clambers through with some muttered invectives against the hostility of the inanimate objects of the world. As soon as he enters the interior, light and sound inside are brought up. Oddly enough, a TV Western is in progress, approaching the climax of an Indian attack or a cattle stampede. It catches* RALPH's *attention. He turns gravely to the TV set, for the moment forgetting* GEORGE *outside. Gunfire subsides and the dialogue is brought up loud:*]

DIALOGUE

– Save your ammunition, they'll come back.
– HOW LONG HAVE WE GOT?
– Till sundown. They'll hit us again after dark.
– Let's make a run for it now!
– We'll have to abandon the wagons if we make a run for it. The Rio Grande is at least five miles south of here.
– Mount the women, one woman behind each man on the hawses, unhitch the hawses! Then stampede the cattle. That'll give us a cover while we make our break.
– What is our chances, you think?
– You want a *honest* answer or a *comforting* answer?
– Give me the honest answer.

– The comforting answer would have been fifty-fifty: I'll leave you to imagine the honest answer.

– Rosemary? Come here, a minute. Take this pistol. There's five shots in it. Save the fifth shot for yourself. Now git on this hawss behind me.

– Oh, Buck! I'm so scared!

– *Git up!* O.K. sweetheart?

– Yes!

– Hold on to me tight. Dusty, when I count ten, start the cattle stampede.

[*He starts counting, slowly.*]

GEORGE [*to himself as he paces the terrace*]: Now I don't even want her. If she asked me for it, I wouldn't give it to her, the way I feel now.

[*Sneezes.*]

Catchin' a cold out here! What's he doing in there, the motherless bastard? BATES! REMEMBER ME?

RALPH [*opening the door*]: I thought you'd gone faw your wife.

[RALPH *chuckles and holds the front door open as* GEORGE *withdraws his head from the window and reappears a moment later on the terrace.* RALPH *lets him in.*]

GEORGE: Will you look at that? A Western on Christmas Eve, even! It's a goddam NATIONAL OBSESSION.

RALPH: Yep, a national homesickness in the American heart for the old wild frontiers with the yelping redskin and the covered wagons on fire and –

GEORGE: Will you look at those miserable shorthorn cattle! Those cows, in this corny Western?

[*They both face the TV. There is a pause.*]

RALPH: Yep – an undignified beast. Man? Buddy? I don't have too much confidence in the project of the Dignified West Texas Longhorn Ranch, even now, but I will go along with you. Don't ask me why. I couldn't tell you why, but I will go along with you. Want to shake on it, Buddy?

GEORGE: That champagne ought to be cold now, let's break out that champagne now.

RALPH: It'll be still colder when you've picked up your wife.

GEORGE: I told you my policy, don't interfere with it, huh?

RALPH: Women are vulnerable creatures.

GEORGE: So's a man.

RALPH [*crosses to the kitchenette door*]: I'll open up the champagne while you pick up your wife.

GEORGE: Ralpho? Man?

RALPH: Huh?

GEORGE: Now I know why I come here. You're a *decent square*!

[*The kitchen door swings closed on them;* CAROLLERS *are singing out front. After a moment* ISABEL *appears before the house with the dog. A* LADY CAROLLER *appears on the terrace with a collection plate.*]

ISABEL: Oh – I'm afraid I don't have any money to give you, but –

[*She knocks at the door.*]

Wait! – till they answer the door, I –

[*Raucous voices are heard within.*]

– Some people regard the celebration of the birthday of Jesus as a, as a – sort of a – occasion, excuse for! – just getting drunk and – *disgusting*! I'll probably have to go round the back to get in . . .

[*Great howls of hilarity have been coming from the back of the cottage, drowning out* ISABEL*'s efforts to draw attention to the front door.*]

I'm very sorry, I just don't have any money.

[*The* CAROLLER *accepts this in good grace and leaves.*
ISABEL *goes around through the carport. A few seconds later* GEORGE, *in a state of Wild West exuberance, comes charging out of the kitchen with the champagne bottle, shouting:*]

GEORGE: POWDER RIVER, POWWWWW-der RIV-errrr! – a mile wide and –

RALPH: TWO INCHES DEEP!

[*He follows him out as* ISABEL*'s head appears through the open window in the dim bedroom; she lifts the dog through and hoists herself over the sill.*]

GEORGE: Git me a pitcher with ice and two cans of that Ballantine's ale and I will make us BLACK VELVET!
RALPH: Huh?
GEORGE: Man, you know Black Velvet!

[*He is back in the kitchen.*]

I made it that time in Hong Kong when we had those girls from the –

[RALPH *has gone in behind him. The door swings shut as* ISABEL *picks up the bedside phone in the bedroom.*]

ISABEL: Operator? I want a cab right away, it's an *emergency, yaiss!*

[*Slight pause.*]

Yellow Cab? Checkered! Well, please send a cab right away to – Oh, my goodness, I can't tell you the address, oh, I'll – I'll find out the address and I'll call you right back, right away . . .

[*She hangs up with a little stricken cry, followed by convulsive sobs that she stifles forcibly. On the bed, in the pink-shaded lamplight, she looks like a little girl making a first discovery of life's sorrow. Instinctively she reaches out for the Infant of Prague; at the same time, the* CAROLLERS *start singing below the terrace: 'I Wonder as I Wander'. This is a sentimental moment, but not 'sticky'.*]

Little Boy Jesus, so lonesome on your birthday. I know how you feel, *exactly!* –

[*She clasps the infant to her breast, tenderly.*]

– just exactly, because I feel the same way . . .

DIM OUT

Act Three

No time lapse.

> [*The men return with an open, foaming bottle of champagne, and pass it back and forth between them before the fireplace, not noticing that the dog has returned or suspecting* ISABEL's *presence in the bedroom.*]

GEORGE: I put them in five categories. Those that worship it, those that love it, those that just like it, those that don't like it, those that just tolerate it, those that *don't* tolerate it, those that can't stand it; and, finally, those that not only can't stand it but want to cut it off you.

RALPH [*following him with glasses, chuckling*]: That's more than five categories.

GEORGE: How many did I name?

RALPH: I don't know. I lost count.

GEORGE: Well, you know what I mean. And I have married into that last category. What scares me is that she has had hospital training and is probably able to do a pretty good cutting job. You know what I mean?

RALPH: Ha, ha, yeah. Wel-l-l . . .

> [*He sets the glasses down and takes the bottle from* GEORGE. *The little parlour is flickering with firelight.*]

GEORGE: Which class did you marry into? Into the same category?

RALPH: No. She got to like it. More than I did even.

GEORGE: Now you're braggin'.

RALPH: Love is a very difficult – occupation. You got to work at it, man. It ain't a thing every Tom, Dick and Harry has got a true aptitude for. Y'know what I mean? Not every Tom, Dick or Harry understands how to use it. It's not a – offensive weapon. It shouldn't be used like one. Too many guys, they use it like a offensive weapon to beat down a woman with. All right. That rouses resistance. Because a woman has pride, even a woman has pride and resents being raped, and most love-making is rape with these self-regarded – experts! That come downstairs yelling, 'Oh man, oh, brother!', and hitching their belts up like they'd accomplished something.

GEORGE [*getting the allusion and resentful*]: You mean me?

RALPH: Naw, naw, will yuh listen a minute? I've got ideas on this subject.

GEORGE: A self-regarded expert!

RALPH: You know goddam right I'm an expert. I know I never had your good looks but made out better.

GEORGE: One man's opinion!

RALPH: Look! Lissen! You got to use – TENDERNESS! – with it, not roughness like raping, snatch-and-grab roughness but true tenderness with it or –

GEORGE: O.K., build yourself up! If that's what you need to!

RALPH: Naw, now, lissen! You know I know what I'm sayin'!

GEORGE: Sure, self-regarded expert!

[*They are both pretty high now.*]

RALPH: I know what went wrong last night at that Cape Girardeau motel as well as if I had seen it all on TV!

GEORGE: What went wrong is that I found myself hitched up with a woman in the 'cut-it-off' category!

[ISABEL *is listening to all this in the bedroom. She stands up and sits down, stands up and sits down, barely able to keep from shouting something.*]

RALPH: Aw, naw, aw, naw. I will tell you what happened. Drink your champagne. What happened, man, is this! You didn't appreciate the natural need for using some tenderness with it. Lacking confidence with it, you wanted to hit her, smash her, clobber her with it. You've got violence in you! That's what made you such a good fighter pilot, the best there was! Sexual violence, that's what gives you the shakes, that's what makes you unstable. That's what made you just sit on the straw mats with the Tokyo dolls, drinking saké with them, teaching them English till it was time to come downstairs and holler, 'Oh, man, oh, brother!' like you had laid them to waste!

[*There is a slight pause.* GEORGE *is sweating, flushed.*]

GEORGE: Who in hell ever told you I –
RALPH: I heard it directly from them. You just sat up there drinkin' saké with 'em an' teachin' 'em English, and then you'd come down shouting, 'Oh, man, oh, brother!' like you had laid 'em to waste.
GEORGE: Which of them told you this story?
RALPH: *Which* of them? ALL! EV'RY ONE!

[*They pause.* ISABEL *sits down on the bed again, raises her hands to either side of her face, slowly shaking her head with a gradual comprehension.*]

GEORGE: Man, at this moment I'd like to bust your face in!
RALPH: I'm tryin' to help you. Don't you know that I am tryin' t' help you?

[*A pause. They look away from each other in solemn reverie for some moments.* ISABEL *rises again from the bed but still doesn't move. After some moments she sits back down. She is crying now.*
RALPH, *continuing gently:*]

You have got this problem.
GEORGE: In Tokyo I never told you –
RALPH: What?
GEORGE: I was choosy. I had a girl on the side. I mean a nice one. One that I wanted to keep to myself, strictly. I didn't want to expose her to a bunch of –
RALPH: Aw, now, man, you don't have to start fabricating some kind of a *Sayonara* fantasy like this!

GEORGE: How about Big Springs, Texas?

RALPH: What about Big Springs, Texas, besides being boring, I mean, what *else* about it?

GEORGE: Plenty. I fixed you up there. You never got nowhere in Big Springs, Texas, till I opened it up for you.

RALPH: Baby, don't be sore.

GEORGE: Sore, I'm not sore. You've done your damnedest to make me feel like a phoney, but I'm not sore. *You're* sore. Not *me*. I'm not sore.

RALPH: You sure are shaking.

GEORGE: Yeah, well, I got this tremor . . . Jesus, my goddam voice is got the shakes too! But you know it's the truth, in Big Springs, Texas, we had the best damn' time you ever had in your life, and I broke the ice there, for you.

RALPH: I don't deny that women naturally like you. Everybody likes you! Don't you know that? People never low-rate you! Don't you know that? I like you. That's for sure. But I hate to see you shaking because of –

GEORGE [*cutting in*]: Look! We're both free now. Like two birds. You're gonna cut out of this High Point over a Cavern. And we'll buy us a piece of ranchland near San Antone and both of us –

RALPH: Yeah, yeah, let's go back to what we wuh tawkin' about. *Tenderness*. With a *woman*.

GEORGE: I don't want to hear a goddam lecture from you about such a thing as that when here you are, night before Christmas, with just a cocker spaniel and presents under a tree, with no one to *take* them from you!

RALPH [*abruptly*]: *Hey!*

GEORGE: *Huh?*

RALPH: Th' *dawg* is back. How *come?*

GEORGE: The dawg come *back*, tha's all . . .

[ISABEL *comes out of the bedroom in coat and hat.*]

ISABEL: Yes, I brought the dog back.

[*A pause, rather long.*]

RALPH: We, uh, we – saw you going up to the wrong – Spanish-type cottage . . .

ISABEL: I haven't discovered the *right* one, Mr Bates.

RALPH: I ain't discovered it either.

GEORGE: What kept you so long in the wrong one?

ISABEL: They invited me in and made me sit down to a lovely buffet supper while they looked up the High Point Bates in the phone book.

[*She pauses.*]

I heard your very enlightening conversation from the bedroom. You're a pair of small boys. Boasting, bragging, showing off to each other . . . I want to call a cab. I'm going downtown, George.

[*He crosses unsteadily to the phone, lifts it and hands it to her with an effort at stateliness.*]

Thank you.

[*To* RALPH.]

Do you know the cab number?

GEORGE: Whacha want, yellow, checkered or what? I'll git it for yuh!

RALPH: Put down th' phone.

ISABEL: I'll get one.

[*She dials the operator.*]

GEORGE: Leave her alone. Let her go downtown. She's free to.

[RALPH *takes the phone from her and puts it back in the cradle.*]

ISABEL: Do I have to walk?

[*She goes to the door, opens it and starts out.*]

There's a car in front of your house, Mr Bates.

RALPH [*rising with sudden energy and rushing to the door*]: YEP! IT'S HER OLD MAN'S CAR! Dorothea's papa, my ex-boss!

ISABEL: Perhaps he'll be kind enough to –

RALPH: Go back in, little lady! Stay in the bedroom till I git through this! Then I'll drive you downtown if you're still determined to go.

[*He has drawn her back in the house.*]

SET DOWN, GEORGE! For Chrissakes. Little lady, will you please wait in the bedroom till I get through this hassle with her old man?

ISABEL: It's all so ridiculous. Yes, all right, I will, but please don't forget your promise to take me downtown right afterwards, Mr Bates!

[*She returns to the bedroom with dignity.* MR *and* MRS MCGILLI-CUDDY *appear before the house.*
They are a pair of old bulls.]

MRS MCGILLICUDDY: The first thing to discuss is their joint savings account.

[MR MCGILLICUDDY *hammers the knocker on the door.*]

I wish you'd listened to me an' brought your lawyer.

MR MCGILLICUDDY: I can handle that boy. You keep your mouth out of it. Just collect the silver and china and let me handle the talk.

[*He knocks again, violently, dislodging the Christmas wreath attached to the knocker.* MRS MCGILLICUDDY *picks it up.*]

Now what are you gonna do with that Christmas wreath? You gonna crown him with it?

[RALPH *opens the door.*]

RALPH: Well, Mr and Mrs *Mac*!

MR MCGILLICUDDY [*handing him the wreath*]: This come off your knocker.

RALPH: Ha, ha, what a surprise!

MRS MCGILLICUDDY: We've come to pick up some things of Dor-othea's.

RALPH: That's O.K. Take out anything that's hers, but don't touch nothing that belongs to us both.

MR MCGILLICUDDY: We've come with a list of things that belong exclusively to Dorothea!

MR MCGILLICUDDY: Is it true that you called up Emory Sparks at the place you quit your job at and asked him to come over here tonight and make you a cash-on-the-barrel offer for everything in this house?

RALPH: Nope.

MR MCGILLICUDDY: Then how come Emory's fiancée called up Dorothea to give her that information?

MRS MCGILLICUDDY [*impatiently*]: Come on in here, Susie.

[SUSIE *is the coloured maid. She enters with a large laundry basket.*]

Is that the biggest basket you could find?

SUSIE: Yes, ma'am, it's the laundry basket.

MRS MCGILLICUDDY: It isn't the large one. You'll have to make several trips up and down those slippery front steps with that little basket.

MR MCGILLICUDDY: Haven't you got any ice-cream salt?

RALPH: You want to make some ice cream?

MR MCGILLICUDDY: Susie, before you go down those steps with my daughter's china, you'd better collect some clinkers out of the furnace in the basement.

RALPH: How is she going to get clinkers out of an oil-burning furnace?

MR MCGILLICUDDY: Oh, that's right. You burn oil. I forgot about that. Well, Susie, you better tote the basket of china down the terrace. Don't try to make the steps with it.

RALPH: She's not takin' no china out of this house.

MR MCGILLICUDDY: You're not going to sell a goddam thing of my daughter's in this house!

RALPH: All I done was call up Emory Sparks because he's about to get married and invited him over to take a look at this place because I've got to unload it and I can't wait a couple of months to –

MR MCGILLICUDDY: Now, hold on a minute, war hero!

RALPH: I don't like the way you always call me war hero!

MR MCGILLICUDDY: *Why?* Ain't that what you *were*?

GEORGE: You're goddam right he was! I flown over seventy bombing missions with this boy in Korea and before that in the –

MR MCGILLICUDDY: Yes, yes, yes, I know it backwards and forwards, and I know who you are. You are Haverstick, ain't you?

GEORGE: Yeah, you got my name right.

MR MCGILLICUDDY: Well, Haverstick, the war's over and you two bombers are grounded. Now, Susie, go in the kitchen and get that Mixmaster and that new Rôtisserie out in the basket while I collect the silver in that sideboard in there.

RALPH: Susie, don't go in my kitchen. You want to be arrested for trespassing, Susie?

MRS MCGILLICUDDY: Stuart, you'd better call that policeman in here.

RALPH: NO KIDDING!

MRS MCGILLICUDDY: We anticipated that you'd make trouble.

RALPH: How does Dorothea feel about you all doing this?

MR MCGILLICUDDY [*at the door*]: OFFICER! – He's coming.

RALPH: How does Dotty feel? What is her attitude towards this kind of –

> [*He is trembling. His voice chokes.* GEORGE *rises and puts a hand on Ralph's shoulder as a young* POLICE OFFICER *enters looking embarrassed.*]

MR MCGILLICUDDY: You know the situation, Lieutenant. We have to remove my daughter's valuables from the house because we've been tipped off this man here, Ralph Bates, is intending to make a quick cash sale of everything in the house and skip out of Memphis tomorrow.

RALPH: THAT'S A GODDAM LIE! WHO TOLD YOU THAT?

MRS MCGILLICUDDY: Emory Sparks's fiancée is Dorothea's good friend! That's how we got the warning. She called to inquire if Dorothea was serious about this matter. How did Dotty feel, how did she FEEL? I'll tell you! SICK AT HER STOMACH! VIOLENTLY SICK AT HER STOMACH.

RALPH: I should think so, goddam it! I should THINK so! She's got many a fault she got from you two, but, hell, she'd never agree to a piece of cheapness like this any more'n she'd believe that story about me callin' –

MR MCGILLICUDDY: How could there be any possible doubt about it when Emory Sparks's fiancée –

RALPH: Will you allow me to speak? I did call Emory Sparks and told him my wife had quit me because I had quit my job, and I merely suggested that he come over and kind of look over the stuff here and see if any of all this goddam electric equipment and so forth would be of any use to him since it isn't to me and since I got to have some financial –

[*He becomes suddenly speechless and breathless.* GEORGE *embraces his shoulder.*]

GEORGE: Now, now, son, this is going to work out. Don't blow a gasket over it.

RALPH: I think you folks had better consider some legal angles of what you're up to here.

MR MCGILLICUDDY [*puffing, red in the face*]: Aw, there's no legal angle about it that I don't know, and if there was, I could cope with that, too. I'm prepared to cope with that trouble. You got no goddam position in this town but what I give you!

RALPH: *Oh!* Uh-huh –

[MRS MCGILLICUDDY *has gone to the bedroom and discovered* ISABEL *in it.*]

MRS MCGILLICUDDY: *Stuart, they have a woman in Dotty's bedroom!*

RALPH: George's wife is in there.

MRS MCGILLICUDDY: How long have you been planning this?

[*She knocks on the bedroom door.*]

Can I come in?

ISABEL: Yes, please.

[MRS MCGILLICUDDY *enters the bedroom.*]

MRS MCGILLICUDDY [*coldly*]: I've come to pick up some things that belong to my daughter.

ISABEL: I told my husband we'd dropped in at the wrong time.

MRS MCGILLICUDDY: May I ask who you are?

ISABEL: I'm Mrs George Haverstick. You probably saw my husband in the front room.

MRS MCGILLICUDDY: Your husband's an old friend of Ralph's, one of his wartime buddies?

ISABEL: Yes, he is, Mrs – I didn't get your name.

MRS MCGILLICUDDY: All I can say is 'Watch out', if he's an old friend of Ralph's!

ISABEL: Why?

MRS MCGILLICUDDY: Birds of a feather, that's all.

[MRS MCGILLICUDDY *opens the closet and starts piling clothes on the bed. In the living-room,* MR MCGILLICUDDY *takes a seat in silence.*]

ISABEL: Are you sure you're doing the right thing?

MRS MCGILLICUDDY [*calling out the door*]: Susie!

SUSIE [*entering*]: Yes, ma'am?

MRS MCGILLICUDDY: Take these clothes of Miss Dotty's out to the car.

[SUSIE *carries out the clothes.*]

ISABEL: I think young people should be given a chance to work things out by themselves.

MRS MCGILLICUDDY: You have no idea at all of the situation. And I'm sure you have your own problems if you have married a friend of my daughter's husband. Is he living on his war record like Ralph Bates is?

ISABEL: He has a distinguished war record and a nervous disability that was a result of seventy-two flying missions in Korea and, and – more than twice that many in –

MRS MCGILLICUDDY: *I'm sick of hearing about past glories! Susie!*

[SUSIE *comes in again*]

Now pick up all Dotty's shoes on the floor of that closet, put 'em in the bottom of the basket, put some paper over them, and then pile her little undies on top of the paper. – Then! If you still have room in the basket, collect some of the china out of the sideboard and cupboards. Be very careful with that. Don't try to carry too much at one time, Susie. That walk and those steps are a hazard.

[*There has been a prolonged silence in the front room during the scene above, which they have been listening to.*]

MR MCGILLICUDDY [*at last*]: Well, you seem to be living the life of Riley. French champagne. Who was the little girl I saw come out and go back in?

RALPH: Mrs George Haverstick.

MR MCGILLICUDDY: That means as much to me as if you said she was a lady from Mars.

RALPH: There's no reason why it should mean anything to you. I just answered your question.

MR MCGILLICUDDY: Why do you feel so superior to me?

RALPH: Aw. Did you notice that?

MR MCGILLICUDDY: From the first time I met you. You have always acted very superior to me for some unknown reason. I'd like to know what it is. You were employed by me till you quit your job today.

RALPH: Does that mean I had to feel inferior to you, Mac?

MR MCGILLICUDDY: You've started calling me 'Mac'?

RALPH: I'm not employed by you, now.

MR MCGILLICUDDY: If there was a war you could be a war hero again, but in a cold war I don't see how you're going to be such a hero. A cold-war hero, ha ha, is not such a hero, at least not in the newspapers.

[*Gathering confidence.*]

Huh? Why don't you answer my question?

RALPH: Which, Mac?

MR MCGILLICUDDY: Why you feel so rutten superior to me.

RALPH: Can I consider that question? For a minute?

MR MCGILLICUDDY: Yeah, consider it, will you? I fail to see anything *special* about you, war hero!

[*He lights a cigar with jerky motions. The two younger men stare at his red, puffy face with intolerant smiles.*]

GEORGE: Let me answer for him. He feels superior to you because you're a big male cow, a spiritual male cow.

RALPH: Shut up, George. Well, Mr Mac? Let me ask you a question. Why did you ask me to marry your daughter?

MR MCGILLICUDDY: DID WHAT? I NEVER! Done any such thing and –

[MRS MCGILLICUDDY *snorts indignantly from the open bedroom door.*]

RALPH: You mean to say you've forgotten that you suggested to me that I marry Dotty?

[MRS MCGILLICUDDY *advances from the bedroom door, bearing a French porcelain clock.*]

MR MCGILLICUDDY: I never forgotten a thing in my adult life, but I never have any such recollections as that. I do remember a conversation I held with you soon after you started to work at Regal Dairy Products an' come to my office to quit because you said you weren't gittin paid well enough an' th' work was monotonous to you.

RALPH: That's right. Five years ago this winter.

MR MCGILLICUDDY: I gave you a fatherly talk. I told you monotony was a part of life. And I said I had an eye on you, which I did at that time.

RALPH: How about the rest of the conversation? In which you said that Dotty was your only child, that you had no son, and Dotty was int'rested in me and if Dotty got married her husband would be the heir to your throne as owner of Regal Dairy an' its subsidiaries such as Royal Ice Cream and Monarch Cheese, huh?

MRS MCGILLICUDDY: HANH!

RALPH: An' you hadn't long for this world because of acute diabetes and so forth and –

MRS MCGILLICUDDY: HANH!

RALPH: And I would be shot right into your shoes when you departed this world? Well, you sure in hell lingered!

MRS MCGILLICUDDY: ARE YOU GOING TO STAND THERE LISTENING TO THIS, STUART? I'M NOT!

MR MCGILLICUDDY: Be still, Mama. I can talk for myself. I did discuss these things with you but how did you arrive at the idea I asked you to marry my daughter?

MRS MCGILLICUDDY: HANH!

[GEORGE *goes to look out of the window as if the scene had ceased to amuse him.*]

RALPH: What other way could it be interpreted, Mac?

[*He is no longer angry.*]

MR MCGILLICUDDY: I offered you a splendid chance in the world which you spit on by your disrespect, your superior –!

RALPH: I respect Dorothea. Always did and still do.

MR MCGILLICUDDY: I'm talkin' about your attitude to me.

RALPH: I know you are. That's all that you care about, not about Dorothea. You don't love Dotty. She let you down by having psychological problems that you brought on her, that you an' Mrs Mac gave her by pushing her socially past her social endowments.

MRS MCGILLICUDDY: WHAT DO YOU MEAN BY THAT?

RALPH: Dotty was never cut out to boost your social position in this city. Which you expected her to. You made her feel inferior all her life.

MRS MCGILLICUDDY: *Me? Me?*

RALPH: Both of yuh. I respected her, though, and sincerely liked her and I married Dotty. Give me credit for that, and provided her with an – offspring. Maybe not much of an offspring, but an offspring, a male one, at least it started a male one. I can't help it if she's turnin' him into a sissy, I –

MRS MCGILLICUDDY: MY GOD, STUART, HOW LONG ARE YOU GONNA STAND THERE AND LISTEN TO THIS WITHOUT –

MR MCGILLICUDDY: *Mama, I told you to keep your mouth outa this!*

RALPH: Yeah, but I MARRIED your baby. Give me credit for that. And provided her with an – offspring!

MRS MCGILLICUDDY: What does he mean by that? That *he* had the baby, not Dotty?

MR MCGILLICUDDY: Mama, I told you to keep your mouth out of this.

MRS MCGILLICUDDY: He talks like he thought he did Dotty a FAVOUR!

RALPH: Now, listen. I don't want to be forced into saying unkind things about Dotty. But you all know damn' well that Dotty was half a year older than me when I married that girl and if I hadn't you would have been stuck with a lonely, unmarried daughter for the rest of your lives!

MRS MCGILLICUDDY: *Oh*, my – GOD!

MR MCGILLICUDDY: Let him talk. I want to hear all, all, all! he has to say about Dotty.

RALPH: You're *going* to hear it, if you stay in my house! I put up a five-year battle between our marriage and your goddam hold on her! You just wouldn't release her! – although I doubt that you wanted her always unmarried.

MRS MCGILLICUDDY: WHAT MAKES YOU THINK SHE WOULD HAVE STAYED UNMARRIED?

RALPH: The indications, past history, when I met her –

MRS MCGILLICUDDY: This is too sickening. I can't stand it, Stuart?

MR MCGILLICUDDY: A bum like you?

RALPH: Don't call *me* a bum!

MR MCGILLICUDDY: What in hell else *are* you? I give you your job which you quit today without warning! Carried you in it despite your indifference to it for – for – for – five –

RALPH: Wait! Like I said. I still respect your daughter, don't want to say anything not kind about her, but let's face facts. Who else but a sucker like me, Ralph Bates, would have married a girl with no looks, a plain, homely girl that probably no one but me had ever felt anything but just – SORRY FOR!

MRS MCGILLICUDDY: OH GOD! STUART, ARE YOU GOING

TO STAND THERE AND LET HIM GO ON WITH THAT
TALK?

RALPH: HOW IN HELL DO YOU FIGURE HE'S GOING TO
STOP ME?

MRS MCGILLICUDDY: OFFICER! CAN'T YOU GET THIS MAN
OUT OF HERE?

OFFICER: No, ma'am. I can't arrest him.

RALPH: ARREST ME FOR WHAT, MRS MAC?

GEORGE: That's right, arrest him for what?

MRS MCGILLICUDDY: Stuart? Take out the silver. I don't know where
Susie is. We should have come here with your lawyer as well as
this – *remarkably* – *incompetent* – *policeman*!

MR MCGILLICUDDY: Susie took out the silver.

GEORGE: Naw, she didn't. I got the goddam silver. I'm sitting on it!

[*He sits on silver, then rises and stuffs it under sofa pillow, having
been discomforted by the forks.*]

MR MCGILLICUDDY: I guess I'll have to call the Chief of Police, who's
a lodge brother of mine, and get a little more police cooperation
than we have gotten so far.

OFFICER: O.K., you do that, Mister.

MR MCGILLICUDDY: He'll call you to the phone and give you exact
instructions.

OFFICER: That's all right. If he gives 'em, I'll take 'em.

[MRS MCGILLICUDDY *has charged back into the bedroom to collect
more things.*]

RALPH: Mr McGillicuddy, you are the worst thing any person can be:
mean-minded, small-hearted, and CHEAP! Outstandingly and
notoriously cheap! It was almost two months before I could *kiss*
Dorothea, sincerely, after meeting her father! That's no crap. It
wasn't the homeliness that threw me, it was the association she
had in my mind with *you*! It wasn't till I found out she despised
you as much as I did that I was able to make real love to Dotty.

MR MCGILLICUDDY: My daughter is *crazy* about me!

RALPH: You're crazy if you *think* so!

[MRS MCGILLICUDDY *comes out of the bedroom.*]

MRS MCGILLICUDDY: All right. All of Dotty's clothes have been taken out. I think we may as well leave now.

MR MCGILLICUDDY: How about the TV? Which I gave Dotty *last* Christmas?

RALPH: You want the TV? O.K.! Here's the TV!

[*He shoves it to the door and pulls the door open.*]

Take the TV out of here – an' git out with it!

MRS MCGILLICUDDY: What is that under the tree? It looks like a new fur coat!

RALPH: That's right. A seven-hundred-and-forty-five-dollar sheared-beaver coat that I'd bought for Dotty for Christmas! – but which I have just now presented to Mrs George Haverstick as her weddin' present.

MR MCGILLICUDDY: The hell you have! How did you git hold of seven hundred and –

RALPH: From my savings account.

MR MCGILLICUDDY: That was a *joint* account!

MRS MCGILLICUDDY: STUART! TAKE THAT COAT! GO ON, PICK UP THAT COAT!

RALPH: By God, if he touches that coat, I'll smash him into next week, and I never hit an old man before in my life.

MRS MCGILLICUDDY: OFFICER! PICK UP THAT COAT!

RALPH: I'll hit any man that tries to pick up that coat!

OFFICER [*putting down the phone, which he has been talking into quietly*]: I talked to my chief. He gave me my instructions. He says not to take any action that might result in publicity, because of Mr Bates having been a very well-known war hero.

MR MCGILLICUDDY: Come on, Mama, I'll just have to refer this whole disgusting business to my lawyer tomorrow, put it all in his hands and get the necessary papers to protect our baby.

MRS MCGILLICUDDY: I just want to say one thing more! Ralph Bates, don't you think for a moment that you are going to escape financial responsibility for the support of your child! Now come on,

Stuart! – Isn't it pitiful? All that little boy's Christmas under the tree?

RALPH: Send him over tomorrow to pick it all up. That can go out of the house, the little boy's Christmas can go . . .

[*They all leave.* ISABEL *enters from bedroom.*]

ISABEL: Mr Bates! I don't believe that this is what your wife wanted. I'll also bet you that she is outside in that car and if you would just stick your head out of the window and call her, she would come running in here.

[DOROTHEA *comes on to the paved terrace and knocks at the door.* RALPH *does not move. She knocks again, harder and longer. He starts to rise, sits down again.*]

George, let his wife in the house.

GEORGE: Let's just keep out of this. I reckon he knows what he's doing.

[*A car honks. A* WOMAN'S VOICE *is heard.*]

WOMAN [*off*]: Dorothea! Come back! We'll get the police!

DOROTHEA [*calling at the door*]: Ralph? Ralph? It's Dotty! I want the child's Christmas things!

RALPH: HE'LL GET THEM HERE OR NOWHERE!

DOROTHEA: *I'm not going to leave here without the child's Christmas things!* – Ralph.

RALPH: *Let him come here alone tomorrow morning.*

DOROTHEA: *You can't do that to a child.* – Ralph!

[*The car honks again, long and loud.*]

RALPH [*shouting back*]: Put the kid in a taxi in the morning and I'll let him in to collect his Christmas presents!

MRS MCGILLICUDDY [*appearing behind Dorothea*]: Dorothea! I will not let you humiliate yourself like this! Come away from that door!

DOROTHEA: Mama, stay in the car!

WOMAN: Your father won't wait any longer. He's started the car. He's determined to get the police.

DOROTHEA: RALPH! [*She has removed the door key from her bag.*] I'M COMING IN!

WOMAN: *Dotty, where is your pride!*

[DOROTHEA *enters and slams the door. The* WOMAN *rushes off, crying 'Stuart!'*

DOROTHEA *stares at* RALPH *from the door. He gazes stubbornly at the opposite wall.*]

DOROTHEA: I could tell you'd been drinkin' by your voice. Who are these people you've got staying in the house?

RALPH: Talk about the police! I could get you all arrested for illegal entry!

DOROTHEA: This is your liquor speaking, not you, Ralph.

RALPH: You have abandoned me. You got no right by law to come back into this house and make insulting remarks about my friends.

DOROTHEA: Ralph? Ralph? I know I acted – impetuously this mawnin' . . .

RALPH: Naw, I think you made the correct decision. You realized that you had tied yourself down to a square peg in a round hole that had now popped out of the hole and consequently would be of no further use to you. You were perfectly satisfied for me to remain at that rutten little desk job, tyrannized over by inferior men, for as long as my – heart kept beating.

DOROTHEA: No, Ralph. I wasn't. MY aim for you was your aim. Independence! A business of your own!

RALPH: Not when you were *faced* with it.

DOROTHEA: You sprung it on me at the wrong moment, Ralph. Our savings account is at a very low ebb.

RALPH: Our savings account is all gone, little woman. It went on Christmas, all of it.

[*He pokes at the fire. There is a pause. The fire crackles and flickers.*]

DOROTHEA: *Mama* says you – bought me a *fur coat* for Christmas.

RALPH: Yeah, she took a look at it. Inquired the price. Wanted to take it off with her.

DOROTHEA: You wouldn't have bought me such a beautiful coat if you didn't still care for me, Ralph. You know that, don't you?

RALPH: I made a decision affecting my whole future life. I know it was a big step, but I had the courage to make it.

DOROTHEA: I've always admired your courage.

RALPH: Hah! – I break the news. You walked right out on me, Dotty, takin' my son that you've turned into a sissy. He won't want these boys' toys under that tree. What he'll want is a doll and a – *tea* set.

DOROTHEA: All of these things are a little too old for Ralph Junior but he'll be delighted with them just the same, Ralph.

[*She takes off her cloth coat.*]

I'm going to try on that wonderful-looking beaver.

RALPH: It's not going out of the house, off you or on you, Dotty.

[*She puts on the beaver-skin coat.*]

DOROTHEA: Oh, how lovely, how lovely! Ralph, it *does* prove you love me!

RALPH: It cleaned out our savings account.

DOROTHEA: Both of us have been guilty of impetuous actions. You must've been awfully lonely, inviting a pair of strangers to occupy our bedroom on Christmas Eve.

RALPH: George Haverstick is not any stranger to me. We both of us died in two wars, repeatedly died in two wars and were buried in suburbs named High Point, but his was hyphenated. H-i-hyphen-Point. Mine was spelled out but was built on a cavern for the daughter and grandchild of Mr and Mrs Stuart McGillicuddy. Oh, I told him something which I should have told you five years ago, Dorothea. I married you without love. I married you for –

DOROTHEA: Ralph? Please don't!

RALPH: I married you for your stingy-fisted old papa's promise to –

DOROTHEA: *Ralphie! Don't! I know!*

RALPH: – to make me his Heir Apparent! Assurances, lies! Even broad hints that he would soon kick off!

DOROTHEA: Ralph?

[*She puts her hand over his mouth, beseechingly.*]

Don't you know I know that?

RALPH: Why d'you accept it? If you –

DOROTHEA: I was so –

[*She covers her face.*]

RALPH: Cut it out, have some pride!

DOROTHEA: I *do*!

RALPH: In *what*?

DOROTHEA: In *you*!

RALPH: Oh, for the love of – In me? Why, I'm telling you I'm nothin'
better'n a goddam –

DOROTHEA: I know, don't tell me again. I always knew it. – I had my
nose done over and my front teeth extracted to look better for
you, Ralphie!

RALPH: 'Ralphie!' *Shoot* . . .

[ISABEL *raps discreetly at the bedroom door.*]

Huh? What is it?

ISABEL: I've made some coffee.

DOROTHEA: I *did* improve my appearance, didn't I, Ralph? It was
extremely painful.

RALPH: Don't claim you done it for me! Every woman wants to
improve on nature any way that she can. Yes! Of course you look
better! You think you've won a *argument*?

DOROTHEA: *Me? What* argument? *No!* I've come back *crawling*! – not
even embarrassed to do so!

[ISABEL *comes in from the kitchenette with coffee.*]

Oh! Hello. I didn't know you were –

ISABEL: Mrs Bates. I'm Isabel Haverstick. I took the liberty of making some coffee in your sweet little kitchen. Mrs Bates, can I give
you some coffee?

DOROTHEA: Thanks, that's awfully sweet of you, Mrs Haverstick. It's
nice of you and your husband to drop in on Ralph, but the situ-

ation between Ralph and me has changed. I guess I don't have to explain it. You see I've come home. We only have one bedroom and Ralph and I have an awful lot to talk over.

ISABEL: I understand perfectly. George and I are going to go right downtown.

DOROTHEA [*softening*]: You don't have to do that. This sofa lets out to a bed and it's actually more comfortable than the beds in the bedroom. I know, because other times when we've had a falling out, less serious than this time, I have – occupied it.

[*With a little, soft, sad, embarrassed laugh.*]

Of course, I usually called Ralph in before mawnin' . . .

ISABEL: Oh, but this is no time for strangers to be here with you!

DOROTHEA [*now really warming*]: You all stay here! I insist! It's really not easy to get a hotel room downtown with so many folks coming into town for Christmas.

ISABEL: Well, if you're sure, if you're absolutely certain our presence wouldn't be inconvenient at all? – I do love this room. The fire is still burning bright – and the Christmas tree is so – pretty.

DOROTHEA: I'll tell my mother and father, they're still outside in the car, to drive home and then we'll all have coffee together.

[*She rushes out in her beaver coat.*]

ISABEL: I like her! She's really nice!

RALPH: She came back for the fur coat.

ISABEL: I think she came back for you.

RALPH: She walked out on me this morning because I had liberated myself from a slave's situation! – and she took the kid with her.

ISABEL: You're just going through a – period of adjustment.

RALPH: We've been married six years.

ISABEL: But all that time you've been under terrible strain, hating what you were doing, and maybe taking it out on your wife, Ralph Bates.

[DOROTHEA *returns.*]

DOROTHEA: All right. I sent them home, much against their objections. I just slammed the car door on them.

RALPH: They comin' back with the police?

DOROTHEA: No. You know they were bluffing.

ISABEL: I think you two should have your coffee alone in your own little bedroom. We'll all get acquainted tomorrow.

DOROTHEA: Ralph?

RALPH [*sadly*]: I don't know. We're living over a cavern . . .

[*He follows* DOROTHEA *into the bedroom. It remains dimly lighted.*]

DOROTHEA: But Mama's took all my things! I forgot to ask them back from her. I'll just have to sleep jay-bird since she took even my nighties.

RALPH: Yes, she was fast and thorough, but didn't get out with that seven-hundred-buck beaver coat.

DOROTHEA: I like your friends. But the girl looks terribly nervous. Well-bred, however, and the boy is certainly very good-looking!

RALPH: Thanks.

[*The bedroom dims out as* DOROTHEA *enters the bathroom. A silence has fallen between the pair in the living-room.*]

ISABEL: Coffee, George?

GEORGE: No, thanks.

ISABEL: Moods change quickly, don't they?

GEORGE: Basic attitudes don't.

ISABEL: Yes, but it takes a long time to form basic attitudes and to know what they are, and meantime you just have to act according to moods.

GEORGE: Is that what you are acting according to, now?

ISABEL: I'm not acting according to anything at all now, I –

[*She sits on a hassock before the fireplace.*]

I don't think she came back just for the coat. Do you?

GEORGE: It's not my business. I don't have any opinion. If that was her reason, Ralph Bates will soon find it out.

ISABEL: Yes . . .

DOROTHEA [*at the door*]: Excuse me, may I come in?

ISABEL: Oh, please.

DOROTHEA [*entering*]: Mama took all my *things*! Have you got an extra nightie that I could borrow?

ISABEL: Of course I have.

DOROTHEA: I forgot to take anything back . . .

[ISABEL *opens her overnight bag and extends a gossamer nightgown to Dorothea.*]

Oh! How exquisite! No! – that's your honeymoon nightie. Just give me any old plain one!

ISABEL: Really, I have two of them, exactly alike. Please take it!

DOROTHEA: Are you sure?

ISABEL: I'm positive. You take it!

[*She holds up another.*]

See? The same thing exactly, just a different colour. I gave you the blue one and kept the pink one for me.

DOROTHEA: Oh. Well, thank you so much.

ISABEL: If you'd prefer the pink one – ?

DOROTHEA: I'm delighted with the blue one! Well, g'night, you folks. Sweet dreams.

[*She returns to the dark bedroom.* RALPH *is prone and motionless on the bed. A tiny light spills from the bathroom door.* DOROTHEA *enters the bathroom and closes the door so the bedroom turns pitch-black.*]

GEORGE [*grimly*]: D'ya want me to go outside while you undress?

ISABEL: No, I, I – I'm – just going to take off my *suit*. I – I, I have a *slip* on, I –

[*She gives him a quick, scared look. The removal of her suit is almost panickily self-conscious and awkward.*]

GEORGE: Well. Ralph and I have decided to –

ISABEL [*fearfully*]: *What?*

GEORGE [*finishes his drink, then goes on*]: Ralph and I have decided to go in the cattle business, near San Antone.

ISABEL: Who is going to finance it?

[*She has turned out the lamp.*]

GEORGE: We think we can work it out. We have to be smart, and lucky. Just smart and lucky.

[ISABEL *drops her skirt to her feet and stands before the flickering fireplace in a slip that the light makes transparent.*]

ISABEL: We all have to be smart and lucky. Or unlucky and silly.

[DOROTHEA *comes out of the bathroom. Light from the bathroom brightens the bedroom, where* RALPH *is slowly undressing.*]

RALPH: All right, you're back. But a lot has been discussed and decided on since you cut out of here, Dotty.

DOROTHEA [*picks up something on the dresser*]: Good! What?

RALPH: Please don't rub that Vick's Vap-O-Rub on your chest.

DOROTHEA: I'm *not*! This is Hind's honey-almond cream for *my hands*!

RALPH: Aw.

[*She starts taking off her shoes.*
In the living-room:]

GEORGE: What're you up to?

ISABEL: Up to?

GEORGE: Standin' in front of that fire with that transparent thing on you. You must know it's transparent.

ISABEL: I honestly didn't even think about that.

[ISABEL *crouches by the fire, holding her delicate hands out to its faint flickering glow.*
In the bedroom:]

RALPH: All right. Here it is. George and me are going to cash in every bit of collateral we possess, including the beaver-skin coat and his fifty-two Caddy to buy a piece of ranchland near San Antone.

DOROTHEA: Oh. What are you planning to do on this –

RALPH: – ranch? Breed cattle. Texas Longhorns.

[*A pause.*]

DOROTHEA: I like animals, Ralph.

RALPH: Cocker spaniels.

DOROTHEA: No, I like horses, too. I took equitation at Sonnie New-comb's. I even learned how to post.

RALPH: Uh-huh.

DOROTHEA: For a little ole Texas girl she sure does have some mighty French taste in nighties!

RALPH: I don't imagine she suffers from psychological frigidity.

DOROTHEA: Honey, I never suffered from that. Did you believe I really suffered from that?

RALPH: When your father proposed to me –

DOROTHEA: Ralph, don't say things like that! Don't, don't humiliate me!

RALPH: Honey, I –

DOROTHEA: PLEASE don't humiliate me by –

RALPH: HONEY!

[*He goes up to her at the dressing table. Sobbing, she presses her head against him.*]

You KNOW I respect you, honey.

ISABEL [*in the other room*]: What an awful, frightening thing it is!

GEORGE: What?

ISABEL: Two people living together, two, two – different worlds! – attempting – existence – together!

[*In the bedroom:*]

RALPH: Honey, will you stop?

DOROTHEA: Respect me, respect me, is that all you can give me when I've loved you so much that sometimes I shake all over at the sight or touch of you? Still? Now? Always?

RALPH: The human heart would never pass the drunk test.

DOROTHEA: Huh?

RALPH: If you took the human heart out of the human body and put a pair of legs on it and told it to walk a straight line, it couldn't do it. It never could pass the drunk test.

DOROTHEA: I love you, baby. And I love animals, too. Hawses, spaniels, longhorns!

RALPH: The Texas Longhorn is a – dignified beast.

DOROTHEA: You say that like you thought it was TOO GOOD FOR
ME!

RALPH: How do I know that you didn't just come back here for that
sheared beaver coat?

[*Living-room:*]

ISABEL: I hope they're getting things ironed out between them.

GEORGE: Why?

ISABEL: They need each other. That's why.

GEORGE: Let's mind our own business, huh?

[*Bedroom:*]

DOROTHEA: You'll just have to WONDER! And WONDER!

[*Living-room:*]

GEORGE: It's a parallel situation. They're going through a period of
adjustment just like us.

[*Bedroom:*]

RALPH: All my life, huh?

DOROTHEA: And I'll have to wonder, too, if you love me, Ralph.
There's an awful lot of wondering between people.

RALPH: Come on. Turn out the light. Let's go to bed-ville, baby.

DOROTHEA [*turning out the light*]: His or hers?

RALPH: In West Texas we'll get a big one called OURS!

[*In the living-room,* GEORGE *has turned on TV and a chorus is singing 'White Christmas'.*]

GEORGE: Aw. You hate 'White Christmas'.

[*He turns it down.*]

ISABEL: I don't hate it now, baby.

[*He turns it back up, but softly.*
Bedroom:]

DOROTHEA: I'm lookin' *forward* to it. I always wanted a big one, OURS!

RALPH: There's more dignity in it.

DOROTHEA: *Yes!*

[*She giggles breathlessly in the dark.*]

ISABEL [*in the living-room*]: I think they've talked things over and are working things out.

[*Bedroom:*]

RALPH: Yes. It makes it easy to know if – I mean, you don't have to wonder if –

[DOROTHEA *giggles in the dark.*]

That long, long, dangerous walk between 'His' and 'Hers' can be accomplished, or not . . .

[*Living-room:*]

ISABEL: I didn't know until now that the shakes are catching! Why do you keep standing up and sitting back down like a big old jack-in-the-box?

[*A low rumble is heard. It builds. Something falls off a shelf in the kitchenette. Crockery rattles together.*]

WHAT'S THIS!?

GEORGE: Aw, nothin', nothin'.

RALPH [*entering the doorway*]: Well, she jus' slipped again!

DOROTHEA [*appearing behind him*]: Did you all feel that tremor?

ISABEL: Yes, it felt like an earthquake.

DOROTHEA: We get those little tremors all the time because it seems that this suburb is built over a huge underground cavern and is sinking into it, bit by bit. That's the secret of how we could afford to buy this nice little home of ours at such a knockdown price.

ISABEL: It isn't likely to fall in the cavern *tonight*?

DOROTHEA: No. They say it's going to be gradual, about half an inch every year. Do you all mind if I turn on the light a second to see if there's any new cracks?

ISABEL: No, I'll – put on my robe.

[*She does. The room is lighted.*]

DOROTHEA: Yais! Ralph? A *new* one! This one is a jimdandy, all the way 'cross the ceiling! See it, honey? All the way 'cross the ceiling! Well –

[*A pause.*]

We will leave you alone now. I still feel badly about you having to sleep on that folding contraption.

RALPH: Anything I can do? Anything I can –

DOROTHEA: Ralph! Leave them alone. Merry Christmas!

[*She shuts the door.
Pause.* ISABEL *stands before fireplace in the fourth wall.
Pause.*]

GEORGE: Isabel? Little Bit? Marriage is a big step for a man to take, especially when he's – nervous. I'm pretty – nervous.

ISABEL: I know.

GEORGE: For a man with the shakes, especially, it's a – big step to take, it's –

ISABEL: I know what you're trying to tell me.

GEORGE [*taking seat on high stool near fire*]: Do you, honey?

[*He looks up at her quickly, then down.*]

ISABEL: Of course I do. I expect all men are a little bit nervous about the same thing.

GEORGE: What?

ISABEL: About how they'll be at love-making.

GEORGE: Yeah, well, they don't have the shakes. I mean, not all the others have got a nervous tremor like I've got.

ISABEL: Inside or outside, they've all got a nervous tremor of some kind, sweetheart. The world is a big hospital, and I am a nurse in it, George. The whole world's a big hospital, a big neurological ward and I am a student nurse in it. I guess that's still my job! – I love this fire. It feels so good on my skin through this little pink slip. I'm glad she left me the *pink* nightie, tonight.

GEORGE [*huskily*]: Yeah, I'm glad she did, too.

[ISABEL *retires to slip into her nightgown.*]

I wish I had that – little electric buzzer I – had at – Barnes . . .

ISABEL: You don't need a buzzer. I'm not way down at the end of a corridor, baby. If you call me, I'll hear you.

[*She returns and hugs her knees, sitting before the fireplace. He rests his head on his cupped hands. She begins to sing softly:*]

'Now the boat goes round the bend,
Good-bye, my lover, good-bye,
It's loaded down with boys and men,
Good-bye, my lover, good-bye.'

RALPH [*in the dark other room*]: She's singin'!

[*Pause.*]

DOROTHEA: Papa said you told him that I was – homely! Did you say that, Ralph? That I was homely?

RALPH: Dotty, you used to be homely but you improved in appearance.

DOROTHEA: You never told me you thought I was homely, Ralph.

RALPH: I just meant you had a off-beat kind of face, honey, but – the rest of you is attractive.

DOROTHEA [*giggles*]: I always knew *I* was homely but you were good enough lookin' to make *up* for it! Baby –

[ISABEL *is singing again, a little forlornly, by the fireplace.*]

ISABEL:

'Bye low, my baby! Bye low, my baby!
Bye low, my baby! Good-bye, my lover, good-bye!'

[GEORGE *whistles softly.*]

Was that for me?

GEORGE: Come here!

ISABEL: No, you come here. It's very nice by the fire.

[*In the other room, as the curtain begins to fall:*]

DOROTHEA: Careful, let me do it! – It isn't mine!

[*She means the borrowed nightgown.*
In the front room, GEORGE *has risen from the bed and is crossing to the fireplace as:*]

THE CURTAIN FALLS

The Night of the Iguana

The Night of the Iguana was presented at the Royale Theater in New York on 28 December 1961 by Charles Bowden, in association with Violla Rubber. It was directed by Frank Corsaro; the stage setting was designed by Oliver Smith; lighting by Jean Rosenthal; costumes by Noel Taylor; audio effects by Edward Beyer. The cast, in order of appearance, was as follows:

MAXINE FAULK	*Bette Davis*
PEDRO	*James Farentino*
PANCHO	*Christopher Jones*
REVEREND SHANNON	*Patrick O'Neal*
HANK	*Theseus George*
HERR FAHRENKOPF	*Heinz Hohenwald*
FRAU FAHRENKOPF	*Lucy Landau*
WOLFGANG	*Bruce Glover*
HILDA	*Laryssa Lauret*
JUDITH FELLOWES	*Patricia Roe*
HANNAH JELKES	*Margaret Leighton*
CHARLOTTE GOODALL	*Lane Bradbury*
JONATHAN COFFIN (NONNO)	*Alan Webb*
JAKE LATTA	*Louis Guss*

Production owned and presented by 'The Night of the Iguana' Joint Venture (the joint venture consisting of Charles Bowden and Two Rivers Enterprises, Inc.)

The play takes place in the summer of 1940 in a rather rustic and very Bohe-mian hotel, the Costa Verde, which, as its name implies, sits on a jungle-covered hilltop overlooking the 'caleta', or 'morning beach' of Puerto Barrio in Mexico. But this is decidedly not the Puerto Barrio of today. At that time – twenty years ago – the west coast of Mexico had not yet become the Las Vegas and Miami Beach of Mexico. The villages were still predomin-antly primitive Indian villages, and the still-water morning beach of Puerto Bar-rio and the rain forests above it were among the world's wildest and loveliest populated places.

The setting for the play is the wide veranda of the hotel. This roofed veranda, enclosed by a railing, runs around all four sides of the somewhat dilapidated, tropical-style frame structure, but on the stage we see only the front and one side. Below the veranda, which is slightly raised above the stage level, are shrubs with vivid trumpet-shaped flowers and a few cactus plants, while at the sides we see the foliage of the encroaching jungle. A tall coconut palm slants upward at one side, its trunk notched for a climber to chop down coconuts for rum-cocos. In the back wall of the veranda are the doors of a line of small cubicle bedrooms which are screened with mosquito-net curtains. For the night scenes they are lighted from within, so that each cubicle appears as a little interior stage, the curtains giving a misty effect to their dim inside light-ing. A path which goes down through the rain forest to the highway and the beach, its opening masked by foliage, leads off from one side of the veranda. A canvas hammock is strung from posts on the veranda and there are a few old wicker rockers and rattan lounging chairs at one side.

Act One

As the curtain rises, there are sounds of a party of excited female tourists arriving by bus on the road down the hill below the Costa Verde Hotel. MRS MAXINE FAULK, the proprietor of the hotel, comes round the turn of the veranda. She is a stout, swarthy woman in her middle forties – affable and rapaciously lusty. She is wearing a pair of levis and a blouse that is half unbuttoned. She is followed by PEDRO, a Mexican of about twenty – slim and attractive. He is an employee in the hotel and also her casual lover. PEDRO is stuffing his shirt under the belt of his pants and sweating as if he had been working hard in the sun. MRS FAULK looks down the hill and is pleased by the sight of someone coming up from the tourist bus below.

MAXINE [*calling out*]: Shannon! [*A man's voice from below answers: 'Hi!'*] Hah! [MAXINE *always laughs with a single harsh, loud bark, opening her mouth like a seal expecting a fish to be thrown to it.*] My spies told me that you were back under the border! [*to* PEDRO] Anda, hombre, anda!

   [MAXINE'S *delight expands and vibrates in her as* SHANNON *labours up the hill to the hotel. He does not appear on the jungle path for a minute or two after the shouting between them starts.*]

   Hah! My spies told me you went through Saltillo last week with a busload of women – a whole busload of females, all females, hah! How many you laid so far? Hah!

SHANNON [*from below, panting*]: Great Caesar's ghost ... stop ... shouting!

MAXINE: No wonder your ass is draggin', hah!

SHANNON: Tell the kid to help me up with this bag.

MAXINE [*shouting directions*]: Pedro! Anda – la maléta. Pancho, no seas flojo! Va y trae el equipaje del señor.

[PANCHO, *another young Mexican, comes around the veranda and trots down the jungle path.* PEDRO *has climbed up a coconut tree with a machete and is chopping down nuts for rum-cocos.*]

SHANNON [*shouting, below*]: Fred? Hey, Fred!

MAXINE [*with a momentary gravity*]: Fred can't hear you, Shannon. [*She goes over and picks up a coconut, shaking it against her ear to see if it has milk in it.*]

SHANNON [*still below*]: Where is Fred – gone fishing?

[MAXINE *lops the end off a coconut with a machete, as* PANCHO *trots up to the veranda with Shannon's bag – a beat-up Gladstone covered with travel stickers from all over the world. Then* SHANNON *appears, in a crumpled white linen suit. He is panting, sweating, and wild-eyed. About thirty-five,* SHANNON *is 'black Irish'. His nervous state is terribly apparent; he is a young man who has cracked up before and is going to crack up again – perhaps repeatedly.*]

MAXINE: Well! Lemme look at you!

SHANNON: Don't look at me; get dressed!

MAXINE: Gee, you look like you had it!

SHANNON: You look like you been having it, too. Get dressed!

MAXINE: Hell, I'm dressed. I never dress in September. Don't you know I never dress in September?

SHANNON: Well, just, just – button your shirt up.

MAXINE: How long you been off it, Shannon?

SHANNON: Off what?

MAXINE: The wagon . . .

SHANNON: Hell, I'm dizzy with fever. Hundred and three this morning in Cuernavaca.

MAXINE: Whatcha got wrong with you?

SHANNON: Fever . . . fever . . . Where's Fred?

MAXINE: Dead.

SHANNON: Did you say *dead*?

MAXINE: That's what I said. Fred is dead.

SHANNON: How?

MAXINE: Less'n two weeks ago, Fred cut his hand on a fishhook, it got infected, infection got in his blood stream, and he was dead inside of forty-eight hours. [*To Pancho*] Vete!

SHANNON: Holy smoke . . .

MAXINE: I can't quite realize it yet . . .

SHANNON: You don't seem – inconsolable about it.

MAXINE: Fred was an old man, baby. Ten years older'n me. We hadn't had sex together in . . .

SHANNON: What's that got to do with it?

MAXINE: Lie down and have a rum-coco.

SHANNON: No, no. I want a cold beer. If I start drinking rum-cocos now I won't stop drinking rum-cocos. So Fred is dead? I looked forward to lying in this hammock and talking to Fred.

MAXINE: Well, Fred's not talking now, Shannon. A diabetic gets a blood infection, he goes like that without a decent hospital in less'n a week. [*A bus horn is heard blowing from below.*] Why don't your busload of women come on up here? They're blowing the bus horn down there.

SHANNON: Let 'em blow it, blow it . . . [*He sways a little.*] I got a fever. [*He goes to the top of the path, divides the flowering bushes and shouts down the hill to the bus.*] Hank! Hank! Get them out of the bus and bring 'em up here! Tell 'em the rates are O.K. Tell 'em the . . . [*His voice gives out, and he stumbles back to the veranda, where he sinks down on to the low steps, panting.*] Absolutely the worst party I've ever been out with in ten years of conducting tours. For God's sake, help me with 'em because I can't go on. I got to rest here a while. [*She gives him a cold beer.*] Thanks. Look and see if they're getting out of the bus. [*She crosses to the masking foliage and separates it to look down the hill.*] Are they getting out of the bus or are they staying in it, the stingy – daughters of – bitches . . . School-teachers at a Baptist Female College in Blowing Rock, Texas. Eleven, eleven of them.

MAXINE: A football squad of old maids . . .

SHANNON: Yea, and I'm the football. Are they out of the bus?

MAXINE: One's gotten out – she's going into the bushes.

SHANNON: Well, I've got the ignition key to the bus in my pocket – this pocket – so they can't continue without me unless they walk.

MAXINE: They're still blowin' that horn.

SHANNON: Fantastic. I can't lose this party. Blake Tours has put me on probation because I had a bad party last month that tried to get me sacked and I am now on probation with Blake Tours. If I lose this party I'll be sacked for sure . . . Ah, my God, are they still all in the bus? [*He heaves himself off the steps and staggers back to the path, dividing the foliage to look down it, then shouts*] Hank! Get them out of the bussss! Bring them up heeee-re!

HANK'S VOICE [*from below*]: They wanta go back in toooooowwwwn.

SHANNON: They *can't* go back in toooowwwwn! – Whew – Five years ago this summer I was conducting round-the-world tours for Cook's. Exclusive groups of retired Wall Street financiers. We travelled in fleets of Pierce Arrows and Hispano Suizas. – Are they getting out of the bus?

MAXINE: You're going to pieces, are you?

SHANNON: No! Gone! Gone! [*He rises and shouts down the hill again.*] Hank! come up here! Come on up here a minute! I wanta talk to you about this situation! – Incredible, fantastic . . . [*He drops back on the steps, his head falling into his hands.*]

MAXINE: They're not getting out of the bus. – Shannon . . . you're not in a nervous condition to cope with this party, Shannon, so let them go and you stay.

SHANNON: You know my situation: I lose this job, what's next? There's nothing lower than Blake Tours, Maxine honey. – Are they getting out of the bus? Are they getting out of it now?

MAXINE: Man's comin' up the hill.

SHANNON: Aw. Hank. You gotta help me with him.

MAXINE: I'll give him a rum-coco.

[HANK *comes grinning on to the veranda.*]

HANK: Shannon, them ladies are not gonna come up here, so you better come on back to the bus.

SHANNON: Fantastic. – I'm not going down to the bus and I've got the ignition key to the bus in my pocket. It's going to stay in my pocket for the next three days.

HANK: You can't get away with that, Shannon. Hell, they'll walk back to town if you don't give up the bus key.

SHANNON: They'd drop like flies from sunstrokes on that road . . . Fantastic, absolutely fantastic . . . [*Panting and sweating, he drops a hand on Hank's shoulder.*] Hank, I want your cooperation. Can I have it? Because when you're out with a difficult party like this, the tour conductor – me – and the guide – you – have got to stick together to control the situations as they come up against us. It's a test of strength between two men, in this case, and a bus-load of old wet *hens*. You know that, don't you?

HANK: Well . . . [*He chuckles.*] There's this kid that's crying on the back seat all the time, and that's what's rucked up the deal. Hell, I don't know if you did or you didn't, but they all think that you did 'cause the kid keeps crying.

SHANNON: *Hank? Look!* I don't care what they think. A tour conducted by T. Lawrence Shannon is in his charge, completely – where to go, when to go, every detail of it. Otherwise I resign. So go on back down there and get them out of that bus before they suffocate in it. Haul them out by force if necessary and herd them up here. Hear me? Don't give me any argument about it. Mrs Faulk, honey? Give him a menu, give him one of your sample menus to show the ladies. She's got a Chinaman cook here, you won't believe the menu. The cook's from Shanghai, handled the kitchen at an exclusive club there. I got him here for her, and he's a bug, a fanatic about – whew! – continental cuisine . . . can even make beef Stroganoff and thermidor dishes. Mrs Faulk, honey? Hand him one of those – whew! – one of those fantastic sample menus. [MAXINE *chuckles, as if perpetrating a practical joke, and she hands him a sheet of paper.*] Thanks. Now, here. Go on back down there and show them this fantastic menu. Describe the view from the hill, and . . . [HANK *accepts the menu with a chuckling shake of the head.*] And have a cold Carta Blanca and . . .

HANK: You better go down with me.

SHANNON: I can't leave this veranda for at least forty-eight hours.

What in blazes is this? A little animated cartoon by Hieronymus Bosch?

[*The German family which is staying at the hotel, the* FAHRENKOPFS, *their daughter and son-in-law, suddenly make a startling, dreamlike entrance upon the scene. They troop around the veranda, then turn down into the jungle path. They are all dressed in the minimal concession to decency and all are pink and gold like baroque cupids in various sizes − Rubensesque, splendidly physical. The bride,* HILDA, *walks astride a big inflated rubber horse which has an ecstatic smile and great winking eyes. She shouts 'Horsey, Horsey, giddap!' as she waddles astride it, followed by her Wagnerian-tenor bridegroom,* WOLFGANG, *and her father,* HERR FAHRENKOPF, *a tank manufacturer from Frankfurt. He is carrying a portable shortwave radio, which is tuned in to the crackle and guttural voices of a German broadcast reporting the Battle of Britain.* FRAU FAHRENKOPF, *bursting with rich, healthy fat and carrying a basket of food for a picnic at the beach, brings up the rear. They begin to sing a Nazi marching song.*]

Aw − Nazis. How come there's so many of them down here lately?

MAXINE: Mexico's the front door to South America − and the back door to the States, that's why.

SHANNON: Aw, and you're setting yourself up here as a receptionist at both doors, now that Fred's dead? [MAXINE *comes over and sits down on him in the hammock.*] Get off my pelvis before you crack it. If you want to crack something, crack some ice for my forehead. [*She removes a chunk of ice from her glass and massages his forehead with it.*] − Ah, God . . .

MAXINE [*chuckling*]: Ha, so you took the young chick and the old hens are squawking about it, Shannon?

SHANNON: The kid asked for it, no kidding, but she's seventeen − less, a month less'n seventeen. So it's serious, it's very serious, because the kid is not just emotionally precocious, she's a musical prodigy, too.

MAXINE: What's that got to do with it?

SHANNON: Here's what it's got to do with it, she's travelling under the wing, the military escort, of this, this – butch vocal teacher who organizes little community sings in the bus. Ah, God! I'm surprised they're not singing now, they must've already suffocated. Or they'd be singing some morale-boosting number like 'She's a Jolly Good Fellow' or 'Pop goes the Weasel'. – Oh, God . . . [MAXINE *chuckles up and down the scale.*] And each night after supper, after the complaints about the supper and the check-up on the checks by the math instructor, and the vomiting of the supper by several ladies, who have inspected the kitchen – then the kid, the canary, will give a vocal recital. She opens her mouth and out flies Carrie Jacobs Bond or Ethelbert Nevin. I mean after a day of one indescribable torment after another, such as three blowouts, and a leaking radi-ator in Tierra Caliente . . . [*He sits up slowly in the hammock as these recollections gather force.*] And an evening climb up sierras, through torrents of rain, around hairpin turns over gorges and chasms measureless to man, and with a thermos-jug under the driver's seat which the Baptist College ladies think is filled with ice-water but which I know is filled with iced tequila – I mean after such a day has finally come to a close, the musical prodigy, Miss Charlotte Goodall, right after supper, before there's a chance to escape, will give a heartbreaking and earsplitting rendition of Carrie Jacobs Bond's 'End of a Perfect Day' – with absolutely no humour . . .

MAXINE: Hah!

SHANNON: Yeah, 'Hah!' Last night – no, night before last, the bus burned out its brake linings in Chilpancingo. This town has a hotel . . . this hotel has a piano, which hasn't been tuned since they shot Maximilian. This Texas song-bird opens her mouth and out flies 'I Love You Truly', and it flies straight at *me*, with *gestures*, all right at *me*, till her chaperon, this Diesel-driven vocal instructor of hers, slams the piano lid down and hauls her out of the mess-hall. But as she's hauled out Miss Bird-Girl opens her mouth and out flies, 'Larry, Larry, I love you, I love you truly!' That night, when I went to my room, I found that I had a room-mate.

MAXINE: The musical prodigy had moved in with you?

SHANNON: The *spook* had moved in with me. In that hot room with

one bed, the width of an ironing board and about as hard, the
spook was up there on it, sweating, stinking, grinning up at me.

MAXINE: Aw, the spook. [*She chuckles.*] So you've got the spook with
you again.

SHANNON: That's right, he's the only passenger that got off the bus
with me, honey.

MAXINE: Is he here now?

SHANNON: Not far.

MAXINE: On the veranda?

SHANNON: He might be on the other side of the veranda. Oh, he's
around somewhere, but he's like the Sioux Indians in the Wild
West fiction, he doesn't attack before sundown, he's an after-
sundown shadow . . .

[SHANNON *wriggles out of the hammock as the bus horn gives one
last, long protesting blast.*]

MAXINE:

> I have a little shadow
> That goes in and out with me,
> And what can be the use of him
> Is more than I can see.
> He's very, very like me,
> From his heels up to his head,
> And he always hops before me
> When I hop into my bed.

SHANNON: That's the truth. He sure hops in the bed with me.

MAXINE: When you're sleeping alone, or . . . ?

SHANNON: I haven't slept in three nights.

MAXINE: Aw, you will tonight, baby.

[*The bus horn sounds again.* SHANNON *rises and squints down the
hill at the bus.*]

SHANNON: How long's it take to sweat the faculty of a Baptist Female
College out of a bus that's parked in the sun when it's hundred
degrees in the shade?

MAXINE: They're staggering out of it now.

SHANNON: Yeah, I've won *this* round, I reckon. What're they doing down there? Can you see?

MAXINE: They're crowding around your pal Hank.

SHANNON: Tearing him to pieces?

MAXINE: One of them's slapped him, he's ducked back into the bus, and she is starting up here.

SHANNON: Oh, Great Caesar's ghost, it's the butch vocal teacher.

MISS FELLOWES [*in a strident voice, from below*]: Shannon! Shannon!

SHANNON: For God's sake, help me with her.

MAXINE: You know I'll help you, baby, but why don't you lay off the young ones and cultivate an interest in normal grown-up women?

MISS FELLOWES [*her voice coming nearer*]: Shannon!

SHANNON [*shouting down the hill*]: Come on up, Miss Fellowes, everything's fixed. [*To Maxine*] Oh, God, here she comes chargin' up the hill like a bull elephant on a rampage!

[MISS FELLOWES *thrashes through the foliage at the top of the jungle path.*]

Miss Fellowes, never do that! Not at high noon in a tropical country in summer. Never charge up a hill like you were leading a troop of cavalry attacking an almost impregnable . . .

MISS FELLOWES [*panting and furious*]: I don't want advice or instructions, I want the *bus* key!

SHANNON: Mrs Faulk, this is Miss Judith Fellowes.

MISS FELLOWES: Is this man making a deal with you?

MAXINE: I don't know what you –

MISS FELLOWES: Is this man getting a *kick-back* out of you?

MAXINE: Nobody gets any kick-back out of me. I turn away more people than –

MISS FELLOWES [*cutting in*]: This isn't the Ambos Mundos. It says in the brochure that in Puerto Barrio we stay at the Ambos Mundos in the heart of the city.

SHANNON: Yes, on the plaza – tell her about the plaza.

MAXINE: What about the plaza?

SHANNON: It's hot, noisy, stinking, swarming with flies. Pariah dogs
dying in the –

MISS FELLOWES: How is this place better?

SHANNON: The view from this veranda is equal and I think better
than the view from Victoria Peak in Hong Kong, the view from
the roof-terrace of the Sultan's palace in –

MISS FELLOWES [*cutting in*]: I want the view of a clean bed, a bathroom with plumbing that works, and food that is eatable and
digestible and not contaminated by filthy –

SHANNON: *Miss Fellowes!*

MISS FELLOWES: Take your hand off my arm.

SHANNON: Look at this sample menu. The cook is a Chinese
imported from Shanghai by *me*! Sent here by *me*, year before last,
in nineteen thirty-eight. He was the chef at the Royal Colonial
Club in –

MISS FELLOWES [*cutting in*]: You got a telephone here?

MAXINE: Sure, in the office.

MISS FELLOWES: I want to use it – I'll call collect. Where's the office?

MAXINE [*to Pancho*]: Llevala al telefono!

[*With* PANCHO *showing her the way,* MISS FELLOWES *stalks off
around the veranda to the office.* SHANNON *falls back, sighing desperately, against the veranda wall.*]

MAXINE: Hah!

SHANNON: Why did you have to . . . ?

MAXINE: Huh?

SHANNON: Come out looking like this! For you it's funny, but for me
it's . . .

MAXINE: This is how I *look*. What's wrong with how I *look*?

SHANNON: I told you to button your shirt. Are you so proud of your
boobs that you won't button your shirt up? – Go in the office and
see if she's calling Blake Tours to get me fired.

MAXINE: She better not unless she pays for the call.

[*She goes around the turn of the veranda.*]

[MISS HANNAH JELKES *appears below the veranda steps and stops short as* SHANNON *turns to the wall, pounding his fist against it with a sobbing sound in his throat.*]

HANNAH: Excuse me.

[SHANNON *looks down at her, dazed.* HANNAH *is remarkable-looking – ethereal, almost ghostly. She suggests a Gothic cathedral image of a medieval saint, but animated. She could be thirty, she could be forty: she is totally feminine and yet androgynous-looking – almost timeless. She is wearing a cotton print dress and has a bag slung on a strap over her shoulder.*]

Is this the Costa Verde Hotel?

SHANNON [*suddenly pacified by her appearance*]: Yes. Yes, it is.

HANNAH: Are you . . . you're not, the hotel manager, are you?

SHANNON: No. She'll be right back.

HANNAH: Thank you. Do you have any idea if they have two vacancies here? One for myself and one for my grandfather who's waiting in a taxi down there on the road. I didn't want to bring him up the hill – till I'd made sure they have rooms for us first.

SHANNON: Well, there's plenty of room here out-of-season – like now.

HANNAH: Good! Wonderful! I'll get him out of the taxi.

SHANNON: Need any help?

HANNAH: No, thank you. We'll make it all right.

[*She gives him a pleasant nod and goes back off down the path through the rain forest. A coconut plops to the ground; a parrot screams at a distance.* SHANNON *drops into the hammock and stretches out. Then* MAXINE *reappears.*]

SHANNON: How about the call? Did she make a phone call?

MAXINE: She called a judge in Texas – Blowing Rock, Texas. Collect.

SHANNON: She's trying to get me fired and she is also trying to pin on me a rape charge, a charge of statutory rape.

MAXINE: What's 'statutory rape'? I've never known what that was.

SHANNON: That's when a man is seduced by a girl under twenty. [*She chuckles.*] It's not funny, Maxine honey.

MAXINE: Why do you want the young ones – or think that you do?

SHANNON: I don't want any, any – regardless of age.

MAXINE: Then why do you take them, Shannon? [*He swallows but does not answer.*] – Huh, Shannon.

SHANNON: People need human contact, Maxine honey.

MAXINE: What size shoe do you wear?

SHANNON: I don't get the point of that question.

MAXINE: These shoes are shot and if I remember correctly, you travel with only one pair. Fred's estate included one good pair of shoes and your feet look about his size.

SHANNON: I loved ole Fred, but I don't want to fill his shoes, honey.

[*She has removed Shannon's beat-up, English-made oxfords.*]

MAXINE: Your socks are shot. Fred's socks would fit you, too, Shannon. [*She opens his collar.*] Aw-aw, I see you got on your gold cross. That's a bad sign, it means you're thinkin' again about goin' back to the Church.

SHANNON: This is my last tour, Maxine. I wrote my old Bishop this morning a complete confession and a complete capitulation.

[*She takes a letter from his damp shirt pocket.*]

MAXINE: If this is the letter, baby, you've sweated through it, so the old bugger couldn't read it even if you mailed it to him this time.

[*She has started around the veranda, and goes off as* HANK *reappears up the hill-path, mopping his face.* SHANNON'S *relaxed position in the hammock aggravates* HANK *sorely.*]

HANK: Will you get your ass out of that hammock?

SHANNON: No, I will not.

HANK: Shannon, git out of that hammock! [*He kicks at Shannon's hips in the hammock.*]

SHANNON: Hank, if you can't function under rough circumstances, you are in the wrong racket, man. I gave you instructions; the instructions were simple. I said get them out of the bus and . . .

[MAXINE *comes back with a kettle of water, a towel and other shaving equipment.*]

HANK: Out of the hammock, Shannon! [*He kicks Shannon again, harder.*]

SHANNON [*warningly*]: That's enough, Hank. A little familiarity goes a long way, but not as far as you're going. [MAXINE *starts lathering his face.*] What's this, what are you . . .

MAXINE: Haven't you ever had a shave-and-haircut by a lady barber?

HANK: The kid has gone into hysterics.

MAXINE: Hold still, Shannon.

SHANNON: Hank, hysteria is a natural phenomenon, the common denominator of the female nature. It's the big female weapon, and the test of a man is his ability to cope with it, and I can't believe you can't. If I believe that you couldn't, I would not be able –

MAXINE: Hold still!

SHANNON: I'm holding still. [*To Hank*] No, I wouldn't be able to take you out with me again. So go on back down there and –

HANK: You want me to go back down there and tell them you're getting a shave up here in a hammock?

MAXINE: Tell them that Reverend Larry is going back to the Church, so they can go back to the Female College in Texas.

HANK: I want another beer.

MAXINE: Help yourself, piggly-wiggly; the cooler's in my office right around there. [*She points around the corner of the veranda.*]

SHANNON [*as HANK goes off*]: It's horrible how you got to bluff and keep bluffing even when hollering 'Help!' is all you're up to, Maxine. *You cut me!*

MAXINE: You didn't hold still.

SHANNON: Just trim the beard a little.

MAXINE: I know. Baby, tonight we'll go night-swimming, whether it storms or not.

SHANNON: Ah, God . . .

MAXINE: The Mexican kids are wonderful night-swimmers . . . Hah, when I found 'em they were taking the two-hundred-foot dives off the Quebrada, but the Quebrada Hotel kicked 'em out for being over-attentive to the lady guests there. That's how I got hold of them.

SHANNON: Maxine, you're bigger than life and twice as unnatural, honey.

MAXINE: No one's bigger than life-size, Shannon, or even ever that big, except maybe Fred. [*She shouts 'Fred?' and gets a faint answering echo from an adjoining hill.*] Little Sir Echo is all that answers for him now, Shannon, but . . . [*She pats some bay rum on his face.*] Dear old Fred was always a mystery to me. He was so patient and tolerant with me that it was insulting to me. A man and a woman have got to challenge each other; y'know what I mean. I mean I hired those diving-boys from the Quebrada six months before Fred died, and did he care? Did he give a damn when I started night-swimming with them? No. He'd go night-*fishing*, all night, and when I got up the next day, he'd be preparing to go out fishing again, but he just caught the fish and threw them back in the sea.

[HANK *returns and sits drinking his beer on the steps.*]

SHANNON: The mystery of old Fred was simple. He was just cool and decent; that's all the mystery of him . . . Get your pair of night-swimmers to grab my ladies' luggage out of the bus before the vocal-teacher gets off the phone and stops them.

MAXINE [*shouting*]: Pedro! Pancho! Muchachos! Trae las maletas al anejo! Pronto! [*The Mexican boys start down the path.* MAXINE *sits in the hammock beside Shannon.*] You I'll put in Fred's old room, next to me.

SHANNON: You want me in his socks and his shoes and in his room next to you? [*He stares at her with a shocked surmise of her intentions towards him, then flops back down in the hammock with an incredulous laugh.*] Oh no, honey. I've just been hanging on till I could get in this hammock on this veranda over the rain forest and the still-water beach; that's all that can pull me through this last tour in a condition to go back to my . . . original . . . vocation.

MAXINE: Hah, you still have some rational moments when you face the fact that churchgoers don't go to church to hear atheistical sermons.

SHANNON: Goddammit, I never preached an atheistical sermon in a church in my life, and . . .

[MISS FELLOWES *has charged out of the office and round the veranda to bear down on* SHANNON *and* MAXINE, *who jumps up out of the hammock.*]

MISS FELLOWES: I've completed my call, which I made collect to Texas.

[MAXINE *shrugs, going by her around the veranda.* MISS FELLOWES *runs across the veranda.*]

SHANNON [*sitting up in the hammock*]: Excuse me, Miss Fellowes, for not getting out of this hammock, but I . . . Miss Fellowes? Please sit down a minute. I want to confess something to you.

MISS FELLOWES: *That* ought to be int'restin'! *What?*

SHANNON: Just that – well, like everyone else, at some point or other in life, my life has cracked up on me.

MISS FELLOWES: How does that compensate *us?*

SHANNON: I don't think I know what you mean by *compensate*, Miss Fellowes. [*He props himself up and gazes at her with the gentlest bewilderment, calculated to melt a heart of stone.*]
I mean I've just confessed to you that I'm at the end of my rope, and you say, 'How does that compensate *us?*' Please, Miss Fellowes. Don't make me feel that any adult human being puts personal compensation before the dreadful, bare fact of a man at the end of his rope who still has to try to go on, to continue, as if he'd never been better or stronger in his whole existence. No, don't do that; it would . . .

MISS FELLOWES: It would *what?*

SHANNON: Shake if not shatter everything left of my faith in essential . . . human . . . *goodness!*

MAXINE [*returning, with a pair of socks*]: Hah!

MISS FELLOWES: Can you sit there, I mean lie there – yeah, I mean *lie* there . . . ! and talk to me about –

MAXINE: Hah!

MISS FELLOWES: 'Essential human goodness?' Why, just plain human decency is beyond your imagination, Shannon, so lie there, lie there and *lie* there, we're *going!*

SHANNON [*rising from the hammock*]: Miss Fellowes, I thought that I
was conducting this party, not you.

MISS FELLOWES: You? You just now *admitted* you're incompetent, as
well as . . .

MAXINE: Hah!

SHANNON: Maxine, will you –

MISS FELLOWES [*cutting in with cold, righteous fury*]: *Shannon,* we girls
have worked and slaved all year at Baptist Female College for this
Mexican tour, and the tour is a cheat!

SHANNON [*to himself*]: Fantastic!

MISS FELLOWES: Yes, *cheat!* You haven't stuck to the schedule and you
haven't stuck to the itinerary advertised in the brochure which
Blake Tours put out. Now, either Blake Tours is cheating us or
you are cheating Blake Tours, and I'm putting wheels in motion
– I don't care *what* it costs me – I'm . . .

SHANNON: Oh, Miss Fellowes, isn't it just as plain to you as it is to me
that your hysterical insults, which are not at all easy for any born
and bred gentleman to accept, are not . . . *motivated, provoked* by
. . . anything as *trivial* as the, the . . . the motivations that you're,
you're . . . *ascribing* them to? Now can't we talk about the *real, true*
cause of . . .

MISS FELLOWES: Cause of *what?*

[CHARLOTTE GOODALL *appears at the top of the hill.*]

SHANNON: – Cause of your *rage,* Miss Fellowes, your –

MISS FELLOWES: *Charlotte!* Stay down the hill in the *bus!*

CHARLOTTE: Judy, they're –

MISS FELLOWES: *Obey me! Down!*

[CHARLOTTE *retreats from view like a well-trained dog.* MISS FEL-
LOWES *charges back to* SHANNON, *who has got out of the hammock. He places a conciliatory hand on her arm.*]

MISS FELLOWES: *Take your hand off my arm!*

MAXINE: Hah!

SHANNON: *Fantastic.* Miss Fellowes, please! No more shouting?
Please? Now I really must ask you to let this party of ladies come

up here and judge the accommodations for themselves and compare them with what they saw passing through town. Miss Fellowes, there is such a thing as charm and beauty in some places, as much as there's nothing but dull, ugly imitation of highway motels in Texas and –

[MISS FELLOWES *charges over to the path to see if* CHARLOTTE *has obeyed her.* SHANNON *follows, still propitiatory.* MAXINE *says 'Hah,' but she gives him an affectionate little pat as he goes by her. He pushes her hand away as he continues his appeal to* MISS FELLOWES.]

MISS FELLOWES: I've taken a look at those rooms and they'd make a room at the 'Y' look like a suite at the Ritz.

SHANNON: Miss Fellowes, I am employed by Blake Tours and so I'm not in a position to tell you quite frankly what mistakes they've made in their advertising brochure. They just don't know Mexico. I do. I know it as well as I know five out of all six continents on the –

MISS FELLOWES: *Continent! Mexico?* You never even studied geography if you –

SHANNON: My degree from Sewanee is *Doctor of Divinity*, but for the past ten years geography's been my *speciality*, Miss Fellowes, honey! Name any tourist agency I haven't worked for! You couldn't! I'm only, now, with Blake Tours because I –

MISS FELLOWES: Because you *what?* Couldn't keep your hands off innocent, under-age girls in your –

SHANNON: Now, Miss Fellowes . . . [*He touches her arm again.*]

MISS FELLOWES: Take your hand off my arm!

SHANNON: For days I've known you were furious and unhappy, but –

MISS FELLOWES: *Oh!* You think it's just *me* that's unhappy. Hauled in that stifling bus over the byways, off the highways, shook up and bumped up so you could get your rake-off, is that what you –

SHANNON: What I know is, all I know is, that you are the *leader of the insurrection!*

MISS FELLOWES: All of the girls in this party have dysentery!

SHANNON: That you can't hold me to blame for.

MISS FELLOWES: I *do* hold you to blame for it.

SHANNON: Before we entered Mexico, at New Laredo, Texas, I called you ladies together in the depot on the Texas side of the border and I passed out mimeographed sheets of instructions on what to eat and what *not* to eat, what to drink, what *not* to drink in the –

MISS FELLOWES: It's not *what* we ate but *where* we ate that gave us dysentery!

SHANNON [*shaking his head like a metronome*]: It is not dysentery.

MISS FELLOWES: The result of eating in places that would be condemned by the Board of Health in –

SHANNON: Now wait a minute –

MISS FELLOWES: For disregarding all rules of sanitation.

SHANNON: It is not dysentery, it is not amoebic, it's nothing at all but –

MAXINE: Montezuma's Revenge! That's what we call it.

SHANNON: I even passed out pills. I passed out bottles of Enteroviaform because I knew that some of you ladies would rather be victims of Montezuma's Revenge than spend cinco centavos on bottled water in stations.

MISS FELLOWES: You sold those pills at a profit of fifty cents per bottle.

MAXINE: Hah-hah! [*She knocks off the end of a coconut with the machete, preparing a rum-coco.*]

SHANNON: Now fun is fun, Miss Fellowes, but an accusation like that –

MISS FELLOWES: I *priced* them in *pharmacies*, because I suspected that –

SHANNON: Miss Fellowes, I am a gentleman, and as a gentleman I can't be insulted like this. I mean I can't accept insults of that kind even from a member of a tour that I am conducting. And Miss Fellowes, I think you might also remember, you might try to remember, that you're speaking to an ordained minister of the Church.

MISS FELLOWES: *De*-frocked! But still trying to pass himself off as a minister!

MAXINE: How about a rum-coco? We give a complimentary rum-coco to all our guests here. [*Her offer is apparently unheard. She shrugs and drinks the rum-coco herself.*]

SHANNON: – Miss Fellowes? In every party there is always one individual that's discontented, that is not satisfied with all I do to make the tour more ... unique – to make it different from the ordinary, to give it a personal thing, the Shannon touch.

MISS FELLOWES: The gyp touch, the touch of a defrocked minister.

SHANNON: Miss Fellowes, don't, don't, don't ... do what ... you're doing! [*He is on the verge of hysteria, he makes some incoherent sounds, gesticulates with clenched fists, then stumbles wildly across the veranda and leans panting for breath against a post.*] Don't! Break! *Human! Pride!*

VOICE FROM DOWN THE HILL [*a very Texan accent*]: Judy? They're taking our luggage!

MISS FELLOWES [*shouting down the hill*]: Girls! Girls! Don't let those boys touch your luggage. Don't let them bring your luggage in this dump!

GIRL'S VOICE [*from below*]: Judy! We can't stop them!

MAXINE: Those kids don't understand English.

MISS FELLOWES [*wild with rage*]: Will you please tell those boys to take that luggage back down to the bus? [*She calls to the party below again.*] Girls! Hold on to your luggage; don't let them take it away! We're going to drive back to A-cap-ul-co! *You hear?*

GIRL'S VOICE: Judy, they want a swim, first!

MISS FELLOWES: I'll be right back. [*She rushes off, shouting at the Mexican boys.*] You! Boys! Muchachos! *You carry that luggage back down!*

[*The voices continue, fading.* SHANNON *moves brokenly across the veranda.* MAXINE *shakes her head.*]

MAXINE: Shannon, give 'em the bus key and let 'em go.

SHANNON: And me do what?

MAXINE: Stay here.

SHANNON: In Fred's old bedroom – yeah, in Fred's old bedroom.

MAXINE: You could do worse.

SHANNON: Could I? Well, then, I'll do worse, I'll ... do worse.

MAXINE: Aw now, baby.

SHANNON: If I could do worse, I'll do worse ... [*He grips the section of railing by the veranda steps and stares with wide lost eyes. His chest heaves like a spent runner's and he is bathed in sweat.*]

MAXINE: Give me that ignition key. I'll take it down to the driver while you bathe and rest and have a rum-coco, baby.

[SHANNON *simply shakes his head slightly. Harsh bird cries sound in the rain forest. Voices are heard on the path.*]

HANNAH: Nonno, you've lost your sun glasses.
NONNO: No. Took them off. No sun.

[HANNAH *appears at the top of the path, pushing her grandfather,* NONNO, *in a wheel-chair. He is a very old man, but has a powerful voice for his age and always seems to be shouting something of importance.* NONNO *is a poet and a showman. There is a good kind of pride and he has it, carrying it like a banner wherever he goes. He is immaculately dressed – a linen suit, white as his thick poet's hair; a black string tie; and he is holding a black cane with a gold crook.*]

Which way is the sea?
HANNAH: Right down below the hill, Nonno. [*He turns in the wheelchair and raises a hand to shield his eyes.*] We can't see it from here. [*The old man is deaf, and she shouts to make him hear.*]
NONNO: I can feel it and smell it. [*A murmur of wind sweeps through the rain forest.*] It's the cradle of life. [*He is shouting, too.*] Life began in the sea.
MAXINE: These two with your party?
SHANNON: No.
MAXINE: They look like a pair of loonies.
SHANNON: Shut up.

[SHANNON *looks at Hannah and Nonno steadily, with a relief of tension almost like that of someone going under hypnosis. The old man still squints down the path, blindly, but* HANNAH *is facing the veranda with a proud person's hope of acceptance when it is desperately needed.*]

HANNAH: How do you do.
MAXINE: Hello.
HANNAH: Have you ever tried pushing a gentleman in a wheel-chair uphill through a rain forest?
MAXINE: Nope, and I wouldn't even try it *downhill*.
HANNAH: Well, now that we've made it, I don't regret the effort.

What a view for a painter! [*She looks about her, panting, digging into her shoulder-bag for a handkerchief, aware that her face is flushed and sweating.*] They told me in town that this was the ideal place for a painter, and they weren't – *whew* – exaggerating!

SHANNON: You've got a scratch on your forehead.

HANNAH: Oh, is that what I felt.

SHANNON: Better put iodine on it.

HANNAH: Yes, I'll attend to that – *whew* – later, thank you.

MAXINE: Anything I can do for you?

HANNAH: I'm looking for the manager of the hotel.

MAXINE: Me – speaking.

HANNAH: Oh, *you're* the manager, *good*! How do you do, I'm Hannah Jelkes, Mrs . . .

MAXINE: Faulk, Maxine Faulk. What can I do for you folks?

[*Her tone indicates no desire to do anything for them.*]

HANNAH [*turning quickly to her grandfather*]: Nonno, the manager is a *lady* from the States.

[NONNO *lifts a branch of wild orchids from his lap, ceremonially, with the instinctive gallantry of his kind.*]

NONNO [*shouting*]: Give the lady these – botanical curiosities! – you picked on the way up.

HANNAH: I believe they're wild orchids, isn't that what they are?

SHANNON: Laelia tibicina.

HANNAH: Oh!

NONNO: But tell her, Hannah, tell her to keep them in the icebox till after dark; they draw bees in the sun! [*He rubs a sting on his chin with a rueful chuckle.*]

MAXINE: Are you all looking for rooms here?

HANNAH: Yes, we are, but we've come without reservations.

MAXINE: Well, honey, the Costa Verde is closed in September – except for a few special guests, so . . .

SHANNON: They're special guests, for God's sake.

MAXINE: I thought you said they didn't come with your party.

HANNAH: Please let us be special guests.

MAXINE: *Watch out!*

[NONNO *has started struggling out of the wheel-chair.* SHANNON *rushes over to keep him from falling.* HANNAH *has started towards him, too, then, seeing that* SHANNON *has caught him, she turns back to Maxine.*]

HANNAH: In twenty-five years of travel this is the first time we've ever arrived at a place without advance reservations.

MAXINE: Honey, that old man ought to be in a hospital.

HANNAH: Oh, no, no, he just sprained his ankle a little in Tasco this morning. He just needs a good night's rest; he'll be on his feet tomorrow. His recuperative powers are absolutely amazing for someone who is ninety-seven years *young*.

SHANNON: Easy, Grampa. Hang on. [*He is supporting the old man up to the veranda.*] Two steps. One! Two! Now you've made it, Grampa.

[NONNO *keeps chuckling breathlessly as* SHANNON *gets him on to the veranda and into a wicker rocker.*]

HANNAH [*breaking in quickly*]: I can't tell you how much I appreciate your taking us in here now. It's – providential.

MAXINE: Well, I can't send that old man back down the hill – right now – but, like I told you, the Costa Verde's practically closed in September. I just take in a few folks as a special accommodation and we operate on a special basis this month.

NONNO [*cutting in abruptly and loudly*]: Hannah, tell the lady that my perambulator is temporary. I will soon be ready to crawl and then to toddle and before long I will be leaping around here like an – old – mountain goat, ha-ha-ha-ha . . .

HANNAH: Yes, I explained that, Grandfather.

NONNO: I don't like being on wheels.

HANNAH: Yes, my grandfather feels that the decline of the western world began with the invention of the wheel.

[*She laughs heartily, but* MAXINE'S *look is unresponsive.*]

NONNO: And tell the manager . . . the, uh, lady . . . that I know some hotels don't want to take dogs, cats, or monkeys and some don't even solicit the patronage of infants in their late nineties who arrive in perambulators with flowers instead of rattles ... [*He chuckles with a sort of fearful, slightly mad quality.* HANNAH *perhaps has the impulse to clap a hand over his mouth at this moment, but must stand there smiling and smiling and smiling.*] ... and a brandy flask instead of a teething ring, but tell her that these, uh, concessions to man's seventh age are only temporary, and ...

HANNAH: Nonno, I told her the wheel-chair's because of a sprained ankle, Nonno!

SHANNON [*to himself*]: Fantastic.

NONNO: And after my siesta, I'll wheel it back down the hill, I'll kick it back down the hill, right into the sea, and tell her ...

HANNAH: Yes? What, Nonno? [*She has stopped smiling now. Her tone and her look are frankly desperate.*] What shall I tell her now, Nonno?

NONNO: Tell her that if she'll forgive my disgraceful longevity and this ... temporary decrepitude ... I will present her with the last signed ... compitty [*he means 'copy'*] of my first volume of verse, published in ... when, Hannah?

HANNAH [*hopelessly*]: The day that President Ulysses S. Grant was inaugurated, Nonno.

NONNO: *Morning Trumpet!* Where is it – you have it, give it to her right now.

HANNAH: Later, a little later! [*Then she turns to Maxine and Shannon.*] My grandfather is the poet Jonathan Coffin. He is ninety-seven years *young* and will be ninety-eight years *young* the fifth of next month, October.

MAXINE: Old folks are remarkable, yep. The office phone's ringing – excuse me, I'll be right back. [*She goes around the veranda.*]

NONNO: Did I talk too much?

HANNAH [*quietly, to Shannon*]: I'm afraid that he did. I don't think she's going to take us.

SHANNON: She'll take you. Don't worry about it.

HANNAH: Nobody would take us in town, and if we don't get in here, I would have to wheel him back down through the rain forest, and then *what*, then *where*? There would just be the road, and no direction to move in, except out to sea – and I doubt that we could make it divide before us.

SHANNON: That won't be necessary. I have a little influence with the patrona.

HANNAH: Oh, then, do use it. Please. Her eyes said *no* in big blue capital letters.

[SHANNON *pours some water from a pitcher on the veranda and hands it to the old man.*]

NONNO: What is this – libation?

SHANNON: Some ice-water, Grampa.

HANNAH: Oh, that's kind of you. Thank you. I'd better give him a couple of salt tablets to wash down with it. [*Briskly she removes a bottle from her shoulder-bag.*] Won't you have some? I see you're perspiring, too. You have to be careful not to become dehydrated in the hot seasons under the Tropic of Cancer.

SHANNON [*pouring another glass of water*]: Are you a little *financially* dehydrated, too?

HANNAH: That's right. Bone-dry, and I think the patrona suspects it. It's a logical assumption, since I pushed him up here myself, and the patrona has the look of a very logical woman. I am sure she knows that we couldn't afford to hire the taxi-driver to help us up here.

MAXINE [*calling from the back*]: Pancho?

HANNAH: A woman's practicality when she's managing something is harder than a man's for another woman to cope with, so if you have influence with her, please do use it. Please try to convince her that my grandfather will be on his feet tomorrow, if not tonight, and with any luck whatsoever, the money situation will be solved just as quickly. Oh, here she comes back, do help us!

[*Involuntarily,* HANNAH *seizes hold of Shannon's wrist as* MAXINE *stalks back on to the veranda, still shouting for* PANCHO. *The Mexican boy reappears, sucking a juicy peeled mango – its juice running down his chin on to his throat.*]

MAXINE: Pancho, run down to the beach and tell Herr Fahrenkopf that the German Embassy's waiting on the phone for him. [PANCHO *stares at her blankly until she repeats the order in Spanish.*] Dile a Herr Fahrenkopf que la embajada alemana lo llama al telefono. Corre, corre! [PANCHO *starts indolently down the path, still sucking noisily on the mango.*] I said run! Corre, corre! [*He goes into a leisurely loping pace and disappears through the foliage.*]

HANNAH: What graceful people they are!

MAXINE: Yeah, they're graceful like cats, and just as dependable, too.

HANNAH: Shall we, uh . . . *register* now?

MAXINE: You all can register later but I'll have to collect six dollars from you first if you want to put your names in the pot for supper. That's how I've got to operate here out of season.

HANNAH: Six? Dollars?

MAXINE: Yeah, three each. In season we operate on the continental plan, but out of season like this we change to the modified American plan.

HANNAH: Oh, what is the, uh . . . modification of it? [*She gives Shannon a quick glance of appeal as she stalls for time, but his attention has turned inward as the bus horn blows down the hill.*]

MAXINE: Just two meals are included instead of all three.

HANNAH [*moving closer to Shannon and raising her voice*]: Breakfast and dinner?

MAXINE: A continental breakfast and a cold lunch.

SHANNON [*aside*]: Yeah, very cold – cracked ice – if you crack it yourself.

HANNAH [*reflectively*]: Not dinner.

MAXINE: No! Not dinner.

HANNAH: Oh, I see, uh, but . . . we, uh, operate on a special basis ourselves. I'd better explain it to you.

MAXINE: How do you mean 'operate' – on what 'basis'?

HANNAH: Here's our card. I think you may have heard of us. [*She presents the card to Maxine.*] We've had a good many write-ups. My grandfather is the oldest living and practising poet. *And* he gives recitations. I . . . paint . . . watercolours and I'm a 'quick sketch artist'. We travel together. We pay our way as we go by my grandfather's recitations and the sale of my watercolours and quick sketches in charcoal or pastel.

SHANNON [*to himself*]: I have fever.

HANNAH: I usually pass among the tables at lunch and dinner in a hotél. I wear an artist's smock – picturesquely dabbled with paint – wide Byronic collar and flowing silk tie. I don't push myself on people. I just display my work and smile at them sweetly and if they invite me to do so sit down to make a quick character sketch in pastel or charcoal. If not? Smile sweetly and go on.

SHANNON: What does Grampa do?

HANNAH: We pass among the tables together slowly. I introduce him as the world's oldest living and practising poet. If invited, he gives a recitation of a poem. Unfortunately, all of his poems were written a long time ago. But do you know, he has started a new poem? For the first time in twenty years he's started another poem!

SHANNON: Hasn't finished it yet?

HANNAH: He still has inspiration, but his power of concentration has weakened a little, of course.

MAXINE: Right now he's not concentrating.

SHANNON: Grampa's catchin' forty winks. Grampa? Let's hit the sack.

MAXINE: Now wait a minute. I'm going to call a taxi for these folks to take them back to town.

HANNAH: Please don't do that. We tried every hotel in town and they wouldn't take us. I'm afraid I have to place myself at your . . . mercy.

[*With infinite gentleness* SHANNON *has roused the old man and is leading him into one of the cubicles back of the veranda. Distant cries of bathers are heard from the beach. The afternoon light is fading very fast now, as the sun has dropped behind an island hilltop out to sea.*]

MAXINE: Looks like you're in for one night. Just one.

HANNAH: Thank you.

MAXINE: The old man's in number 4. You take 3. Where's your luggage – no luggage?

HANNAH: I hid it behind some palmettos at the foot of the path.

SHANNON [*shouting to Pancho*]: Bring up her luggage. Tu, flojo . . . las maletas . . . baja las palmas. Vamos! [*The Mexican boys rush down the path.*] Maxine honey, would you cash a post-dated cheque for me?

MAXINE [*shrewdly*]: Yeah – mañana, maybe.

SHANNON: Thanks – generosity is the cornerstone of your nature.

[MAXINE *utters her one-note bark of a laugh as she marches around the corner of the veranda.*]

HANNAH: I'm dreadfully afraid my grandfather had a slight stroke in those high passes through the sierras. [*She says this with the coolness of someone saying that it may rain before nightfall. An instant later, a long, long sigh of wind sweeps the hillside. The bathers are heard shouting below.*]

SHANNON: Very old people get these little 'cerebral accidents', as they call them. They're not regular strokes, they're just little cerebral . . . incidents. The symptoms clear up so quickly that sometimes the old people don't even know they've had them.

[*They exchange this quiet talk without looking at each other. The Mexican boys crash back through the bushes at the top of the path, bearing some pieces of ancient luggage fantastically plastered with hotel and travel stickers indicating a vast range of wandering. The boys deposit the luggage near the steps.*]

How many times have you been around the world?

HANNAH: Almost as many times as the world's been around the sun, and I feel as if I had gone the whole way on foot.

SHANNON [*picking up her luggage*]: What's your cell number?

HANNAH [*smiling faintly*]: I believe she said it was cell number 3.

SHANNON: She probably gave you the one with the leaky roof. [*He carries the bags into the cubicle.* MAXINE *is visible to the audience only as she appears outside the door to her office on the wing of the veranda.*] But you won't find out till it rains and then it'll be too late to do much about it but swim out of it. [HANNAH *laughs wanly. Her fatigue is now very plain.* SHANNON *comes back out with her luggage.*] Yep, she gave you the one with the leaky roof so you take mine and . . .

HANNAH: Oh, no, no, Mr Shannon, I'll find a dry spot if it rains.

MAXINE [*from around the corner of the veranda*]: Shannon!

[*A bit of pantomime occurs between* HANNAH *and* SHANNON. *He wants to put her luggage in cubicle number 5. She catches hold of his arm, indicating by gesture towards the back that it is necessary to avoid displeasing the proprietor.* MAXINE *shouts his name louder.* SHANNON *surrenders to* HANNAH'S *pleading and puts her luggage back in the leaky cubicle number 3.*]

HANNAH: Thank you so much, Mr Shannon. [*She disappears behind the mosquito netting.* MAXINE *advances to the veranda angle as* SHANNON *starts towards his own cubicle.*]

MAXINE [*mimicking Hannah's voice*]: 'Thank you so much, Mr Shannon.'

SHANNON: Don't be bitchy. Some people say thank you sincerely. [*He goes past her and down the steps from the end of the veranda.*] I'm going down for a swim now.

MAXINE: The water's blood temperature this time of day.

SHANNON: Yeah; well, I have a fever, so it'll seem cooler to me. [*He crosses rapidly to the jungle path leading to the beach.*]

MAXINE [*following him*]: Wait for me. I'll . . .

[*She means she will go down with him, but he ignores her call and disappears into the foliage.* MAXINE *shrugs angrily and goes back on to the veranda. She faces out, gripping the railings tightly and glaring into the blaze of the sunset as if it were a personal enemy. Then the ocean breathes a long, cooling breath up the hill, as* NONNO'S *voice is heard from his cubicle.*]

NONNO:

How calmly does the orange branch
Observe the sky begin to blanch.
Without a cry, without a prayer.
With no expression of despair . . .

[*And from a beach cantina in the distance a marimba band is heard playing a popular song of that summer of 1940, 'Palabras de Mujer' – which means 'Words of Women'.*]

SLOW DIM OUT AND SLOW CURTAIN

Act Two

Several hours later: near sunset.
The scene is bathed in a deep golden, almost coppery light; the heavy trop-
ical foliage gleams with wetness from a recent rain.

> [MAXINE *comes around the turn of the veranda. To the formalities*
> *of evening she has made the concession of changing from levis to*
> *clean white cotton pants, and from a blue work shirt to a pink one.*
> *She is about to set up the folding card-tables for the evening meal,*
> *which is served on the veranda. All the while she is talking, she is*
> *setting up tables, etc.*]

MAXINE: Miss Jelkes?

> [HANNAH *lifts the mosquito net over the door of cubicle number 3.*]

HANNAH: Yes, Mrs Faulk?
MAXINE: Can I speak to you while I set up these tables for supper?
HANNAH: Of course, you may. I wanted to speak to you, too.

> [*She comes out. She is now wearing her artist's smock.*]

MAXINE: Good.
HANNAH: I just wanted to ask you if there's a tub-bath Grandfather
    could use. A shower is fine for me – I prefer a shower to a tub – but
    for my grandfather there is some danger of falling down in a shower
    and at his age, although he says he is made out of indiarubber, a
    broken hip-bone would be a very serious matter, so I . . .
MAXINE: What I wanted to say is I called up the Casa de Huéspedes
    about you and your Grampa, and I can get you in there.
HANNAH: Oh, but we don't want to *move*!

MAXINE: The Costa Verde isn't the right place for you. Y'see, we cater to folks that like to rough it a little, and – well, frankly, we cater to younger people.

[HANNAH *has started unfolding a card-table.*]

HANNAH: Oh yes . . . uh . . . well . . . the, uh, Casa de Huéspedes, that means a, uh, sort of a rooming-house, Mrs Faulk?

MAXINE: Boarding-house. They feed you, they'll even feed you on credit.

HANNAH: Where is it located?

MAXINE: It has a central location. You could get a doctor there quick if the old man took sick on you. You got to think about that.

HANNAH: Yes, I – [*She nods gravely, more to herself than* MAXINE.] – I *have* thought about that, but . . .

MAXINE: What are you doing?

HANNAH: Making myself useful.

MAXINE: Don't do that. I don't accept help from guests here.

[HANNAH *hesitates, but goes on setting the tables.*]

HANNAH: Oh, please, let me. Knife and fork on one side, spoon on the . . . ? [*Her voice dies out.*]

MAXINE: Just put the plates on the napkins so they don't blow away.

HANNAH: Yes, it is getting breezy on the veranda. [*She continues setting the table.*]

MAXINE: Hurricane winds are already hitting up coast.

HANNAH: We've been through several typhoons in the Orient. Sometimes *outside* disturbances like that are an almost welcome distraction from *inside* disturbances, aren't they? [*This is said almost to herself. She finishes putting the plates on the paper napkins.*] When do you want us to leave here, Mrs Faulk?

MAXINE: The boys'll move you in my station wagon tomorrow – no charge for the service.

HANNAH: That is very kind of you. [MAXINE *starts away.*] Mrs Faulk?

MAXINE [*turning back to her with obvious reluctance*]: Huh?

HANNAH: Do you know jade?

MAXINE: Jade?

HANNAH: Yes.

MAXINE: Why?

HANNAH: I have a small but interesting collection of jade pieces. I asked if you know jade because in jade it's the craftsmanship, the carving of the jade, that's most important about it. [*She has removed a jade ornament from her blouse.*] This one, for instance – a miracle of carving. Tiny as it is, it has two figures carved on it – the legendary Prince Ahk and Princess Angh, and a heron flying above them. The artist that carved it probably received for this miraculously delicate workmanship, well, I would say perhaps the price of a month's supply of rice for his family, but the merchant who employed him sold it, I would guess, for at least three hundred pounds sterling to an English lady who got tired of it and gave it to me, perhaps because I painted her not as she was at that time, but as I could see she must have looked in her youth. Can you see the carving?

MAXINE: Yeah, honey, but I'm not operating a hock-shop here. I'm trying to run a hotel.

HANNAH: I know, but couldn't you just accept it as security for a few days' stay here?

MAXINE: You're completely broke, are you?

HANNAH: Yes, we are – completely.

MAXINE: You say that like you're proud of it.

HANNAH: I'm not proud of it or ashamed of it either. It just happens to be what's happened to us, which has never happened before in all our travels.

MAXINE [*grudgingly*]: You're telling the truth, I reckon, but I told you the truth, too, when I told you, when you came here, that I had just lost my husband and he'd left me in such a financial hole that if living didn't mean more to me than money, I'd might as well have been dropped in the ocean with him.

HANNAH: Ocean?

MAXINE [*peacefully philosophical about it*]: I carried out his burial instructions exactly. Yep, my husband, Fred Faulk, was the greatest game fisherman on the West Coast of Mexico – he'd racked up unbeatable records in sailfish, tarpon, kingfish, barracuda – and on his deathbed, last week, he requested to be dropped in the sea, yeah, right out there in that bay, not even sewed up in canvas, just in his fisherman's outfit. So now old Freddie the Fisherman is feeding the fish – fishes' revenge on old Freddie. How about that, I ask you?

HANNAH [*regarding* MAXINE *sharply*]: I doubt that he regrets it.

MAXINE: I do. It gives me the shivers.

[*She is distracted by the German party singing a marching song on the path up from the beach.* SHANNON *appears at the top of the path, a wet beachrobe clinging to him.* MAXINE'*s whole concentration shifts abruptly to him. She freezes and blazes with it like an exposed power line. For a moment the 'hot light' is concentrated on her tense, furious figure.* HANNAH *provides a visual counterpoint. She clenches her eyes shut for a moment, and when they open, it is on a look of stoical despair of the refuge she has unsuccessfully fought for. Then* SHANNON *approaches the veranda and the scene is his.*]

SHANNON: Here they come up, your conquerors of the world, Maxine honey, singing 'Horst Wessel'. [*He chuckles fiercely, and starts towards the veranda steps.*]

MAXINE: Shannon, wash that sand off you before you come on the veranda.

[*The Germans are heard singing the 'Horst Wessel' marching song. Soon they appear, trooping up from the beach like an animated canvas by Rubens. They are all nearly nude, pinked and bronzed by the sun. The women have decked themselves with garlands of pale green seaweed, glistening wet, and the Munich-opera bridegroom is blowing on a great conch shell. His father-in-law, the tank manufacturer, has his portable radio, which is still transmitting a shortwave broadcast about the Battle of Britain, now at its climax.*]

HILDA [*capering, astride her rubber horse*]: Horsey, horsey, horsey!

HERR FAHRENKOPF [*ecstatically*]: London is burning, the heart of London's on fire! [WOLFGANG *turns a handspring on to the veranda and walks on his hands a few paces, then tumbles over with a great whoop.* MAXINE *laughs delightedly with the Germans.*] Beer, beer, beer!

FRAU FAHRENKOPF: Tonight champagne!

[*The euphoric horseplay and shouting continue as they gambol around the turn of the veranda.* SHANNON *has come on to the porch.* MAXINE'*s laughter dies out a little sadly, with envy.*]

SHANNON: You're turning this place into the Mexican Berchtesgaden, Maxine honey?

MAXINE: I told you to wash that sand off. [*Shouts for beer from the Germans draw her around the veranda corner.*]

HANNAH: Mr Shannon, do you happen to know the Casa de Huéspedes, or anything about it, I mean? [SHANNON *stares at her somewhat blankly.*] We are, uh, thinking of . . . *moving* there tomorrow. Do you, uh, recommend it?

SHANNON: I recommend it along with the Black Hole of Calcutta and the Siberian salt-mines.

HANNAH [*nodding reflectively*]: I suspected as much. Mr Shannon, in your touring party, do you think there might be anyone interested in my watercolours? Or in my character sketches?

SHANNON: I doubt it. I doubt that they're corny enough to please my ladies. *Oh-oh! Great Caesar's ghost . . .*

[*This exclamation is prompted by the shrill, approaching call of his name.* CHARLOTTE *appears from the rear, coming from the hotel annex, and rushes like a teen-age Medea towards the veranda.* SHANNON *ducks into his cubicle, slamming the door so quickly that a corner of the mosquito netting is caught and sticks out, flirtatiously.* CHARLOTTE *rushes on to the veranda.*]

CHARLOTTE: *Larry!*

HANNAH: Are you looking for someone, dear?

CHARLOTTE: Yeah, the man conducting our tour, Larry Shannon.

HANNAH: Oh, Mr Shannon. I think he went down to the beach.

CHARLOTTE: I just now saw him coming up from the beach.

[*She is tense and trembling, and her eyes keep darting up and down the veranda.*]

HANNAH: Oh. Well . . . But . . .

CHARLOTTE: Larry? Larry! [*Her shouts startle the rain forest birds into a clamorous moment.*]

HANNAH: Would you like to leave a message for him, dear?

CHARLOTTE: No. I'm staying right here till he comes out of wherever he's hiding.

HANNAH: Why don't you just sit down, dear. I'm an artist, a painter. I was just sorting out my watercolours and sketches in this portfolio, and look what I've come across.

[*She selects a sketch and holds it up.*]

SHANNON [*from inside his cubicle*]: Oh, God!

CHARLOTTE [*darting to the cubicle*]: Larry, let me in there!

[*She beats on the door of the cubicle as* HERR FAHRENKOPF *comes around the veranda with his portable radio. He is bug-eyed with excitement over the news broadcast in German.*]

HANNAH: Guten abend.

[HERR FAHRENKOPF *jerks his head with a toothy grin, raising a hand for silence.* HANNAH *nods agreeably and approaches him with her portfolio of drawings. He maintains the grin as she displays one picture after another.* HANNAH *is uncertain whether the grin is for the pictures or the news broadcast. He stares at the pictures, jerking his head from time to time. It is rather like the pantomime of showing lantern slides.*]

CHARLOTTE [*suddenly crying out again*]: Larry, open this door and let me in! I know you're in there, Larry!

HERR FAHRENKOPF: Silence, please, for one moment! This is a recording of Der Führer addressing the Reichstag just . . . [*He glances at his wristwatch*] . . . eight hours ago, today, transmitted by Deutsches Nachrichtenbüro to Mexico City. Please! Quiet, bitte!

[*A human voice like a mad dog's bark emerges from the static momentarily.* CHARLOTTE *goes on pounding on Shannon's door.* HANNAH *suggests in pantomime that they go to the back veranda, but* HERR FAHRENKOPF *despairs of hearing that broadcast. As he rises to leave, the light catches his polished glasses so that he appears for a moment to have electric light bulbs in his forehead. Then he ducks his head in a genial little bow and goes out beyond the veranda, where he performs some muscle-flexing movements of a formalized nature, like the preliminary stances of Japanese Sumo wrestlers.*]

HANNAH: May I show you my work on the other veranda?

[HANNAH *has started to follow Herr Fahrenkopf with her portfolio, but the sketches fall out, and she stops to gather them from the floor with the sad, preoccupied air of a lonely child picking flowers.* SHAN-NON's *head slowly, furtively, appears through the window of his cubicle. He draws quickly back as* CHARLOTTE *darts that way, stepping on Hannah's spilt sketches.* HANNAH *utters a soft cry of protest, which is drowned by* CHARLOTTE'*s renewed clamour.*]

CHARLOTTE: Larry, Larry, Judy's looking for me. Let me come in, Larry, before she finds me here!
SHANNON: You can't come in. Stop shouting and I'll come out.
CHARLOTTE: All right, come out.
SHANNON: Stand back from the door so I *can*.

[*She moves a little aside and he emerges from his cubicle like a man entering a place of execution. He leans against the wall, mopping the sweat off his face with a handkerchief.*]

How does Miss Fellowes know what happened that night? Did you tell her?
CHARLOTTE: I didn't tell her; she guessed.
SHANNON: Guessing isn't knowing. If she is just guessing, that means she doesn't know – I mean if you're not lying, if you didn't tell her.

[HANNAH *has finished picking up her drawings and moves quietly over to the far side of the veranda.*]

CHARLOTTE: Don't talk to me like that.
SHANNON: Don't complicate my life now, please, for God's sake; don't complicate my life now.
CHARLOTTE: Why have you changed like this?

SHANNON: I have a fever. Don't complicate me . . . fever.

CHARLOTTE: You act like you hated me now.

SHANNON: You're going to get me kicked out of Blake Tours, Charlotte.

CHARLOTTE: Judy is, not me.

SHANNON: Why did you sing 'I Love You Truly' at me?

CHARLOTTE: Because I do love you truly!

SHANNON: Honey girl, don't you know that nothing worse could happen to a girl in your, your . . . unstable condition . . . than to get emotionally mixed up with a man in my unstable condition, huh?

CHARLOTTE: No, no, no I –

SHANNON [*cutting through*]: Two unstable conditions can set a whole world on fire, can blow it up, past repair, and that is just as true between two people as it's true between . . .

CHARLOTTE: All I know is you've got to marry me, Larry, after what happened between us in Mexico City!

SHANNON: A man in my condition can't marry; it isn't decent or legal. He's lucky if he can even hold on to his job. [*He keeps catching hold of her hands and plucking them off his shoulders.*] I'm almost out of my mind. Can't you see that, honey?

CHARLOTTE: I don't believe you don't love me.

SHANNON: Honey, it's almost impossible for anybody to believe they're not loved by someone they believe they love, but, honey, I love *nobody*. I'm like that; it isn't my fault. When I brought you home that night I told you good night in the hall, just kissed you on the cheek like the little girl that you are, but the instant I opened my door, you rushed into my room and I couldn't get you out of it, not even when I, oh God, tried to scare you out of it by, oh God, don't you remember?

[MISS FELLOWES' *voice is heard from back of the hotel calling,* 'Charlotte!']

CHARLOTTE: Yes, I remember that after making love to me, you hit me, Larry, you struck me in the face, and you twisted my arm to make me kneel on the floor and pray with you for forgiveness.

SHANNON: I do that, I do that always when I, when . . . I don't have a dime left in my nervous emotional bank account – I can't write a cheque on it, now.

CHARLOTTE: Larry, let me help you!

MISS FELLOWES [*approaching*]: Charlotte, Charlotte, Charlie!

CHARLOTTE: Help me and let me help you!

SHANNON: The helpless can't help the helpless!

CHARLOTTE: Let me in. Judy's coming!

SHANNON: Let me go. Go away!

[*He thrusts her violently back and rushes into his cubicle, slamming and bolting the door – though the gauze netting is left sticking out. As* MISS FELLOWES *charges on to the veranda,* CHARLOTTE *runs into the next cubicle, and* HANNAH *moves over from where she has been watching and meets her in the centre.*]

MISS FELLOWES: Shannon, Shannon! Where are you?

HANNAH: I think Mr Shannon has gone down to the beach.

MISS FELLOWES: Was Charlotte Goodall with him? A young blonde girl in our party – was she with him?

HANNAH: No, nobody was with him; he was completely alone.

MISS FELLOWES: I heard a door slam.

HANNAH: That was mine.

MISS FELLOWES [*pointing to the door with the gauze sticking out*]: Is this yours?

HANNAH: Yes, mine. I rushed out to catch the sunset.

[*At this moment* MISS FELLOWES *hears* CHARLOTTE *sobbing in Hannah's cubicle. She throws the door open.*]

MISS FELLOWES: Charlotte! Come out of there, Charlie! [*She has seized* CHARLOTTE *by the wrist.*] What's your word worth – nothing? You promised you'd stay away from him! [CHARLOTTE *frees her arm, sobbing bitterly.* MISS FELLOWES *seizes her again, tighter, and starts dragging her away.*] I have talked to your father about this man by long-distance and he's getting out a warrant for his arrest, if he dare try coming back to the States after this!

CHARLOTTE: I don't care.

MISS FELLOWES: I do! I'm responsible for you.

CHARLOTTE: I don't want to go back to Texas.

MISS FELLOWES: Yes, you do! And you will!

[*She takes* CHARLOTTE *firmly by the arm and drags her away behind the hotel.* HANNAH *comes out of her cubicle, where she had gone when* MISS FELLOWES *pulled* CHARLOTTE *out of it.*]

SHANNON [*from his cubicle*]: Ah, God . . .

[HANNAH *crosses to his cubicle and knocks by the door.*]

HANNAH: The coast is clear now, Mr Shannon.

[SHANNON *does not answer or appear. She sets down her portfolio to pick up Nonno's white linen suit, which she had pressed and hung on the veranda. She crosses to his cubicle with it, and calls in.*]

Nonno? It's almost time for supper! There's going to be a lovely, stormy sunset in a few minutes.

NONNO [*from within*]: Coming!

HANNAH: So is Christmas, Nonno.

NONNO: So is the Fourth of July!

HANNAH: We're past the Fourth of July. Hallowe'en comes next and then Thanksgiving. I hope you'll come forth sooner.

[*She lifts the gauze net over his cubicle door.*] Here's your suit, I've pressed it. [*She enters the cubicle.*]

NONNO: It's mighty dark in here, Hannah.

HANNAH: I'll turn the light on for you.

[SHANNON *comes out of his cubicle, like the survivor of a plane crash, bringing out with him several pieces of his clerical garb. The black heavy silk bib is loosely fastened about his panting, sweating chest. He hangs over it a heavy gold cross with an amethyst centre and attempts to fasten on a starched round collar. Now* HANNAH *comes back out of Nonno's cubicle, adjusting the flowing silk tie which goes with her 'artist' costume. For a moment they both face front, adjusting their two outfits. They are like two actors in a play which is about to fold on the road, preparing gravely for a performance which may be the last one.*]

HANNAH [*glancing at Shannon*]: Are you planning to conduct church services of some kind here tonight, Mr Shannon?

SHANNON: Goddammit, please help me with this! [*He means the round collar.*]

HANNAH [*crossing behind him*]: If you're not going to conduct a church service, why get into that uncomfortable outfit?

SHANNON: Because I've been accused of being defrocked and of lying about it, that's why. I want to show the ladies that I'm still a clocked – *frocked!* – minister of the . . .

HANNAH: Isn't that lovely gold cross enough to convince the ladies?

SHANNON: No; they know I redeemed it from a Mexico City pawnshop, and they suspect that that's where I got it in the first place.

HANNAH: Hold still just a minute. [*She is behind him, trying to fasten the collar.*] There now; let's hope it stays on. The buttonhole is so frayed I'm afraid that it won't hold the button. [*Her fear is instantly confirmed: the button pops out.*]

SHANNON: Where'd it go?

HANNAH: Here, right under . . .

[*She picks it up.* SHANNON *rips the collar off, crumples it and hurls it off the veranda. Then he falls into the hammock, panting and twisting.* HANNAH *quietly opens her sketch-pad and begins to sketch him. He doesn't at first notice what she is doing.*]

HANNAH [*as she sketches*]: How long have you been inactive in the, uh, Church, Mr Shannon?

SHANNON: What's that got to do with the price of rice in China?

HANNAH [*gently*]: Nothing.

SHANNON: What's it got to do with the price of coffee beans in Brazil?

HANNAH: I retract the question. With apologies.

SHANNON: To answer your question politely, I have been inactive in the Church for all but one year since I was ordained a minister of the Church.

HANNAH [*sketching rapidly and moving forward a bit to see his face better*]: Well, that's quite a sabbatical, Mr Shannon.

SHANNON: Yeah, that's . . . quite a . . . sabbatical.

[NONNO's *voice is heard from his cubicle repeating a line of poetry several times.*]

SHANNON: Is your grandfather talking to himself in there?

HANNAH: No; he composes out loud. He has to commit his lines to memory because he can't see to write them or read them.

SHANNON: Sounds like he's stuck on one line.

HANNAH: Yes. I'm afraid his memory is failing. Memory failure is his greatest dread. [*She says this almost coolly, as if it didn't matter.*]

SHANNON: Are you drawing me?

HANNAH: Trying to. You're a very difficult subject. When the Mexican painter Siqueiros did his portrait of the American poet Hart Crane he had to paint him with closed eyes because he couldn't paint his eyes open – there was too much suffering in them and he couldn't paint it.

SHANNON: Sorry, but I'm not going to close my eyes for you. I'm hypnotizing myself – at least trying to – by looking at the light on the orange tree . . . leaves.

HANNAH: That's all right. I can paint your eyes open.

SHANNON: I had one parish one year and then I wasn't defrocked, but I was . . . locked out of my church.

HANNAH: Oh . . . Why did they lock you out of it?

SHANNON: Fornication and heresy . . . in the same week.

HANNAH [*sketching rapidly*]: What were the circumstances of the . . . uh . . . first offence?

SHANNON: Yeah, the fornication came first, preceded the heresy by several days. A very young Sunday-school teacher asked to see me privately in my study. A pretty little thing – no chance in the world – only child, and both of her parents were spinsters, almost identical spinsters wearing clothes of the opposite sexes. Fooling some of the people some of the time, but not me – none of the time . . . [*He is pacing the veranda with gathering agitation, and the all-inclusive mockery that his guilt produces.*] Well, she declared herself to me – wildly.

HANNAH: A declaration of love?

SHANNON: Don't make *fun* of me, honey!

HANNAH: I wasn't.

SHANNON: The natural, or unnatural, attraction of one . . . lunatic for . . . another . . . that's all it was. I was the god-damnedest prig in those days that even you could imagine. I said, let's kneel down together and pray, and we did; we knelt down, but all of a sudden the kneeling position turned to a reclining position on the rug of my study and . . . When we got up? I struck her. Yes, I did, I struck her in the face and called her a damned little tramp. So she ran home. I heard the next day she'd cut herself with her father's straight-blade razor. Yeah, the paternal spinster shaved.

HANNAH: Fatally?

SHANNON: Just broke the skin surface enough to bleed a little but it made a scandal.

HANNAH: Yes, I can imagine that it . . . provoked some comment.

SHANNON: That it did, it did that. [*He pauses a moment in his fierce pacing as if the recollection still appalled him.*] So the next Sunday when I climbed into the pulpit and looked down over all of those smug, disapproving, accusing faces uplifted, I had an impulse to shake them – so I shook them. I had a prepared sermon – meek, apologetic – I threw it away, tossed it into the chancel. Look here, I said, I shouted, I'm tired of conducting services in praise and worship of a senile delinquent – yeah, that's what I said, I shouted! All your Western theologies, the whole mythology of them, are based on the concept of God as a *senile delinquent*, by God, I will not and cannot continue to conduct services in praise and worship of this, this . . . this . . .

HANNAH [*quietly*]: Senile delinquent?

SHANNON: Yeah, this angry, petulant old man. I mean He's represented like a bad-tempered childish old, old, sick, peevish man – I mean like the sort of old man in a nursing-home that's putting together a jigsaw puzzle and can't put it together and gets furious at it and kicks over the table. Yes, I tell you they *do* that, all our theologies do it – accuse God of being a cruel, senile delinquent, blaming the world and brutally punishing all He created for His own faults in construction, and then, ha-ha, yeah – a thunderstorm broke that Sunday . . .

HANNAH: You mean *outside* the church?

SHANNON: Yep; it was wilder than I was! And out they slithered, they slithered out of their pews to their shiny black cockroach sedans, ha-ha, and I shouted after them, hell, I even followed them half-way out of the church, shouting after them as they . . . [*He stops with a gasp for breath.*]

HANNAH: Slithered out?

SHANNON: I shouted after them, go on, go home and close your house windows, all your windows and doors, against the truth about God!

HANNAH: Oh, my heavens. Which is just what they did – poor things.

SHANNON: Miss Jelkes honey, Pleasant Valley, Virginia, was an exclusive suburb of a large city and these poor things were not poor – materially speaking.

HANNAH [*smiling a bit*]: What was the, uh, upshot of it?

SHANNON: Upshot of it? Well, I wasn't defrocked. I was just locked out of the church in Pleasant Valley, Virginia, and put in a nice little private asylum to recuperate from a complete nervous breakdown, as they preferred to regard it, and then, and then I . . . I entered my present line – tours of God's world conducted by a minister of God with a cross and a round collar to prove it. Collecting evidence!

HANNAH: Evidence of what, Mr Shannon?

SHANNON [*a touch shyly now*]: My personal idea of God, not as a senile delinquent, but as a . . .

HANNAH: Incomplete sentence.

SHANNON: It's going to storm tonight – a terrific electric storm. Then you will see the Reverend T. Lawrence Shannon's conception of God Almighty paying a visit to the world He created. I want to go back to the Church and preach the gospel of God as Lightning and Thunder . . . and also stray dogs vivisected and . . . and . . . and . . . [*He points out suddenly towards the sea.*] That's him! There he is now! [*He is pointing out at a blaze, a majestic apocalypse of gold light, shafting the sky as the sun drops into the Pacific.*] His oblivious majesty – and *here I am* on this . . . dilapidated veranda of a cheap hotel, out of season, in a country caught and destroyed in its flesh and corrupted in its spirit by its gold-hungry Conquistadors that bore the flag of the Inquisition along with the Cross of Christ. Yes . . . and . . . [*There is a pause.*]

HANNAH: Mr Shannon . . . ?

SHANNON: Yes . . . ?

HANNAH [*smiling a little*]: I have a strong feeling you will go back to the Church with this evidence you've been collecting, but when you do and it's a black Sunday morning, look out over the congregation, over the smug, complacent faces for a few old, very old faces, looking up at you, as you begin your sermon, with eyes like a piercing cry for something to still look up to, something to still believe in. And then I think you'll not shout what you say you shouted that black Sunday in Pleasant Valley, Virginia. I think you will throw away the violent, furious sermon, you'll toss *it* into the chancel, and talk about . . . no, maybe talk about . . . nothing . . . just . . .

SHANNON: What?

HANNAH: Lead them beside still waters because you know how badly they need the still waters, Mr Shannon.

[*There is a moment of silence between them.*]

SHANNON: Lemme see that thing. [*He seizes the sketch-pad from her and is visibly impressed by what he sees. There is another moment which is prolonged to* HANNAH's *embarrassment.*]

HANNAH: Where did you say the patrona put your party of ladies?

SHANNON: She had her . . . Mexican concubines put their luggage in the annex.

HANNAH: Where is the annex?

SHANNON: Right down the hill back of here, but all of my ladies except the teen-age Medea and the older Medea have gone out in a glass-bottomed boat to observe the submarine marvels.

HANNAH: Well, when they come back to the annex they're going to observe my watercolours with some marvellous submarine prices marked on the mattings.

SHANNON: By God, you're a hustler, aren't you; you're a fantastic, cool hustler.

HANNAH: Yes, like *you*, Mr Shannon. [*She gently removes her sketch-pad from his grasp.*] Oh, Mr Shannon, if Nonno, Grandfather, comes out of his cell number 4 before I get back, will you please look out for him for me? I won't be longer than three shakes of a lively sheep's tail. [*She snatches up her portfolio and goes briskly off the veranda.*]

SHANNON: Fantastic, absolutely fantastic.

[*There is a windy sound in the rain forest and a flicker of gold light like a silent scattering of gold coins on the veranda; then the sound of shouting voices. The Mexican boys appear with a wildly agitated creature – a captive iguana tied up in a shirt. They crouch down by the cactus clumps that are growing below the veranda and hitch the iguana to a post with a piece of rope. MAXINE is attracted by the commotion and appears on the veranda above them.*]

PEDRO: Tenemos fiesta!

PANCHO: Comeremos bien.

PEDRO: Damela, damela! Yo la ataré.

PANCHO: Yo la cojí – yo la ataré!

PEDRO: Lo que was a *bacer* es dejarla escapar.

MAXINE: Ammarla fuerte! Ole, ole! No la dejes escapar. Dejala moverse!* [*To Shannon.*] They caught an iguana.

SHANNON: I've noticed they did that, Maxine.

[*She is holding her drink deliberately close to him. The Germans have heard the commotion and crowd on to the veranda.* FRAU FAHRENKOPF *rushes over to Maxine.*]

FRAU FAHRENKOPF: What is it? What's going on? A snake? Did they catch a snake?

MAXINE: No. *Lizard.*

FRAU FAHRENKOPF [*with exaggerated revulsion*]: Ouuu . . . lizard! [*She strikes a grotesque attitude of terror as if she were threatened by Jack the Ripper.*]

---

* We're going to have a feast! / We'll eat good. / Give it to me! I'll tie it up. / I caught it – *I'll* tie it up! / You'll only let it get away. / Tie it up tight! Ole, ole! Don't let it get away. Give it enough room!

SHANNON [*to Maxine*]: You like iguana meat, don't you?

FRAU FAHRENKOPF: Eat? *Eat?* A big *lizard?*

MAXINE: Yep, they're mighty good eating – taste like white meat of chicken.

[FRAU FAHRENKOPF *rushes back to her family. They talk excitedly in German about the iguana.*]

SHANNON: If you mean Mexican chicken, that's no recommendation. Mexican chickens are scavengers and they taste like what they scavenge.

MAXINE: Naw; I mean Texas chicken.

SHANNON [*dreamily*]: Texas . . . Chicken . . .

[*He paces restlessly down the veranda.* MAXINE *divides her attention between his lean figure, that seems incapable of stillness, and the wriggling bodies of the Mexican boys lying on their stomachs half under the veranda – as if she were mentally comparing two opposite attractions to her simple, sensual nature.* SHANNON *turns at the end of the veranda and sees her eyes fixed on him.*]

SHANNON: What is the sex of this iguana, Maxine?

MAXINE: Hah, who cares about the sex of an iguana . . . [*He passes close by her.*] . . . except another . . . iguana?

SHANNON: Haven't you heard the limerick about iguanas? [*He removes her drink from her hand and it seems as if he might drink it, but he only sniffs it, with an expression of repugnance. She chuckles.*]

There was a young gaucho named Bruno
Who said about love, This I do know:
Women are fine, and sheep are divine,
But iguanas are – *Numero Uno!*

[*On 'Numero Uno'* SHANNON *empties Maxine's drink over the railing, deliberately on to the humped, wriggling posterior of* PEDRO, *who springs up with angry protests.*]

PEDRO: Me cágo . . . hijo de la . . .

SHANNON: Qué? Qué?

MAXINE: Véte!

[SHANNON *laughs viciously. The iguana escapes and both boys rush shouting after it. One of them dives on it and recaptures it at the end of the jungle.*]

PANCHO: La iguana se escapé.

MAXINE: Cojela, cojela! La cojíste? So no la cojes, te moderá el culo. La cojíste?

PEDRO: La cojí.*

[*The boys wriggle back under the veranda with the iguana.*]

MAXINE [*returning to Shannon*]: I thought you were gonna break down and take a drink, Reverend.

SHANNON: Just the odour of liquor makes me feel nauseated.

MAXINE: You couldn't smell it if you got it in you. [*She touches his sweating forehead. He brushes her hand off like an insect.*] Hah! [*She crosses over to the liquor cart, and he looks after her with a sadistic grin.*]

SHANNON: Maxine honey, whoever told you that you look good in tight pants was not a sincere friend of yours.

[*He turns away. At the same instant, a crash and a hoarse, startled outcry are heard from Nonno's cubicle.*]

MAXINE: I knew it! I *knew* it! The old man's took a fall!

[SHANNON *rushes into the cubicle, followed by* MAXINE. *The light has been gradually, steadily dimming during the incident of the iguana's escape. There is, in effect, a division of scenes here, though it is accomplished without a blackout or curtain. As* SHANNON *and* MAXINE *enter* NONNO'S *cubicle,* HERR FAHRENKOPF *appears on the now twilit veranda. He turns on an outsize light fixture that is suspended from overhead, a full pearly-moon of a light globe that gives an unearthly lustre to the scene. The great pearly globe is decorated by night insects, large but gossamer moths that have immolated themselves on its surface: the light through their wings gives them an opalescent colour, a touch of fantasy.*

---

* The iguana's escaped. / Get it, get it! Have you got it? If you don't, it'll bite your behind. Have you got it? / He's got it.

Now SHANNON *leads the old poet out of his cubicle, on to the facing veranda. The old man is impeccably dressed in snow-white linen with a black string tie. His leonine mane of hair gleams like silver as he passes under the globe.*]

NONNO: No bones broken. I'm made out of indiarubber!

SHANNON: A traveller-born falls down many times in his travels.

NONNO: Hannah? [*His vision and other senses have so far deteriorated that he thinks he is being led out by* HANNAH.] I'm pretty sure I'm going to finish it here.

SHANNON [*shouting, gently*]: I've got the same feeling, Grampa.

[MAXINE *follows them out of the cubicle.*]

NONNO: I've never been surer of anything in my life.

SHANNON [*gently and wryly*]: I've never been surer of anything in mine either.

[HERR FAHRENKOPF *has been listening with an expression of entrancement to his portable radio, held close to his ear, the sound un-realistically low. Now he turns it off and makes an excited speech.*]

HERR FAHRENKOPF: The London fires have spread all the way from the heart of London to the Channel coast! Goering, Field-Marshal Goering, calls it 'the new phase of conquest!' *Super-fire-bombs! Each night!*

[NONNO *catches only the excited tone of this announcement and interprets it as a request for a recitation. He strikes the floor with his cane, throws back his silver-maned head and begins the delivery in a grand, declamatory style.*]

NONNO:

Youth must be wanton, youth must be quick,
Dance to the candle while lasteth the wick,

Youth must be foolish and . . .

[NONNO *falters on the line, a look of confusion and fear on his face. The Germans are amused.* WOLFGANG *goes up to* NONNO *and shouts into his face.*]

WOLFGANG: Sir? What is your age? How old?

[HANNAH, *who has just returned to the veranda, rushes up to her grandfather and answers for him.*]

HANNAH: He is ninety-seven years *young!*
HERR FAHRENKOPF: How old?
HANNAH: Ninety-seven – almost a *century young!*

[HERR FAHRENKOPF *repeats this information to his beaming wife and* HILDA *in German.*]

NONNO [*cutting in on the Germans*]:

> Youth must be foolish and mirthful and blind,
> Gaze not before and glance not behind,
>
> Mark not . . .

[*He falters again.*]

HANNAH [*prompting him, holding tightly on to his arm*]:
> Mark not the shadow that darkens the way –

[*They recite the next lines together.*]

> Regret not the glitter of any lost day,
> But laugh with no reason except the red wine,
> For youth must be youthful and foolish and blind!

[*The Germans are loudly amused.* WOLFGANG *applauds directly in the old poet's face.* NONNO *makes a little unsteady bow, leaning forward precariously on his cane.* SHANNON *takes a firm hold of his arm as* HANNAH *turns to the Germans, opening her portfolio of sketches and addressing* WOLFGANG.]

HANNAH: Am I right in thinking you are on your honeymoon? [*There is no response, and she repeats the question in German while* FRAU

FAHRENKOPF *laughs and nods vehemently.*] Habe ich recht dass Sie auf Ihrer Hochzeitsreise sind! Was für eine hübsche junge Braut! Ich mache Pastell-Skizzen . . . darf ich, würden Sie mir erlauben . . . ? Würden Sie, bitte . . . bitte . . .

[HERR FAHRENKOPF *bursts into a Nazi marching song and leads his party to the champagne bucket on the table at the left.* SHANNON *has steered* NONNO *to the other table.*]

NONNO [*exhilarated*]: Hannah! What was the take?

HANNAH [*embarrassed*]: Grandfather, sit down, please stop shouting!

NONNO: Hah? Did they cross your palm with silver or paper, Hannah?

HANNAH [*almost desperately*]: Nonno! No more shouting! Sit down at the table. It's time to *eat*!

SHANNON: Chow time, Grampa.

NONNO [*confused but still shouting*]: How much did they come across with?

HANNAH: Nonno! *Please!*

NONNO: Did they, did you . . . sell 'em a . . . watercolour?

HANNAH: No sale, Grandfather!

MAXINE: Hah!

[HANNAH *turns to Shannon, her usual composure shattered, or nearly so.*]

HANNAH: He won't sit down or stop shouting.

NONNO [*blinking and beaming with the grotesque suggestion of an old coquette*]: Hah? How rich did we strike it, Hannah?

SHANNON: *You* sit down, Miss Jelkes. [*He says it with gentle authority, to which she yields. He takes hold of the old man's forearm and places in his hand a crumpled Mexican bill.*] Sir? Sir? [*He is shouting.*] Five! Dollars! I'm putting it in your pocket.

HANNAH: We can't accept . . . gratuities, Mr Shannon.

SHANNON: Hell, I gave him five pesos.

NONNO: Mighty good for one poem!

SHANNON: Sir? Sir? The *pecuniary rewards* of a *poem* are *grossly inferior* to its *merits, always!*

[*He is being fiercely, almost mockingly tender with the old man — a thing we are when the pathos of the old, the ancient, the dying is such a wound to our own (savagely beleaguered) nerves and sensibilities that this outside demand on us is beyond our collateral, our emotional reserve. This is as true of Hannah as it is of Shannon, of course. They have both overdrawn their reserves at this point of the encounter between them.*]

NONNO: Hah? Yes . . . [*He is worn out now, but still shouting.*] We're going to clean up in this place!

SHANNON: You bet you're going to clean up here!

[MAXINE *utters her one-note bark of a laugh.* SHANNON *throws a hard roll at her. She wanders amiably back towards the German table.*]

NONNO [*tottering, panting, hanging on to* SHANNON'S *arm, thinking it is* HANNAH'S]: Is the, the . . . dining-room . . . *crowded*? [*He looks blindly about with wild surmise.*]

SHANNON: Yep, it's filled to capacity! There's a big crowd at the door! [*His voice doesn't penetrate the old man's deafness.*]

NONNO: If there's a cocktail lounge, Hannah, we ought to . . . work that . . . first. Strike while the iron is hot, ho, ho, while it's hot . . . [*This is like a delirium — only as strong a woman as* HANNAH *could remain outwardly impassive.*]

HANNAH: He thinks you're me, Mr Shannon. Help him into a chair. Please stay with him a minute. I . . .

[*She moves away from the table and breathes as if she has just been dragged up half-drowned from the sea.* SHANNON *eases the old man into a chair. Almost at once* NONNO'S *feverish vitality collapses and he starts drifting back towards half-sleep.*]

SHANNON [*crossing to Hannah*]: What're you breathing like that for?

HANNAH: Some people take a drink, some take a pill. I just take a few deep breaths.

SHANNON: You're making too much out of this. It's a natural thing in a man as old as Grampa.

HANNAH: I know, I know. He's had more than one of these little 'cerebral accidents' as you call them, and all in the last few months. He was amazing till lately. I had to show his passport to prove that he was the oldest living and practising poet on earth. We did well, we made expenses and *more!* But . . . when I saw he was failing, I tried to persuade him to go back to Nantucket, but he conducts our tours. He said, 'No; *Mexico!*' So here we are on this windy hilltop like a pair of scarecrows . . . The bus from Mexico City broke down at an altitude of 15,000 feet above sea-level. That's when I think the latest cerebral incident happened. It isn't so much the loss of hearing and sight but the . . . dimming out of the mind that I can't bear, because until lately, just lately, his mind was amazingly clear. But yesterday? In Tasco? I spent nearly all we had left on the wheel-chair for him and still he insisted that we go on with the trip till we got to the sea, the . . . cradle of life as he calls it . . . [*She suddenly notices* NONNO, *sunk in his chair as if lifeless. She draws a sharp breath, and goes quietly to him.*]

SHANNON [*to the Mexican boys*]: Servicio! Aqui! [*The force of his order proves effective: they serve the fish course.*]

HANNAH: What a kind man you are. I don't know how to thank you, Mr Shannon. I'm going to wake him up now. Nonno! [*She claps her hands quietly at his ear. The old man rouses with a confused, breathless chuckle.*] Nonno, linen napkins. [*She removes a napkin from the pocket of her smock.*] I always carry one with me, you see, in case we run into paper napkins, as sometimes happens, you see . . .

NONNO: Wonderful place here . . . I hope it is à la carte, Hannah. I want a very light supper so I won't get sleepy. I'm going to work after supper. I'm going to finish it here.

HANNAH: Nonno? We've made a friend here. Nonno, this is the Reverend Mr Shannon.

NONNO [*struggling out of his confusion*]: Reverend?

HANNAH [*shouting to him*]: Mr Shannon's an Episcopal clergyman, Nonno.

NONNO: A man of God?

HANNAH: A man of God, on vacation.

NONNO: Hannah, tell him I'm too old to baptize and too young to bury, but on the market for marriage to a rich widow, fat, fair, and forty.

> [NONNO *is delighted by all of his own little jokes. One can see him exchanging these pleasantries with the rocking-chair brigades of summer hotels at the turn of the century – and with professors' wives at little colleges in New England. But now it has become some-what grotesque in a touching way, this desire to please, this playful manner, these venerable jokes.* SHANNON *goes along with it. The old man touches something in him which is outside of his concern with himself. This part of the scene, which is played in a 'scherzo' mood, has an accompanying windy obbligato on the hilltop – all through it we hear the wind from the sea gradually rising, sweeping up the hill through the rain forest, and there are fitful glimmers of lightning in the sky.*]

NONNO: But very few ladies ever go past forty if you believe 'em, ho, ho! Ask him to . . . give the blessing. Mexican food needs blessing.

SHANNON: Sir, you give the blessing. I'll be right with you. [*He has broken one of his shoe-laces.*]

NONNO: Tell him I will oblige him on one condition.

SHANNON: What condition, sir?

NONNO: That you'll keep my daughter company when I retire after dinner. I go to bed with the chickens and get up with the roosters, ho, ho! So you're a man of God. A benedict or a bachelor?

SHANNON: Bachelor, sir. No sane and civilized woman would have me, Mr Coffin.

NONNO: What did he say, Hannah?

HANNAH [*embarrassed*]: Nonno, give the blessing.

NONNO [*not hearing this*]: I call her my daughter, but she's my daugh-ter's daughter. We've been in charge of each other since she lost both her parents in the very first automobile crash on the island of Nantucket.

HANNAH: Nonno, give the blessing.

NONNO: She isn't a modern flapper, she isn't modern and she – doesn't flap, but she was brought up to be a wonderful wife and mother. But . . . I'm a selfish old man, so I've kept her all to myself.

HANNAH [*shouting in his ear*]: Nonno, Nonno, the blessing!

NONNO [*rising with an effort*]: Yes, the blessing. Bless this food to our use, and ourselves to Thy service. Amen. [*He totters back into his chair.*]

SHANNON: Amen.

[NONNO's *mind starts drifting, his head drooping forward. He murmurs to himself.*]

How good is the old man's poetry?

HANNAH: My grandfather was a fairly well-known minor poet before the First World War and for a little while after.

SHANNON: In the minor league, huh?

HANNAH: Yes, a minor league poet with a major league spirit. I'm proud to be his granddaughter . . . [*She draws a pack of cigarettes from her pocket, then replaces it immediately without taking a cigarette.*]

NONNO [*very confused*]: Hannah, it's too hot for . . . hot cereals this . . . morning . . . [*He shakes his head several times with a rueful chuckle.*]

HANNAH: He's not quite back, you see; he thinks it's morning. [*She says this as if making an embarrassing admission, with a quick, frightened smile at Shannon.*]

SHANNON: Fantastic – *fantastic.*

HANNAH: That word 'fantastic' seems to be your favourite word, Mr Shannon.

SHANNON [*looking out gloomily from the veranda*]: Yeah, well, you know we – live on two levels, Miss Jelkes, the realistic level and the fantastic level, and which is the real one, really? . . .

HANNAH: I would say both, Mr Shannon.

SHANNON: But when you live on the fantastic level as I have lately but have got to operate on the realistic level, that's when you're spooked, that's the spook . . . [*This is said as if it were a private reflection.*] I thought I'd shake the spook here but conditions have changed here. I didn't know the patrona had turned to a widow, a sort of bright widow spider. [*He chuckles almost like* NONNO.]

[MAXINE *has pushed one of those gay little brass-and-glass liquor carts around the corner of the veranda. It is laden with an ice bucket, coconuts and a variety of liquors. She hums gaily to herself as she pushes the cart close to the table.*]

MAXINE: Cocktails, anybody?

HANNAH: No, thank you, Mrs Faulk, I don't think we care for any.

SHANNON: People don't drink cocktails between the fish and the entrée, Maxine honey.

MAXINE: Grampa needs a toddy to wake him up. Old folks need a toddy to pick 'em up. [*She shouts into the old man's ear.*] Grampa! How about a toddy? [*Her hips are thrust out at Shannon.*]

SHANNON: Maxine, your ass – excuse me, Miss Jelkes – your hips, Maxine, are too fat for this veranda.

MAXINE: Hah! Mexicans like 'em, if I can judge by the pokes and pinches I get in the buses to town. And so do the Germans. Ev'ry time I go near Herr Fahrenkopf he gives me a pinch or a goose.

SHANNON: Then go near him again for another goose.

MAXINE: Hah! I'm mixing Grampa a Manhattan with two cherries in it so he'll live through dinner.

SHANNON: Go on back to your Nazis. I'll mix the Manhattan for him. [*He goes to the liquor cart.*]

MAXINE [*to Hannah*]: How about you, honey – a little soda with lime juice?

HANNAH: Nothing for me, thank you.

SHANNON: Don't make nervous people more nervous, Maxine.

MAXINE: You better let me mix that toddy for Grampa; you're making a mess of it, Shannon.

[*With a snort of fury, he thrusts the liquor cart like a battering ram at her belly. Some of the bottles fall off it; she thrusts it right back at him.*]

HANNAH: Mrs Faulk, Mr Shannon, this is childish; please stop it!

[*The Germans are attracted by the disturbance. They cluster around, laughing delightedly.* SHANNON *and* MAXINE *seize opposite ends of the rolling liquor cart and thrust it towards each other, both grinning fiercely as gladiators in mortal combat. The Germans shriek with laughter and chatter in German.*]

HANNAH: Mr Shannon, stop it! [*She appeals to the Germans.*] Bitte! Nehmen Sie die Spirituosen weg. Bitte, nehmen Sie die weg.

[SHANNON *has wrested the cart from Maxine and pushed it at the Germans. They scream delightedly. The cart crashes into the wall of the veranda.* SHANNON *leaps down the steps and runs into the foliage. Birds scream in the rain forest. Then sudden quiet returns to the veranda as the Germans go back to their own table.*]

MAXINE: Crazy, black Irish protestant son of a . . . protestant!

HANNAH: Mrs Faulk, he's putting up a struggle not to drink.

MAXINE: Don't interfere. You're an interfering woman.

HANNAH: Mr Shannon is dangerously . . . disturbed.

MAXINE: I know how to handle him, honey – you just met him today. Here's Grampa's Manhattan cocktail with two cherries in it.

HANNAH: Please don't call him Grampa.

MAXINE: Shannon calls him Grampa.

HANNAH [*taking the drink*]: He doesn't make it sound condescending, but you *do*. My grandfather is a gentleman in the true sense of the word; he is a *gentle man*.

MAXINE: What are you?

HANNAH: I am his granddaughter.

MAXINE: Is that all you are?

HANNAH: I think it's enough to be.

MAXINE: Yeah, but you're also a dead-beat, using that dying old man for a front to get in places without the cash to pay even one day in advance. Why, you're dragging him around with you like Mexican beggars carry around a sick baby to put the touch on the tourists.

HANNAH: I told you I had no money.

MAXINE: Yes, and I told you that I was a widow – recent. In such a financial hole they might as well have buried me with my husband.

[SHANNON *reappears from the jungle foliage, but remains unnoticed by Hannah and Maxine.*]

HANNAH [*with forced calm*]: Tomorrow morning, at daybreak, I will go in town. I will set up my easel in the plaza and peddle my watercolours and sketch tourists. I am not a weak person; my failure here isn't typical of me.

MAXINE: I'm not a weak person either.

HANNAH: No. By no means, no. Your strength is awe-inspiring.

MAXINE: You're goddam right about that, but how do you think you'll get to Acapulco without the cab-fare or even the bus-fare there?

HANNAH: I will go on shanks's mare, Mrs Faulk – islanders are good walkers. And if you doubt my word for it, if you really think I came here as a dead-beat, then I will put my grandfather back in his wheel-chair and push him back down this hill to the road and all the way back into town.

MAXINE: Ten miles, with a storm coming up?

HANNAH: Yes, I would – I will. [*She is dominating* MAXINE *in this exchange. Both stand beside the table.* NONNO'*s head is drooping back into sleep.*]

MAXINE: I wouldn't let you.

HANNAH: But you've made it clear that you don't want us to stay here for one night even.

MAXINE: The storm would blow that old man out of his wheel-chair like a dead leaf.

HANNAH: He would prefer that to staying where he's not welcome, and I would prefer it for him, and for myself, Mrs Faulk. [*She turns to the Mexican boys.*] Where is his wheel-chair? Where is my grand-father's wheel-chair?

[*This exchange has roused the old man. He struggles up from his chair, confused, strikes the floor with his cane and starts declaiming a poem.*]

NONNO:

Love's an old remembered song

A drunken fiddler plays,
Stumbling crazily along

Crooked alleyways.
When his heart is mad with music
He will play the –

HANNAH: Nonno, not now, Nonno! He thought someone asked for a poem. [*She gets him back into the chair.* HANNAH *and* MAXINE *are still unaware of Shannon.*]

MAXINE: Calm down, honey.

HANNAH: I'm perfectly calm, Mrs Faulk.

MAXINE: I'm *not*. That's the trouble.

HANNAH: I understand that, Mrs Faulk. You lost your husband just lately. I think you probably miss him more than you know.

MAXINE: No, the trouble is Shannon.

HANNAH: You mean his nervous state and his . . . ?

MAXINE: No, I just mean Shannon. I want you to lay off him, honey. You're not for Shannon and Shannon isn't for you.

HANNAH: Mrs Faulk, I'm a New England spinster who is pushing forty.

MAXINE: I got the vibrations between you – I'm very good at catching vibrations between people – and there sure was a vibration between you and Shannon the moment you got here. That, just that, believe me, nothing but that has made this . . . misunderstanding between us. So if you just don't mess with Shannon, you and your Grampa can stay on here as long as you want to, honey.

HANNAH: Oh, Mrs Faulk, do I look like a *vamp*?

MAXINE: They come in all types. I've had all types of them here.

[SHANNON *comes over to the table.*]

SHANNON: Maxine, I told you don't make nervous people more nervous, but you wouldn't listen.

MAXINE: What you need is a drink.

SHANNON: Let me decide about that.

HANNAH: Won't you sit down with us, Mr Shannon, and eat something? Please. You'll feel better.

SHANNON: I'm not hungry right now.

HANNAH: Well, just sit down with us, won't you?

[SHANNON *sits down with* HANNAH.]

MAXINE [*warningly to Hannah*]: O.K., O.K . . .

NONNO [*rousing a bit and mumbling*]: Wonderful . . . wonderful place here.

[MAXINE *retires from the table and wheels the liquor cart over to the German party.*]

SHANNON: Would you have gone through with it?

HANNAH: Haven't you ever played poker, Mr Shannon?

SHANNON: You mean you were bluffing?

HANNAH: Let's say I was drawing to an inside straight. [*The wind rises and sweeps up the hill like a great waking sigh from the ocean.*] It *is* going to storm. I hope your ladies aren't still out in that, that . . . glass-bottomed boat, observing the submarine . . . marvels.

SHANNON: That's because you don't know these ladies. However they're back from the boat trip. They're down at the cantina dancing together to the juke-box and hatching new plots to get me kicked out of Blake Tours.

HANNAH: What would you do if you . . . ?

SHANNON: Got the sack? Go back to the Church or take the long swim to China. [HANNAH *removes a crumpled pack of cigarettes from her pocket. She discovers only two left in the pack and decides to save them for later. She returns the pack to her pocket.*] May I have one of your cigarettes, Miss Jelkes? [*She offers him the pack. He takes it from her and crumples it and throws it off the veranda.*] Never smoke those; they're made out of tobacco from cigarette stubs that beggars pick up off sidewalks and out of gutters in Mexico City. [*He produces a tin of English cigarettes.*] Have these – Benson and Hedges, imported, in an airtight tin, my luxury in my life.

HANNAH: Why – thank you, I will, since you have thrown mine away.

SHANNON: I'm going to tell you something about yourself. You are a lady, a *real* one and a *great* one.

HANNAH: What have I done to merit that compliment from you?

SHANNON: It isn't a compliment; it's just a report on what I've noticed about you at a time when it's hard for me to notice anything outside myself. You took out those Mexican cigarettes, you found you just had two left, you can't afford to buy a new pack of even that cheap brand, so you put them away for later. Right?

HANNAH: Mercilessly accurate, Mr Shannon.

SHANNON: But when I asked you for one, you offered it to me without a sign of reluctance.

HANNAH: Aren't you making a big point out of a small matter?

SHANNON: Just the opposite, honey. I'm making a small point out of a very large matter. [SHANNON *has put a cigarette in his lips, but has no matches.* HANNAH *has some, and she lights his cigarette for him.*] How'd you learn how to light a match in the wind?

HANNAH: Oh, I've learned lots of useful things like that. I wish I'd learned some *big* ones.

SHANNON: Such as what?

HANNAH: How to help you, Mr Shannon . . .

SHANNON: Now I know why I came here!

HANNAH: To meet someone who can light a match in the wind?

SHANNON [*looking down at the table, his voice choking*]: To meet someone who wants to *help me*, Miss Jelkes . . . [*He makes a quick, embarrassed turn in the chair, as if to avoid her seeing that he has tears in his eyes. She regards him steadily and tenderly, as she would her grandfather.*]

HANNAH: Has it been so long since anyone has wanted to help you, or have you just . . .

SHANNON: Have I – what?

HANNAH: Just been so much involved with a struggle in yourself that you haven't noticed when people have wanted to help you, the little they can? I know people torture each other many times like devils, but sometimes they do see and know each other, you know, and then, if they're decent, they do want to help each other all that they can. Now will you please help *me*? Take care of Nonno while I remove my watercolours from the annex veranda because the storm is coming up by leaps and bounds now.

[*He gives a quick, jerky nod, dropping his face briefly into the cup of his hands. She murmurs 'Thank you' and springs up, starting along the veranda. Halfway across, as the storm closes in upon the hilltop with a thunderclap and a sound of rain coming,* HANNAH *turns to look back at the table.* SHANNON *has risen and gone around the table to* NONNO.]

SHANNON: Grampa? Nonno? Let's get up before the rain hits us, Grampa.

NONNO: What? What?

[SHANNON *gets the old man out of his chair and shepherds him to the back of the veranda as* HANNAH *rushes towards the annex. The Mexican boys hastily clear the table, fold it up and lean it against the wall.* SHANNON *and* NONNO *turn and face towards the storm, like brave men facing a firing squad.* MAXINE *is excitedly giving orders to the boys.*]

MAXINE: Pronto, pronto, muchachos! Pronto, pronto! Llevaros todas las cosas! Pronto, pronto! Recoje los platos! Apurate con el mantel!

PEDRO: Nos estamos dando prisa!

PANCHO: Que el chubasco lave los platos!*

[*The German party look on the storm as a Wagnerian climax. They rise from their table as the boys come to clear it, and start singing exultantly. The storm, with its white convulsions of light, is like a giant white bird attacking the hilltop of the Costa Verde.* HANNAH *reappears with her watercolours clutched against her chest.*]

SHANNON: Got them?

HANNAH: Yes, just in time. Here is your God, Mr Shannon.

SHANNON [*quietly*]: Yes, I see Him, I hear Him, I know Him. And if He doesn't know that I know Him, let Him strike me dead with a bolt of His lightning.

---

* Hurry, hurry, boys! Pick everything up! Get the plates! Hurry with the table cloth! / We *are* hurrying! / Let the storm wash the plates!

[*He moves away from the wall to the edge of the veranda as a fine silver sheet of rain descends off the sloping roof, catching the light and dimming the figures behind it. Now everything is silver, delicately lustrous.* SHANNON *extends his hands under the rainfall, turning them in it as if to cool them. Then he cups them to catch the water in his palms and bathes his forehead with it. The rainfall increases. The sound of the marimba band at the beach cantina is brought up the hill by the wind.* SHANNON *lowers his hands from his burning forehead and stretches them out through the rain's silver sheet as if he were reaching for something outside and beyond himself. Then nothing is visible but these reaching-out hands. A pure white flash of lightning reveals* HANNAH *and* NONNO *against the wall, behind* SHANNON, *and the electric globe suspended from the roof goes out, the power extinguished by the storm. A clear shaft of light stays on Shannon's reaching-out hands till the stage curtain has fallen, slowly.**]

INTERVAL

**Note:* In staging, the plastic elements should be restrained so that they don't take precedence over the more important human values. It should not seem like an 'effect curtain'. The faint, windy music of the marimba band from the cantina should continue as the houselights are brought up for the intermission.

Act Three

The veranda, several hours later. Cubicles numbers 3, 4, and 5 are dimly lighted within. We see HANNAH *in number 3, and* NONNO *in number 4.* SHANNON, *who has taken off his shirt, is seated at a table on the veranda, writing a letter to his Bishop. All but this table have been folded and stacked against the wall and* MAXINE *is putting the hammock back up which had been taken down for dinner. The electric power is still off and the cubicles are lighted by oil lamps. The sky has cleared completely, the moon is making for full and it bathes the scene in an almost garish silver which is intensified by the wetness from the recent rainstorm. Everything is drenched – there are pools of silver here and there on the floor of the veranda. At one side a smudge-pot is burning to repel the mosquitoes, which are particularly vicious after a tropical downpour when the wind is exhausted.*

[SHANNON *is working feverishly on the letter to the Bishop, now and then slapping a mosquito on his bare torso. He is shiny with perspiration, still breathing like a spent runner, muttering to himself as he writes and sometimes suddenly drawing a loud deep breath and simultaneously throwing back his head to stare up wildly at the night sky.* HANNAH *is seated on a straight-back chair behind the mosquito-netting in her cubicle – very straight herself, holding a small book in her hands, but looking steadily over it at Shannon, like a guardian angel. Her hair has been let down.* NONNO *can be seen in his cubicle rocking back and forth on the edge of the narrow bed as he goes over and over his lines of his first new poem in 'twenty-some years' – which he knows is his last one.*

Now and then the sound of distant music drifts up from the beach cantina.]

MAXINE: Workin' on your sermon for next Sunday, Rev'rend?

SHANNON: I'm writing a very important letter, Maxine. [*He means don't disturb me.*]

MAXINE: Who to, Shannon?

SHANNON: The Dean of the Divinity School at Sewanee. [MAXINE *repeats 'Sewanee' to herself, tolerantly.*] Yes, and I'd appreciate it very much, Maxine honey, if you'd get Pedro or Pancho to drive into town with it tonight so it will go out first thing in the morning.

MAXINE: The kids took off in the station wagon already – for some cold beers and hot whores at the cantina.

SHANNON: 'Fred's dead' – he's lucky . . .

MAXINE: Don't misunderstand me about Fred, baby. I miss him, but we'd not only stopped sleeping together, we'd stopped talking together except in grunts – no quarrels, no misunderstandings, but if we exchanged two grunts in the course of a day, it was a long conversation we'd had that day between us.

SHANNON: Fred knew when I was spooked – wouldn't have to tell him. He'd just look at me and say, 'Well, Shannon, you're spooked.'

MAXINE: Yeah, well, Fred and me'd reached the point of just grunting.

SHANNON: Maybe he thought you'd turned into a pig, Maxine.

MAXINE: Hah! You know damn well that Fred respected me, Shannon, like I did Fred. We just, well, you know . . . age difference . . .

SHANNON: Well, you've got Pedro and Pancho.

MAXINE: Employees. They don't respect me enough. When you let employees get too free with you, personally, they stop respecting you, Shannon. And it's, well, it's . . . humiliating – not to be . . . respected.

SHANNON: Then take more bus trips to town for the Mexican pokes and the pinches, or get Herr Fahrenkopf to 'respect' you, honey.

MAXINE: Hah! You kill me. I been thinking lately of selling out here and going back to the States, to Texas, and operating a tourist camp outside some live town like Houston or Dallas, on a highway, and renting out cabins to business executives wanting a comfortable little intimate little place to give a little after-hours' dictation to their cute little secretaries that can't type or write shorthand. Complimentary rum-cocos – bathrooms with bidets. I'll introduce the bidet to the States.

SHANNON: Does everything have to wind up on that level with you, Maxine?

MAXINE: Yes and no, baby. I know the difference between loving someone and just sleeping with someone – even I know about that. [*He starts to rise.*] We've both reached a point where we've got to settle for something that works for us in our lives – even if it isn't on the highest kind of level.

SHANNON: I don't want to rot.

MAXINE: You wouldn't. I wouldn't let you! I know your psychological history. I remember one of your conversations on this veranda with Fred. You was explaining to him how your problems first started. You told him that Mama, your Mama, used to send you to bed before you was ready to sleep – so you practised the little boy's vice, you amused yourself with yourself. And once she caught you at it and whaled your backside with the backside of a hairbrush because she said she had to punish you for it because it made God mad as much as it did Mama, and she had to punish you for it so God wouldn't punish you for it harder than she would.

SHANNON: I was talking to Fred.

MAXINE: Yeah; but I heard it, all of it. You said you loved God and Mama and so you quit it to please them, but it was your secret pleasure and you harboured a secret resentment against Mama and God for making you give it up. And so you got back at God by preaching atheistical sermons and you got back at Mama by starting to lay young girls.

SHANNON: I have never delivered an atheistical sermon, and never would or could when I go back to the Church.

MAXINE: You're not going back to no Church. Did you mention the charge of statutory rape to the Divinity Dean?

SHANNON [*thrusting his chair back so vehemently that it topples over*]: Why don't you *let up* on me? You haven't let up on me since I got here this morning! *Let up on me!* Will you please *let up* on me?

MAXINE [*smiling serenely into his rage*]: Aw, baby . . .

247

SHANNON: What do you mean by 'aw baby'? What do you want out of me, Maxine honey?

MAXINE: Just to do this. [*She runs her fingers through his hair. He thrusts her hand away.*]

SHANNON: Ah, God. [*Words fail him. He shakes his head with a slight, helpless laugh and goes down the steps from the veranda.*]

MAXINE: The Chinaman in the kitchen says, 'No sweat.' . . . 'No sweat.' He says that's all his philosophy. All the Chinese philosophy in three words, 'Mei yoo gaunchi' – which is Chinese for 'No sweat.' . . . With your record and a charge of statutory rape hanging over you in Texas, how could you go to a church except to the Holy Rollers with some lively young female rollers and a bushel of hay on the church floor?

SHANNON: I'll drive into town in the bus to post this letter tonight. [*He has started towards the path. There are sounds below. He divides the masking foliage with his hands and looks down the hill.*]

MAXINE [*descending the steps from the veranda*]: Watch out for the spook; he's out there.

SHANNON: My ladies are up to something. They're all down there on the road, around the bus.

MAXINE: They're running out on you, Shannon.

[*She comes up beside him. He draws back and she looks down the hill. The light in number 3 cubicle comes on and HANNAH rises from the little table that she had cleared for letter-writing. She removes her Kabuki robe from a hook and puts it on as an actor puts on a costume in his dressing-room. NONNO's cubicle is also lighted dimly. He sits on the edge of his cot, rocking slightly back and forth, uttering an indistinguishable mumble of lines from his poem.*]

Yeah. There's a little fat man down there that looks like Jake Latta to me. Yep, that's Jake, that's Latta. I reckon Blake Tours has sent him here to take over your party, Shannon. [SHANNON *looks out over the jungle and lights a cigarette with jerky fingers.*] Well, let him do it. No sweat! He's coming up here now. Want me to handle it for you?

SHANNON: I'll handle it for myself. You keep out of it, please.

[*He speaks with a desperate composure.* HANNAH *stands just behind the curtain of her cubicle, motionless as a painted figure, during the scene that follows.* JAKE LATTA *comes up the veranda steps, beaming genially.*]

LATTA: Hi there, Larry.

SHANNON: Hello, Jake. [*He folds his letter into an envelope.*] Mrs Faulk honey, this goes air special.

MAXINE: First you'd better address it.

SHANNON: Oh!

[SHANNON *laughs and snatches the letter back, fumbling in his pocket for an address book, his fingers shaking uncontrollably.* LATTA *winks at Maxine. She smiles tolerantly.*]

LATTA: How's our boy doin', Maxine?

MAXINE: He'd feel better if I could get him to take a drink.

LATTA: Can't you get a drink down him?

MAXINE: Nope; not even a rum-coco.

LATTA: Let's have a rum-coco, Larry.

SHANNON: You have a rum-coco, Jake. I have a party of ladies to take care of. And I've discovered that situations come up in this business that call for cold, sober judgement. How about you? Haven't you ever made that discovery, Jake? What're you doing here? Are you here with a party?

LATTA: I'm here to pick up your party, Larry boy.

SHANNON: That's interesting! On whose authority, Jake?

LATTA: Blake Tours wired me in Cuernavaca to pick up your party here and put them together with mine 'cause you'd had this little nervous upset of yours and . . .

SHANNON: Show me the wire! Huh?

LATTA: The bus-driver says you took the ignition key to the bus.

SHANNON: That's right. I have the ignition key to the bus and I have this party and neither the bus or the party will pull out of here till I say so.

LATTA: Larry, you're a sick boy. Don't give me trouble.

SHANNON: What jail did they bail you out of, you fat zero?

LATTA: Let's have the bus key, Larry.

SHANNON: Where did they dig you up? You've got no party in Cuernavaca, you haven't been out with a party since 'thirty-seven.

LATTA: Just give me the bus key, Larry.

SHANNON: In a pig's snout – like yours!

LATTA: Where is the reverend's bedroom, Mrs Faulk?

SHANNON: The bus key is in my pocket. [*He slaps his pants pocket fiercely.*] Here, right here, in my pocket! Want it? Try and get it, Fatso!

LATTA: What language for a reverend to use, Mrs Faulk . . .

SHANNON [*holding up the key*]: See it? [*He thrusts it back into his pocket.*] Now go back wherever you crawled from. My party of ladies is staying here three more days because several of them are in no condition to travel, and neither – neither am I.

LATTA: They're getting in the bus now.

SHANNON: How are you going to start it?

LATTA: Larry, don't make me call the bus-driver up here to hold you down while I get that key away from you. You want to see the wire from Blake Tours? [*He produces the wire.*] Read it.

SHANNON: You sent that wire to yourself.

LATTA: From Houston?

SHANNON: You had it sent you from Houston. What's that prove? Why, Blake Tours was nothing, *nothing*! – till they got me. You think they'd let me go? – Ho, ho! Latta, it's caught up with you, Latta, all the whores and tequila have hit your brain now, Latta. [LATTA *shouts down the hill for the bus-driver.*] Don't you realize what I mean to Blake Tours? Haven't you seen the brochure in which they mention, they brag, that special parties are conducted by the Reverend T. Lawrence Shannon, D.D., noted world traveller, lecturer, son of a minister and grandson of a bishop, and the direct descendant of two colonial governors? [MISS FELLOWES *appears at the veranda steps.*] Miss Fellowes has read the brochure, she's memorized the brochure. She knows what it says about me.

MISS FELLOWES [*to Latta*]: Have you got the bus key?

LATTA: Bus-driver's going to get it away from him, lady. [*He lights a cigar with dirty, shaky fingers.*]

SHANNON: Ha-ha-ha-ha-ha! [*His laughter shakes him back against the veranda wall.*]

LATTA: He's gone. [*He touches his forehead.*]

SHANNON: Why, those ladies . . . have had . . . some of them, most of them if not all of them . . . for the first time in their lives the advantage of contact, social contact, with a gentleman born and bred, whom under no other circumstances they could have possibly met . . . let alone be given the chance to insult and accuse and . . .

MISS FELLOWES: Shannon! The girls are in the bus and we want to go now, so give up that key. Now!

[HANK, *the bus-driver, appears at the top of the path, whistling casually: he is not noticed at first.*]

SHANNON: If I didn't have a decent sense of responsibility to these parties I take out, I would gladly turn over your party – because I don't like your party – to this degenerate here, this Jake Latta of the gutter-rat Lattas. Yes, I would – I would surrender the bus key in my pocket, even to Latta, but I am not that irresponsible, no, I'm not, to the parties that I take out, regardless of the party's treatment of me. I still feel responsible for them till I get them back wherever I picked them up. [HANK *comes on to the veranda.*] Hi, Hank. Are you friend or foe?

HANK: Larry, I got to get that ignition key now so we can get moving down there.

SHANNON: Oh! Then *foe!* I'm disappointed, Hank. I thought you were friend, not foe. [HANK *puts a wrestler's armlock on Shannon and* LATTA *removes the bus key from his pocket.* HANNAH *raises a hand to her eyes.*] O.K., O.K., you've got the bus key. By force. I feel exonerated now of all responsibility. Take the bus and the ladies in it and go. Hey, Jake, did you know they had lesbians in Texas – without the dikes the plains of Texas would be engulfed by the Gulf. [*He nods his head violently towards* MISS FELLOWES, *who springs forward and slaps him.*] Thank you, Miss Fellowes. Latta, hold on a minute. I will not be stranded here. I've had unusual expenses on this trip. Right now I don't have my fare back to Houston or even to Mexico City. Now if there's any truth in your statement that Blake Tours have really authorized you to take over my party, then I am sure they have . . . [*He draws a breath, almost gasping.*] . . . I'm sure they must have given you something in the . . . the nature of . . . *severance* pay? Or at least enough to get me back to the States?

LATTA: I got no money for you.

SHANNON: I hate to question your word, but . . .

LATTA: We'll drive you back to Mexico City. You can sit up front with the driver.

SHANNON: *You* would do that, Latta. *I'd* find it *humiliating*. Now! Give me my severance pay!

LATTA: Blake Tours is having to refund those ladies half the price of the tour. That's your severance pay. And Miss Fellowes tells me you got plenty of money out of this young girl you seduced in . . .

SHANNON: Miss Fellowes, did you really make such a . . . ?

MISS FELLOWES: When Charlotte returned that night, she'd cashed two traveller's cheques.

SHANNON: After I had spent all my own cash.

MISS FELLOWES: On what? Whores in the filthy places you took her through?

SHANNON: Miss Charlotte cashed two ten-dollar traveller's cheques because I had spent all the cash I had on me. And I've never had to, I've certainly never desired to, have relations with whores.

MISS FELLOWES: You took her through ghastly places, such as . . .

SHANNON: I showed her what she wanted me to show her. Ask her! I showed her San Juan de Letran, I showed her Tenampa and some other places not listed in the Blake Tours brochure. I showed her more than the floating gardens at Xochimilco, Maximilian's Palace, and the mad Empress Carlotta's little homesick chapel, Our Lady of Guadalupe, the monument to Juarez, the relics of the Aztec civilization, the sword of Cortez, the head-dress of Montezuma. I showed her what she told me she wanted to see. Where is she? Where is Miss . . . oh, down there with the ladies. [*He leans over the rail and shouts down.*] Charlotte! Charlotte! [MISS FELLOWES *seizes his arm and thrusts him away from the veranda rail.*]

MISS FELLOWES: Don't you dare!

SHANNON: Dare what?

MISS FELLOWES: Call her, speak to her, go near her, you, you . . . filthy!

> [MAXINE *reappears at the corner of the veranda; with the ceremonial rapidity of a cuckoo bursting from a clock to announce the hour. She just stands there with an incongruous grin, her big eyes unblinking, as if they were painted on her round beaming face.* HANNAH *holds a gold-lacquered Japanese fan motionless but open in one hand; the other hand touches the netting at the cubicle door as if she were checking an impulse to rush to* SHANNON'S *defence. Her attitude has the style of a Kabuki dancer's pose.* SHANNON'S *manner becomes courtly again.*]

SHANNON: Oh, all right, I won't. I only wanted her to confirm my story that I took her out that night at her request, not at my . . . suggestion. All that I did was offer my services to her when *she* told *me* she'd like to see things not listed in the brochure, not usually witnessed by ordinary tourists, such as . . .

MISS FELLOWES: Your hotel bedroom? Later? That too? She came back *flea*-bitten!

SHANNON: Oh, now, don't exaggerate, please. Nobody ever got any fleas off Shannon.

MISS FELLOWES: Her clothes had to be fumigated!

SHANNON: I understand your annoyance, but you are going too far when you try to make out that I gave Charlotte fleas. I don't deny that . . .

MISS FELLOWES: Wait till they get my *report*!

SHANNON: I don't deny that it's possible to get flea-bites on a tour of inspection of what lies under the public surface of cities, off the grand boulevards, away from the night-clubs, even away from Diego Rivera's murals, but . . .

MISS FELLOWES: Oh, preach that in a pulpit, Reverend Shannon-*de*-frocked!

SHANNON [*ominously*]: You've said that once too often. [*He seizes her arm.*] This time before witnesses. Miss Jelkes? Miss Jelkes!

> [HANNAH *opens the curtain of her cubicle.*]

HANNAH: Yes, Mr Shannon, what is it?

SHANNON: You heard what this . . .

MISS FELLOWES: Shannon! Take your hand off my arm!

SHANNON: Miss Jelkes, just tell me, did you hear what she . . . [*His voice stops oddly with a choked, sobbing sound. He runs at the wall and pounds it with his fists.*]

MISS FELLOWES: I spent this entire afternoon and over twenty dollars checking up on this impostor, with long-distance phone-calls.

HANNAH: Not impostor – you mustn't say things like that.

MISS FELLOWES: You were locked out of your church! – for atheism and seducing of girls!

SHANNON [*turning about*]: In front of God and witnesses, you are lying, lying!

LATTA: Miss Fellowes, I want you to know that Blake Tours was deceived about this character's background, and Blake Tours will see that he is blacklisted from now on at every travel agency in the States.

SHANNON: How about Africa, Asia, Australia? The whole world, Latta, God's world, has been the range of my travels. I haven't stuck to the schedules of the brochures and I've always allowed the ones that were willing to see, to *see*! – the underworlds of all places, and if they had hearts to be touched, feelings to feel with, I gave them a priceless chance to feel and be touched. And none will ever forget it, none of them, ever, never [*The passion of his speech imposes a little stillness.*]

LATTA: Go on, lie back in your hammock; that's all you're good for, Shannon. [*He goes to the top of the path and shouts down the hill.*] O.K. Let's get cracking. Get that luggage strapped on top of the bus. We're moving! [*He starts down the hill with* MISS FELLOWES.]

NONNO [*incongruously, from his cubicle*]:

> How calmly does the orange branch
> Observe the sky begin to blanch . . .

[SHANNON *sucks in his breath with an abrupt, fierce sound. He rushes off the veranda and down the path towards the road.* HANNAH *calls after him, with a restraining gesture.* MAXINE *appears on the* veranda. *Then a great commotion commences below the hill, with shrieks of outrage and squeals of shocked laughter.*]

MAXINE [*rushes to the path*]: Shannon! Shannon! Get back up here, get back up here. Pedro, Pancho, traerme a Shannon. Que está haciendo allí? Oh, my God! Stop him, for God's sake, somebody stop him!

[SHANNON *returns, panting and spent. He is followed by* MAXINE.]

MAXINE: Shannon, go in your room and stay there until that party's gone.

SHANNON: Don't give me orders.

MAXINE: You do what I tell you to do or I'll have you removed – you know where.

SHANNON: Don't push me, don't pull at me, Maxine.

MAXINE: All right; do as I say.

SHANNON: Shannon obeys only Shannon.

MAXINE: You'll sing a different tune if they put you where they put you in 'thirty-six. Remember 'thirty-six, Shannon?

SHANNON: O.K., Maxine, just . . . let me breathe alone, please. I won't go, but I will lie in the . . . hammock.

MAXINE: Go into Fred's room where I can watch you.

SHANNON: Later, Maxine, not yet.

MAXINE: Why do you always come here to crack up, Shannon?

SHANNON: It's the hammock, Maxine, the hammock by the rain forest.

MAXINE: Shannon, go in your room and stay there until I get back. Oh, my God, the money. They haven't paid the mother-grabbin' bill. I got to go back down there and collect their goddam bill before they . . . Pancho, vijilalo, entiendes? [*She rushes back down the hill, shouting* 'Hey! Just a minute down there!']

SHANNON: What did I do? [*He shakes his head, stunned.*] I don't know what I did.

[HANNAH *opens the screen of her cubicle, but doesn't come out. She is softly lighted so that she looks, again, like a medieval sculpture of a saint. Her pale gold hair catches the soft light. She has let it down and still holds the silver-backed brush with which she was brushing it.*]

God almighty, I . . . what did I do? I don't know what I did. [*He turns to the Mexican boys, who have come back up the path.*] Que hice? Que hice?

[*There is breathless, spasmodic laughter from the boys as* PANCHO *informs him that he pissed on the ladies' luggage.*]

PANCHO: Tú measte en las maletas de las señoras!

[SHANNON *tries to laugh with the boys, while they bend double with amusement.* SHANNON'S *laughter dies out in little choked spasms. Down the hill,* MAXINE'S *voice is raised in angry altercation with* JAKE LATTA, MISS FELLOWES' *voice is lifted and then there is a general rhubarb, to which is added the roar of the bus motor.*]

SHANNON: There go my ladies, ha, ha! There go my . . . [*He turns about to meet* HANNAH'S *grave, compassionate gaze. He tries to laugh again. She shakes her head with a slight restraining gesture and drops the curtain so that her softly luminous figure is seen as through a mist.*] . . . ladies, the last of my – ha, ha! – ladies. [*He bends far over the veranda rail, then straightens violently and with an animal outcry begins to pull at the chain suspending the gold cross about his neck.* PANCHO *watches indifferently as the chain cuts the back of Shannon's neck.* HANNAH *rushes out to him.*]

HANNAH: Mr Shannon, stop that! You're cutting yourself doing that. That isn't necessary, so stop it! [*To Pancho.*] Agarrale las manos! [PANCHO *makes a half-hearted effort to comply, but* SHANNON *kicks at him and goes on with the furious self-laceration.*] Shannon, let me do it, let me take it off you. Can I take it off you? [*He drops his arms. She struggles with the clasp of the chain, but her fingers are too shaky to work it.*]

SHANNON: No, no, it won't come off, I'll have to break it off me.

HANNAH: No, no, wait – I've got it. [*She has now removed it.*]

SHANNON: Thanks. Keep it. Good-bye! [*He starts towards the path down to the beach.*]

HANNAH: Where are you going? What are you going to do?

SHANNON: I'm going swimming. I'm going to swim out to China!

HANNAH: No, no, not tonight, Shannon! Tomorrow . . . tomorrow, Shannon!

[*But he divides the trumpet-flowered bushes and passes through them.* HANNAH *rushes after him, screaming for 'Mrs Faulk.'* MAXINE *can be heard shouting for the Mexican boys.*]

MAXINE: Muchachos, cojerlo! Atarlo! Está loco. Traerlo aqui. Catch him, he's crazy. Bring him back and tie him up!

[*In a few moments* SHANNON *is hauled back through the bushes and on to the veranda by* MAXINE *and the boys. They rope him into the hammock. His struggle is probably not much of a real struggle – histrionics mostly. But* HANNAH *stands wringing her hands by the steps as* SHANNON, *gasping for breath, is tied up.*]

HANNAH: The ropes are too tight on his chest!

MAXINE: No, they're not. He's acting, acting. He likes it! I know this black Irish bastard like nobody ever knowed him, so you keep out of it, honey. He cracks up like this so regular that you can set a calendar by it. Every eighteen months he does it, and twice he's done it here and I've had to pay for his medical care. Now I'm going to call in town to get a doctor to come out here and give him a knockout injection, and if he's not better tomorrow he's going into the Casa de Locos again, like he did the last time he cracked up on me!

[*There is a moment of silence.*]

SHANNON: Miss Jelkes?

HANNAH: Yes.

SHANNON: Where are you?

HANNAH: I'm right here behind you. Can I do anything for you?

SHANNON: Sit here where I can see you. Don't stop talking. I have to fight this panic.

[*There is a pause. She moves a chair beside his hammock. The Germans troop up from the beach. They are delighted by the drama that*

SHANNON *has provided. In their scanty swim-suits they parade on to the veranda and gather about* SHANNON'S *captive figure as if they were looking at a funny animal in a zoo. Their talk is in German except when they speak directly to* SHANNON *or* HANNAH. *Their heavily handsome figures gleam with oily wetness and they keep chuckling lubriciously.*]

HANNAH: Please! Will you be so kind as to leave him alone?

[*They pretend not to understand her.* FRAU FAHRENKOPF *bends over Shannon in his hammock and speaks to him loudly and slowly in English.*]

FRAU FAHRENKOPF: Is this true you make pee-pee all over the suit-cases of the ladies from Texas? Hah? Hah? You run down there to the bus and right in front of the ladies you pees all over the luggage of the ladies from Texas?

[HANNAH'S *indignant protest is drowned in the Rabelaisian laughter of the Germans.*]

HERR FAHRENKOPF: Thees is vunderbar, vunderbar! Hah? Thees is a *epic gesture*! Hah? Thees is the way to demonstrate to ladies that you are a American *gentleman*! Hah?

[*He turns to the others and makes a ribald comment. The two women shriek with amusement,* HILDA *falling back into the arms of* WOLF-GANG, *who catches her with his hands over her almost nude breasts.*]

HANNAH [*calling out*]: Mrs Faulk! Mrs Faulk! [*She rushes to the veranda angle as* MAXINE *appears there.*] Will you please ask these people to leave him alone. They're tormenting him like an animal in a trap.

[*The Germans are already trooping around the veranda, laughing and capering gaily.*]

SHANNON [*suddenly, in a great shout*]: Regression to infantilism, ha, ha, regression to infantilism . . . The infantile protest, ha, ha, ha, the infantile expression of rage at Mama and rage at God and

rage at the goddam crib, and rage at the everything, rage at the
. . . everything . . . Regression to infantilism . . .

[*Now all have left but* HANNAH *and* SHANNON.]

SHANNON: Untie me.

HANNAH: Not yet.

SHANNON: I can't stand being tied up.

HANNAH: You'll have to stand it a while.

SHANNON: It makes me panicky.

HANNAH: I know.

SHANNON: A man can die of panic.

HANNAH: Not if he enjoys it as much as you, Mr Shannon.

[*She goes into her cubicle directly behind his hammock. The cubicle is
lighted and we see her removing a small teapot and a tin of tea from
her suitcase on the cot, then a little alcohol burner. She comes back
out with these articles.*]

SHANNON: What did you mean by that insulting remark?

HANNAH: What remark, Mr Shannon?

SHANNON: That I enjoy it.

HANNAH: Oh . . . that.

SHANNON: Yes. That.

HANNAH: That wasn't meant as an insult, just an observation. I don't
judge people; I draw them. That's all I do, just draw them, but in
order to draw them I have to observe them, don't I?

SHANNON: And you've observed, you think you've observed, that I
like being tied in this hammock, trussed up in it like a hog being
hauled off to the slaughter-house, Miss Jelkes.

HANNAH: Who wouldn't like to suffer and atone for the sins of himself and the world if it could be done in a hammock with ropes
instead of nails, on a hill that's so much lovelier than Golgotha,
the Place of the Skull, Mr Shannon? There's something almost
voluptuous in the way that you twist and groan in that hammock
– no nails, no blood, no death. Isn't that a comparatively comfortable, almost voluptuous kind of crucifixion to suffer for the guilt
of the world, Mr Shannon?

[*She strikes a match to light the alcohol burner. A pure blue jet of flame springs up to cast a flickering, rather unearthly glow on their section of the veranda. The glow is delicately refracted by the subtle, faded colours of her robe – a robe given to her by a Kabuki actor who posed for her in Japan.*]

SHANNON: Why have you turned against me all of a sudden, when I need you the most?

HANNAH: I haven't turned against you at all, Mr Shannon. I'm just attempting to give you a character sketch of yourself, in words instead of pastel crayons or charcoal.

SHANNON: You're certainly suddenly very sure of some New England spinsterish attitudes that I didn't know you had in you. I thought that you were an *emancipated* Puritan, Miss Jelkes.

HANNAH: Who is . . . ever . . . completely?

SHANNON: I thought you were sexless, but you've suddenly turned into a woman. Know how I know that? Because you, not me – not me – are taking pleasure in my tied-up condition. All women, whether they face it or not, want to see a man in a tied-up situation. They work at it all their lives, to get a man in a tied-up situation. Their lives are fulfilled, they're satisfied at last, when they get a man, or as many men as they can, in the tied-up situation. [HANNAH *leaves the alcohol burner and teapot and moves to the railing, where she grips a veranda post and draws a few deep breaths.*] You don't like this observation of you? The shoe's too tight for comfort when it's on your own foot, Miss Jelkes? Some deep breaths again – feeling panic?

HANNAH [*recovering and returning to the burner*]: I'd like to untie you right now, but let me wait till you've passed through your present disturbance. You're still indulging yourself in your . . . your Passion Play performance. I can't help observing this self-indulgence in you.

SHANNON: What rotten indulgence?

HANNAH: Well, your busload of ladies from the female college in Texas. I don't like those ladies any more than you do, but after all, they did save up all year to make this Mexican tour, to stay in stuffy hotels and eat the food they're used to. They want to be at home away from home, but you . . . you indulged yourself, Mr Shannon. You did conduct the tour as if it was just for you, for your own pleasure.

SHANNON: Hell, what pleasure – going through hell all the way?

HANNAH: Yes, but comforted, now and then, weren't you, by the little musical prodigy under the wing of the college vocal instructor?

SHANNON: Funny, ha-ha funny! Nantucket spinsters have their wry humour, don't they?

HANNAH: Yes, they do. They have to.

SHANNON [*becoming progressively quieter under the cool influence of her voice behind him*]: I can't see what you're up to, Miss Jelkes honey, but I'd almost swear you're making a pot of tea over there.

HANNAH: That is just what I'm doing.

SHANNON: Does this strike you as the right time for a tea party?

HANNAH: This isn't plain tea; this is poppy-seed tea.

SHANNON: Are you a slave to the poppy?

HANNAH: It's a mild, sedative drink that helps you get through nights that are hard for you to get through, and I'm making it for my grandfather and myself as well as for you, Mr Shannon. Because, for all three of us, this won't be an easy night to get through. Can't you hear him in his cell number 4, mumbling over and over and over the lines of his new poem? It's like a blind man climbing a staircase that goes to nowhere, that just falls off into space, and I hate to say what it is . . . [*She draws a few deep breaths behind him.*]

SHANNON: Put some hemlock in his poppy-seed tea tonight so he won't wake up tomorrow for the removal to the Casa de Huéspedes. Do that act of mercy. Put in the hemlock and I will consecrate it, turn it to God's blood. Hell, if you'll get me out of this hammock I'll serve it to him myself, I'll be your accomplice in this act of mercy. I'll say, 'Take and drink this, the blood of our –'

HANNAH: Stop it! Stop being childishly cruel! I can't stand for a person that I respect to talk and behave like a small, cruel boy, Mr Shannon.

SHANNON: What've you found to respect in me, Miss . . . Thin-Standing-Up-Female-Buddha?

HANNAH: I respect a person that has had to fight and howl for his
decency and his –

SHANNON: *What* decency?

HANNAH: Yes, for his decency and his bit of goodness, much more
than I respect the lucky ones that just had theirs handed out to
them at birth and never afterwards snatched from them by . . .
unbearable . . . torments, I . . .

SHANNON: You *respect* me?

HANNAH: I do.

SHANNON: But you just said that I'm taking pleasure in a . . . voluptuous crucifixion without nails. A . . . what? . . . painless atonement
for the –

HANNAH [*cutting in*]: Yes, but I think –

SHANNON: Untie me!

HANNAH: Soon, soon. Be patient.

SHANNON: Now!

HANNAH: Not quite yet, Mr Shannon. Not till I'm reasonably sure
that you won't swim out to China, because, you see, I think you
think of the . . . 'the long swim to China' as another painless atonement. I mean I don't think you think you'd be intercepted by sharks
and barracudas before you got far past the barrier reef. And I'm
afraid you *would be*. It's as simple as that, if that is simple.

SHANNON: What's simple?

HANNAH: Nothing, except for simpletons, Mr Shannon.

SHANNON: Do you believe in people being tied up?

HANNAH: Only when they might take the long swim to China.

SHANNON: All right, Miss Thin-Standing-Up-Female-Buddha, just
light a Benson and Hedges cigarette for me and put it in my mouth
and take it out when you hear me choking on it – if that doesn't
seem to you like another bit of voluptuous self-crucifixion.

HANNAH [*looking about the veranda*]: I will, but . . . where did I put
them?

SHANNON: I have a pack of my own in my pocket.

HANNAH: Which pocket?

SHANNON: I don't know which pocket, you'll have to frisk me for it.

[*She pats his jacket pocket.*]

HANNAH: They're not in your coat-pocket.

SHANNON: Then look for them in my pants' pockets.

[*She hesitates to put her hand in his pants' pockets, for a moment.* HANNAH *has always had a sort of fastidiousness, a reluctance, towards intimate physical contact. But after the momentary fastidious hesitation, she puts her hands in his pants' pocket and draws out the cigarette pack.*]

Now light it for me and put it in my mouth.

[*She complies with these directions. Almost at once he chokes and the cigarette is expelled.*]

HANNAH: You've dropped it on you – where is it?

SHANNON [*twisting and lunging about in the hammock*]: It's under me, under me, burning. Untie me, for God's sake, will you – it's burning me through my pants!

HANNAH: Raise your hips so I can –

SHANNON: I can't; the ropes are too tight. Untie me, untieeeee meeeeee!

HANNAH: I've found it. I've got it!

[*But* SHANNON's *shout has brought* MAXINE *out of her office. She rushes on to the veranda and sits on Shannon's legs.*]

MAXINE: Now hear this, you crazy black Irish mick, you! You Protestant black Irish looney. I've called up Lopez, Doc Lopez. Remember him – the man in the dirty white jacket that come here the last time you cracked up here? And hauled you off to the Casa de Locos? Where they threw you into that cell with nothing in it but a bucket and straw and a water-pipe? That you crawled up the water-pipe? And dropped head-down on the floor and got a concussion? Yeah, and I told him you were back here to crack up again and if you didn't quiet down here tonight you should be hauled out in the morning.

SHANNON [*cutting in, with the honking sound of a panicky goose*]: Off, off, off, off, off!

HANNAH: Oh, Mrs Faulk, Mr Shannon won't quiet down till he's left alone in the hammock.

MAXINE: Then why don't *you* leave him alone?

HANNAH: I'm not sitting on him and he . . . has to be cared for by someone.

MAXINE: And that someone is *you*?

HANNAH: A long time ago, Mrs Faulk, I had experience with someone in Mr Shannon's condition, so I know how necessary it is to let them be quiet for a while.

MAXINE: He wasn't quiet; he was shouting.

HANNAH: He will quiet down again. I'm preparing a sedative tea for him, Mrs Faulk.

MAXINE: Yeah, I see. Put it out. Nobody cooks here but the China-man in the kitchen.

HANNAH: This is just a little alcohol burner, a spirit lamp, Mrs Faulk.

MAXINE: I know what it is. It goes out! [*She blows out the flame under the burner.*]

SHANNON: Maxine honey? [*He speaks quietly now.*] Stop persecuting this lady. You can't intimidate her. A bitch is no match for a lady except in a brass bed, honey, and sometimes not even there.

[*The Germans are heard shouting for beer – a case of it to take down to the beach.*]

WOLFGANG: Eine Kiste Carta Blanca.

FRAU FAHRENKOPF: Wir haben genug gehabt . . . vielleicht nicht.

HERR FAHRENKOPF: Nein! Niemals genug.

HILDA: Mutter du bist dick . . . aber wir sind es nicht.

SHANNON: Maxine, you're neglecting your duties as a beer-hall wait-ress. [*His tone is deceptively gentle.*] They want a case of Carta Blanca to carry down to the beach, so give it to 'em . . . and tonight, when the moon's gone down, if you'll let me out of this hammock, I'll try to imagine you as a . . . as a nymph in her teens.

MAXINE: A fat lot of good you'd be in your present condition.

SHANNON: Don't be a sexual snob at your age, honey.

MAXINE: Hah! [*But the unflattering offer has pleased her realistically mod-est soul, so she goes back to the Germans.*]

SHANNON: Now let me try a bit of your poppy-seed tea, Miss Jelkes.

HANNAH: I ran out of sugar, but I had some ginger, some sugared ginger. [*She pours a cup of tea and sips it.*] Oh, it's not well brewed yet, but try to drink some now and the – [*she lights the burner again*] – the second cup will be better. [*She crouches by the hammock and presses the cup to his lips. He raises his head to sip it, but he gags and chokes.*]

SHANNON: *Caesar's ghost!* – it could be chased by the witches' brew from Macbeth.

HANNAH: Yes, I know; it's still bitter.

[*The Germans appear on the wing of the veranda and go trooping down to the beach for a beer festival and a moonlight swim. Even in the relative dark they have a luminous colour, an almost phosphorescent pink and gold colour of skin. They carry with them a case of Carta Blanca beer and the fantastically painted rubber horse. On their faces are smiles of euphoria as they move like a dream-image, starting to sing a marching song as they go.*]

SHANNON: Fiends out of hell with the . . . voices of . . . angels.

HANNAH: Yes, they call it 'the logic of contradictions', Mr Shannon.

SHANNON [*lunging suddenly forward and undoing the loosened ropes*]: Out! Free! Unassisted!

HANNAH: Yes, I never doubted that you could get loose, Mr Shannon.

SHANNON: Thanks for your help, anyhow.

HANNAH: Where are you going?

[*He has crossed to the liquor cart.*]

SHANNON: Not far. To the liquor cart to make myself a rum-coco.

HANNAH: Oh . . .

SHANNON [*at the liquor cart*]: Coconut? Check. Machete? Check. Rum? Double check! Ice? The ice bucket's empty. O.K., it's a night for warm drinks. Miss Jelkes? Would you care to have your complimentary rum-coco?

HANNAH: No thank you, Mr Shannon.

SHANNON: You don't mind me having mine?

HANNAH: Not at all, Mr Shannon.

SHANNON: You don't disapprove of this weakness, this self-indulgence?

HANNAH: Liquor isn't your problem, Mr Shannon.

SHANNON: What is my problem, Miss Jelkes?

HANNAH: The oldest one in the world – the need to believe in something or in someone – almost anyone – almost anything . . . something.

SHANNON: Your voice sounds hopeless about it.

HANNAH: No, I'm not hopeless about it. In fact, I've discovered something to believe in.

SHANNON: Something like . . . God?

HANNAH: No.

SHANNON: What?

HANNAH: Broken gates between people so they can reach each other, even if it's just for one night only.

SHANNON: One-night stands, huh?

HANNAH: One night . . . communication between them on a veranda outside their . . . separate cubicles, Mr Shannon.

SHANNON: You don't mean physically, do you?

HANNAH: No.

SHANNON: I didn't think so. Then what?

HANNAH: A little understanding exchanged between them, a wanting to help each other through nights like this.

SHANNON: Who was the someone you told the widow you'd helped long ago to get through a crack-up like this one I'm going through?

HANNAH: Oh . . . that. Myself.

SHANNON: You?

HANNAH: Yes. I can help you because I've been through what you are going through now. I had something like your spook – I just had a different name for him. I called him the blue devil, and . . . oh . . . we had quite a battle, quite a contest between us.

SHANNON: Which you obviously won.

HANNAH: I couldn't afford to lose.

SHANNON: How'd you beat your blue devil?

HANNAH: I showed him that I could endure him and I made him respect my endurance.

SHANNON: How?

HANNAH: Just by, just by . . . enduring. Endurance is something that spooks and blue devils respect. And they respect all the tricks that panicky people use to outlast and outwit their panic.

SHANNON: Like poppy-seed tea?

HANNAH: Poppy-seed tea or rum-cocos or just a few deep breaths. Anything, everything, that we take to give them the slip, and so to keep on going.

SHANNON: To where?

HANNAH: To somewhere like this, perhaps. This veranda over the rain forest and the still-water beach, after long, difficult travels. And I don't mean just travels about the world, the earth's surface. I mean . . . subterranean travels, the . . . the journeys that the spooked and bedevilled people are forced to take through the . . . the *unlighted* sides of their natures.

SHANNON: Don't tell me you have a dark side to your nature. [*He says this sardonically.*]

HANNAH: I'm sure I don't have to tell a man as experienced and knowledgeable as you, Mr Shannon, that everything has its shadowy side?

[*She glances up at him and observes that she doesn't have his attention. He is gazing tensely at something off the veranda. It is the kind of abstraction, not vague but fiercely concentrated, that occurs in madness. She turns to look where he's looking. She closes her eyes for a moment and draws a deep breath, then goes on speaking in a voice like a hypnotist's, as if the words didn't matter, since he is not listening to her so much as to the tone and the cadence of her voice.*]

Everything in the whole solar system has a shadowy side to it except the sun itself – the sun is the single exception. You're not listening, are you?

SHANNON [*as if replying to her*]: The spook is in the rain forest. [*He suddenly hurls his coconut shell with great violence off the veranda creating a commotion among the jungle birds.*] Good shot – it caught him right on the kisser and his teeth flew out like popcorn from a popper.

HANNAH: Has he gone off – to the dentist?

SHANNON: He's retreated a little way away for a little while, but when I buzz for my breakfast tomorrow, he'll bring it in to me with a grin that'll curdle the milk in the coffee and he'll stink like a . . . gringo drunk in a Mexican jail who's slept all night in his vomit.

HANNAH: If you wake up before I'm out, I'll bring your coffee in to you . . . if you call me.

SHANNON [*his attention returns to her*]: No, you'll be gone, God help me.

HANNAH: Maybe and maybe not. I might think of something tomorrow to placate the widow.

SHANNON: The widow's implacable, honey.

HANNAH: I think I'll think of something because I have to. I can't let Nonno be moved to the Casa de Huéspedes, Mr Shannon. Not any more than I could let you take the long swim out to China. You know that. Not if I can prevent it, and when I have to be resourceful, I can be very resourceful.

SHANNON: How'd you get over your crack-up?

HANNAH: I never cracked up, I couldn't afford to. Of course, I nearly did once. I was young once, Mr Shannon, but I was one of those people who can be young without really having their youth, and not to have your youth when you are young is naturally very disturbing. But I was lucky. My work, this occupational therapy that I gave myself – painting and doing quick character sketches – made me look out of myself, not in, and gradually, at the far end of the tunnel that I was struggling out of I began to see this faint, very faint grey light – the light of the world outside me – and I kept climbing towards it. I had to.

SHANNON: Did it stay a grey light?

HANNAH: No, no, it turned white.

SHANNON: Only white, never gold?

HANNAH: No, it stayed only white, but white is a very good light to see at the end of a long black tunnel you thought would be never ending, that only God or Death could put a stop to, especially when you . . . since I was . . . far from sure about God.

SHANNON: You're still unsure about him?

HANNAH: Not as unsure as I was. You see, in my profession I have to look hard and close at human faces in order to catch something in them before they get restless and call out, 'Waiter, the check, we're leaving'. Of course sometimes, a few times, I just see blobs of wet dough that pass for human faces, with bits of jelly for eyes. Then I cue in Nonno to give a recitation, because I can't draw such faces. But those aren't the usual faces, I don't think they're even real. Most times I *do* see something, and I can catch it – I *can*, like I caught something in your face when I sketched you this afternoon with your eyes open. Are you still listening to me? [*He crouches beside her chair, looking up at her intently.*] In Shanghai, Shannon, there is a place that's called the House for the Dying – the old and penniless dying, whose younger, penniless living children and grandchildren take them there for them to get through with their dying on pallets, on straw mats. The first time I went there it shocked me, I ran away from it. But I came back later and I saw that their children and grandchildren and the custodians of the place had put little comforts beside their death-pallets, little flowers and opium candies and religious emblems. That made me able to stay to draw their dying faces. Sometimes only their eyes were still alive, but, Mr Shannon, those eyes of the penniless dying with those last little comforts beside them, I tell you, Mr Shannon, those eyes looked up with their last dim life left in them as clear as the stars in the Southern Cross, Mr Shannon. And now . . . now I am going to say something to you that will sound like something that only the spinster granddaughter of a minor romantic poet is likely to say . . . Nothing I've ever seen has seemed as beautiful to me, not even the view from this veranda between the sky and the still-water beach, and lately . . . lately my grandfather's eyes have looked up at me like that . . . [*She rises abruptly and crosses to the front of the veranda.*] Tell me, what is that sound I keep hearing down there?

SHANNON: There's a marimba band at the cantina on the beach.

HANNAH: I don't mean that, I mean that scraping, scuffling sound that I keep hearing under the veranda.

SHANNON: Oh, that. The Mexican boys that work here have caught an iguana and tied it up under the veranda, hitched it to a post, and naturally, of course, it's trying to scramble away. But it's got to the end of its rope, and get any further it cannot. Ha-ha – that's it. [*He quotes from* NONNO'S *poem:* 'And still the orange,' etc.] Do you have any life of your own – besides your watercolours and sketches and your travels with Grampa?

HANNAH: We make a home for each other, my grandfather and I. Do you know what I mean by a home? I don't mean a regular home. I mean I don't mean what other people mean when they speak of a home, because I don't regard a home as a . . . well, as a place, a building . . . a house . . . of wood, bricks, stone. I think of a home as being a thing that two people have between them in which each can . . . well, nest – rest – live in, emotionally speaking. Does that make any sense to you, Mr Shannon?

SHANNON: Yeah, complete. But . . .

HANNAH: Another incomplete sentence.

SHANNON: We better leave it that way. I might've said something to hurt you.

HANNAH: I'm not thin-skinned, Mr Shannon.

SHANNON: No, well, then, I'll say it . . . [*He moves to the liquor cart.*] When a bird builds a nest to rest in and live in, it doesn't build it in a . . . a falling-down tree.

HANNAH: I'm not a bird, Mr Shannon.

SHANNON: I was making an analogy, Miss Jelkes.

HANNAH: I thought you were making yourself another rum-coco, Mr Shannon.

SHANNON: Both. When a bird builds a nest, it builds it with an eye for the . . . the relative permanence of the location, and also for the purpose of mating and propagating its species.

HANNAH: I still say that I'm not a bird, Mr Shannon, I'm a human being and when a member of that fantastic species builds a nest in the heart of another, the question of permanence isn't the first or even the last thing that's considered . . . necessarily? . . . always? Nonno and I have been continuously reminded of the impermanence of things lately. We go back to an hotel where we've been many times before and it isn't there any more. It's been demolished and there's one of those glassy, brassy new ones. Or if the old one's still there, the manager or the Maître D' who always welcomed us back so cordially before has been replaced by someone new who looks at us with suspicion.

SHANNON: Yeah, but you still had each other.

HANNAH: Yes. We did.

SHANNON: But when the old gentleman goes?

HANNAH: Yes?

SHANNON: What will you do? Stop?

HANNAH: Stop or go on . . . probably go on.

SHANNON: Alone? Checking into hotels alone, eating alone at tables for one in a corner, the tables waiters call aces?

HANNAH: Thank you for your sympathy, Mr Shannon, but in my profession I'm obliged to make quick contacts with strangers who turn to friends very quickly.

SHANNON: Customers aren't friends.

HANNAH: They turn to friends, if they're friendly.

SHANNON: Yeah, but how will it seem to be travelling alone after so many years of travelling with . . .

HANNAH: I will know how it feels when I feel it – and don't say alone as if nobody had ever gone on alone. For instance, you.

SHANNON: I've always travelled with train-loads, plane-loads and bus-loads of tourists.

HANNAH: That doesn't mean you're still not really alone.

SHANNON: I never fail to make an intimate connection with someone in my parties.

HANNAH: Yes, the youngest young lady, and I was on the veranda this afternoon when the latest of these young ladies gave a demonstration of how lonely the intimate connection has always been for you. The episode in the cold, inhuman hotel room, Mr Shannon, for which you despise the lady almost as much as you despise yourself. Afterwards you are so polite to the lady that I'm sure it must chill her to the bone, the scrupulous little attentions that you pay her in return for your little enjoyment of her. The gentleman-of-Virginia act that you put on for her, your noblesse oblige treatment of her . . . Oh no, Mr Shannon, don't kid yourself that you ever travel with someone. You have always travelled alone except for your spook, as you call it. He's your travelling companion. Nothing, nobody else has travelled with you.

SHANNON: Thank you for your sympathy, Miss Jelkes.

HANNAH: You're welcome, Mr Shannon. And now I think I had better warm up the poppy-seed tea for Nonno. Only a good night's sleep could make it possible for him to go on from here tomorrow.

SHANNON: Yes, well, if the conversation is over – I think I'll go down for a swim now.

HANNAH: To China?

SHANNON: No, not to China, just to the little island out here with the sleepy bar on it . . . called the Cantina Serena.

HANNAH: Why?

SHANNON: Because I'm not a nice drunk and I was about to ask you a not nice question.

HANNAH: Ask it. There's no set limit on questions here tonight.

SHANNON: And no set limits on answers?

HANNAH: None I can think of between you and me, Mr Shannon.

SHANNON: That I will take you up on.

HANNAH: Do.

SHANNON: It's a bargain.

HANNAH: Only do lie back down in the hammock and drink a full cup of poppy-seed tea this time. It's warmer now and the sugared ginger will make it easier to get down.

SHANNON: All right. The question is this: have you never had in your life any kind of a love life? [HANNAH *stiffens for a moment.*] I thought you said there was no limit set on questions.

HANNAH: We'll make a bargain – I will answer your question *after* you've had a full cup of the poppy-seed tea so you'll be able to get the good night's sleep you need, too. It's fairly warm now and the sugared ginger's made it much more – [*she sips the cup*] – palatable.

SHANNON: You think I'm going to drift into dreamland so you can welch on the bargain? [*He accepts the cup from her.*]

HANNAH: I'm not a welcher on bargains. Drink it all. All. *All!*

SHANNON [*with a disgusted grimace as he drains the cup*]: *Great* Caesar's ghost! [*He tosses the cup off the veranda and falls into the hammock, chuckling.*] The Oriental idea of a Mickey Finn, huh? Sit down where I can see you, Miss Jelkes, honey. [*She sits down in a straight-back chair, some distance from the hammock.*] Where I can *see* you! I don't have an X-ray eye in the back of my head, Miss Jelkes. [*She moves the chair alongside the hammock.*] Further, further, up further. [*She complies.*] There now. Answer the question now, Miss Jelkes honey.

HANNAH: Would you mind repeating the question?

SHANNON [*slowly, with emphasis*]: Have you never had in all your life and your travels any experience, any encounter with what Larry-the-crackpot Shannon thinks of as a love life?

HANNAH: There are . . . worse things than chastity, Mr Shannon.

SHANNON: Yeah, lunacy and death are both a little worse, *maybe!* But chastity isn't a thing that a beautiful woman or an attractive man falls into like a booby trap or an overgrown gopher hole, is it? [*There is a pause.*] I still think you are welching on the bargain and I . . . [*He starts out of the hammock.*]

HANNAH: Mr Shannon, this night is just as hard for me to get through as it is for you to get through. But it's you that are welching on the bargain; you're not staying in the hammock. Lie back down in the hammock. Now. Yes. Yes, I have had two experiences, well, encounters, with . . .

SHANNON: *Two*, did you say?

HANNAH: Yes, I said two. And I wasn't exaggerating and don't you say 'fantastic' before I've told you both stories. When I was sixteen, your favourite age, Mr Shannon, each Saturday afternoon my grandfather Nonno would give me thirty cents, my allowance, my pay for my secretarial and housekeeping duties. Twenty-five cents for admission to the Saturday matinée at the Nantucket movie theatre and five cents extra for a bag of popcorn, Mr Shannon. I'd sit at the almost empty back of the movie theatre so that the popcorn munching wouldn't disturb the other movie patrons. Well

. . . one afternoon a young man sat down beside me and pushed his . . . knee against mine and . . . I moved over two seats, but he moved over beside me and continued this . . . pressure! I jumped up and screamed, Mr Shannon. He was arrested for molesting a minor.

SHANNON: Is he still in the Nantucket jail?

HANNAH: No. I got him out. I told the police that it was a Clara Bow picture – it *was* a Clara Bow picture – and I was just over-excited.

SHANNON: Fantastic.

HANNAH: Yes, very! The second experience is much more recent, only two years ago, when Nonno and I were operating at the Raffles Hotel in Singapore, and doing very well there, making expenses and more. One evening in the Palm Court of the Raffles we met this middle-aged, sort of nondescript Australian salesman. You know – plump, bald-spotted, with a bad attempt at speaking with an upper-class accent and terribly over-friendly. He was alone and looked lonely. Grandfather said him a poem and I did a quick character sketch that was shamelessly flattering of him. He paid me more than my usual asking price and gave my grandfather five Malayan dollars, yes, and he even purchased one of my water-colours. Then it was Nonno's bedtime. The Aussie salesman asked me out in a sampan with him. Well, he'd been so generous . . . I accepted. I did, I accepted. Grandfather went up to bed and I went out in the sampan with this ladies' underwear salesman. I noticed that he became more and more . . .

SHANNON: What?

HANNAH: Well . . . *agitated* . . . as the afterglow of the sunset faded out on the water. [*She laughs with a delicate sadness.*] Well, finally, eventually, he leaned towards me . . . we were vis-à-vis in the sampan . . . and he looked intensely, passionately into my eyes. [*She laughs again.*] And he said to me: 'Miss Jelkes? Will you do me a favour? Will you do something for me?' 'What?' said I. 'Well,' said he, 'if I turn my back, if I look the other way, will you take off some piece of your clothes and let me hold it, just hold it?'

SHANNON: Fantastic!

HANNAH: Then he said, 'It will just take a few seconds.' 'Just a few seconds for what?' I asked him. [*She gives the same laugh again.*] He didn't say for what, but . . .

SHANNON: His satisfaction?

HANNAH: Yes.

SHANNON: What did you do – in a situation like that?

HANNAH: I . . . gratified his request, I did! And he kept his promise. He did keep his back turned till I said ready and threw him . . . the part of my clothes.

SHANNON: What did he do with it?

HANNAH: He didn't move, except to seize the article he'd requested. I looked the other way while his satisfaction took place.

SHANNON: Watch out for commercial travellers in the Far East. Is that the moral, Miss Jelkes honey?

HANNAH: Oh, no, the moral is Oriental. Accept whatever situation you cannot improve.

SHANNON: 'When it's inevitable, lean back and enjoy it' – is that it?

HANNAH: He'd bought a watercolour. The incident was embarrassing, not violent. I left and returned unmolested. Oh, and the funniest part of all is that when we got back to the Raffles Hotel, he took the piece of apparel out of his pocket like a bashful boy producing an apple for his school-teacher and tried to slip it into my hand in the elevator. I wouldn't accept it. I whispered, 'Oh, please keep it, Mr Willoughby!' He'd paid the asking price for my watercolour and somehow the little experience had been rather touching. I mean it was so *lonely*, out there in the sampan with violet streaks in the sky and this little middle-aged Australian making sounds like he was dying of asthma! And the planet Venus coming serenely out of a fair-weather cloud, over the Straits of Malacca . . .

SHANNON: And that experience . . . you call that a . . .

HANNAH: A love experience? Yes. I do call it one.

[*He regards her with incredulity, peering into her face so closely that she is embarrassed and becomes defensive.*]

SHANNON: That, that . . . sad, dirty little episode, you call it a . . . ?

HANNAH [*cutting in sharply*]: Sad it certainly was – for the odd little man – but why do you call it 'dirty'?

SHANNON: How did you feel when you went into your bedroom?

HANNAH: Confused, I . . . a little confused, I suppose . . . I'd known about loneliness – but not that degree or . . . depth of it.

SHANNON: You mean it didn't *disgust* you?

HANNAH: Nothing human disgusts me unless it's unkind, violent. And I told you how gentle he was – apologetic, shy, and really very, well, *delicate* about it. However, I do grant you it was on the rather fantastic level.

SHANNON: You're . . .

HANNAH: I am *what*? 'Fantastic'?

[*While they have been talking,* NONNO's *voice has been heard now and then, mumbling, from his cubicle. Suddenly it becomes loud and clear.*]

NONNO: And finally the broken stem,
The plummeting to earth and then . . .

[*His voice subsides to its mumble.* SHANNON, *standing behind Hannah, places his hand on her throat.*]

HANNAH: What is that for? Are you about to strangle me, Mr Shannon?

SHANNON: You can't stand to be touched?

HANNAH: Save it for the widow. It isn't for me.

SHANNON: Yes, you're right. [*He removes his hand.*] I could do it with Mrs Faulk, the inconsolable widow, but I couldn't with you.

HANNAH [*dryly and lightly*]: Spinster's loss, widow's gain, Mr Shannon.

SHANNON: Or widow's loss, spinster's gain. Anyhow it sounds like some old parlour game in a Virginia or Nantucket Island parlour. But . . . I wonder something . . .

HANNAH: What do you wonder?

SHANNON: If we couldn't . . . *travel* together, I mean just *travel* together?

HANNAH: Could we? In your opinion?

SHANNON: Why not? I don't see why not.

HANNAH: I think the impracticality of the idea will appear much clearer to you in the morning, Mr Shannon. [*She folds her dimly gold-lacquered fan and rises from her chair.*] Morning can always be counted on to bring us back to a more realistic level . . . Good night, Mr Shannon. I have to pack before I'm too tired to.

SHANNON: Don't leave me out here alone yet.

HANNAH: I have to pack now so I can get up at daybreak and try my luck in the plaza.

SHANNON: You won't sell a watercolour or sketch in that blazing hot plaza tomorrow. Miss Jelkes honey, I don't think you're operating on the realistic level.

HANNAH: Would I be if I thought we could travel together?

SHANNON: I still don't see why we couldn't.

HANNAH: Mr Shannon, you're not well enough to travel anywhere with anybody right now. Does that sound cruel of me?

SHANNON: You mean that I'm stuck here for good? Winding up with the . . . inconsolable widow?

HANNAH: We all wind up with something or with someone, and if it's someone instead of just something, we're lucky, perhaps . . . unusually lucky. [*She starts to enter her cubicle, then turns to him again in the doorway.*] Oh, and tomorrow . . . [*She touches her forehead, as if a little confused as well as exhausted.*]

SHANNON: What about tomorrow?

HANNAH [*with difficulty*]: I think it might be better, tomorrow, if we avoid showing any particular interest in each other, because Mrs Faulk is a morbidly jealous woman.

SHANNON: *Is* she?

HANNAH: Yes; she seems to have misunderstood our . . . sympathetic interest in each other. So I think we'd better avoid any more long talks on the veranda. I mean till she's thoroughly reassured it might be better if we just say good morning or good night to each other.

SHANNON: We don't even have to say that.

HANNAH: I will, but you don't have to answer.

SHANNON [*savagely*]: How about wall-tappings between us by way of communication? You know, like convicts in separate cells communicate with each other by tapping on the walls of the cells? One tap: I'm here. Two taps: are you there? Three taps: yes, I am. Four taps: that's good, we're together. *Christ!* . . . Here, take this. [*He snatches the gold cross from his pocket.*] Take my gold cross and hock it; it's 22-carat gold.

HANNAH: What do you, what are you . . . ?

SHANNON: There's a fine amethyst in it; it'll pay your travel expenses back to the States.

HANNAH: Mr Shannon, you're making no sense at all now.

SHANNON: Neither are you, Miss Jelkes, talking about tomorrow, and . . .

HANNAH: All I was saying was . . .

SHANNON: You won't *be* here tomorrow! Had you forgotten you won't be here tomorrow?

HANNAH [*with a slight, shocked laugh*]: Yes, I *had*, I'd *forgotten*!

SHANNON: The widow wants you out, and out you'll go, even if you sell your watercolours like hot cakes to the pariah dogs in the plaza. [*He stares at her, shaking his head hopelessly.*]

HANNAH: I suppose you're right, Mr Shannon. I must be too tired to think or I've contracted your fever . . . It had actually slipped my mind for a moment that –

NONNO [*abruptly, from his cubicle*]: Hannah!

HANNAH [*rushing to his door*]: Yes; what is it, Nonno? [*He doesn't hear her and repeats her name louder.*] Here I am, I'm here.

NONNO: Don't come in yet, but stay where I can call you.

HANNAH: Yes, I'll *hear* you, Nonno. [*She turns towards Shannon, drawing a deep breath.*]

SHANNON: Listen, if you don't take this gold cross that I never want on me again, I'm going to pitch it off the veranda at the spook in the rain forest. [*He raises an arm to throw it, but she catches his arm to restrain him.*]

HANNAH: All right, Mr Shannon, I'll take it. I'll hold it for you.

SHANNON: Hock it, honey, you've got to.

HANNAH: Well, if I do, I'll mail the pawn ticket to you so you can redeem it, because you'll want it again, when you've gotten over your fever. [*She moves blindly down the veranda and starts to enter the wrong cubicle.*]

SHANNON: That isn't your cell; you went past it. [*His voice is gentle again.*]

HANNAH: I did. I'm sorry. I've never been this tired in all my life. [*She turns to face him again. He stares into her face. She looks blindly out, past him.*] Never! [*There is a slight pause.*] What did you say is making that constant, dry, scuffling sound beneath the veranda?

SHANNON: I told you.

HANNAH: I didn't hear you.

SHANNON: I'll get my flashlight. I'll show you. [*He lurches rapidly into his cubicle and back out with a flashlight.*] It's an iguana. I'll show you . . . See? The iguana? At the end of its rope? Trying to go on past the end of its goddam rope? Like *you*! Like *me*! Like Grampa with his last poem!

[*In the pause which follows singing is heard from the beach.*]

HANNAH: What is a – what – iguana?

SHANNON: It's a kind of lizard – a big one, a giant one. The Mexican kids caught it and tied it up.

HANNAH: Why did they tie it up?

SHANNON: Because that's what they do. They tie them up and fatten them up and then eat them up, when they're ready for eating. They're a delicacy. Taste like white meat of chicken. At least the Mexicans think so. And also the kids, the Mexican kids, have a lot of fun with them, poking out their eyes with sticks and burning their tails with matches. You know? Fun? Like that?

HANNAH: Mr Shannon, please go down and cut it loose!

SHANNON: I can't do that.

HANNAH: Why can't you?

SHANNON: Mrs Faulk wants to eat it. I've got to please Mrs Faulk. I am at her mercy. I am at her disposal.

HANNAH: I don't understand. I mean I don't understand how anyone could eat a big lizard.

SHANNON: Don't be so critical. If you got hungry enough you'd eat it too. You'd be surprised what people will eat if hungry. There's a lot of hungry people still in the world. Many have died of starvation, but a lot are still living and hungry, believe you me, if you will take my word for it. Why, when I was conducting a party of – *ladies?* – yes, ladies . . . through a country that shall be nameless but in this world, we were passing by rubberneck bus along a tropical coast when we saw a great mound of ... well, the smell was unpleasant. One of my ladies said, 'Oh, Larry, what is that?' My name being Lawrence, the most familiar ladies sometimes call me Larry. I didn't use the four-letter word for what the great mound was. I didn't think it was necessary to say it. Then she noticed, and I noticed too, a pair of very old natives of this nameless country, practically naked except for a few filthy rags, creeping and crawling about this mound of ... and ... occasionally stopping to pick something out of it, and pop it into their mouths. What? Bits of undigested ... food particles, Miss Jelkes. [*There is silence for a moment. She makes a gagging sound in her throat and rushes the length of the veranda to the wooden steps and disappears for a while.* SHANNON *continues, to himself and the moon.*] Now why did I tell her that? Because it's true? That's no reason to tell her, because it's true. Yeah. Because it's true was a good reason not to tell her. Except ... I think I first *faced* it in that nameless country. The gradual, rapid, natural, unnatural – predestined, accidental – cracking up and going to pieces of young Mr T. Lawrence Shannon, yes, still *young* Mr T. Lawrence Shannon, by which rapid-slow process ... his final tour of ladies through tropical countries ... Why did I say 'tropical'? Hell! Yes! It's always been tropical countries I took ladies through. Does that, does that – huh? – signify something, I wonder? Maybe. Fast decay is a thing of hot climates, steamy, hot, wet climates, and I run back to them like a ... Incomplete sentence ... Always seducing a lady or two, or three or four or five ladies in the party, but really ravaging her first by pointing out to her the – what? – horrors? Yes, horrors! – of the tropical country being conducted a tour through. My ... brain's going out now, like a failing – power ... So I stay here, I reckon, and live off la patrona for the rest of my life. Well, she's old enough to predecease me. She could check out of here first, and I imagine that after a couple of years of having to satisfy her I might be prepared for the shock of her passing on ... Cruelty ... pity. What is it? ... Don't know, all I know is ...

HANNAH [*from below the veranda*]: You're talking to yourself.

SHANNON: No. To you. I knew you could hear me out there, but not being able to see you I could say it easier, you know ...

NONNO: A chronicle no longer gold,
A bargaining with mist and mould . . .

HANNAH [*coming back on to the veranda*]: I took a closer look at the iguana down there.

SHANNON: You did? How did you like it? Charming? Attractive?

HANNAH: No; it's not an attractive creature. Nevertheless, I think it should be cut loose.

SHANNON: Iguanas have been known to bite their tails off when they're tied up by their tails.

HANNAH: This one is tied by its throat. It can't bite its own head off to escape from the end of the rope, Mr Shannon. Can you look at me and tell me truthfully that you don't know it's able to feel pain and panic?

SHANNON: You mean it's one of God's creatures?

HANNAH: If you want to put it that way, yes, it is. Mr Shannon, will you please cut it loose, set it free? Because if you don't I will.

SHANNON: Can you look at *me* and tell *me* truthfully that this reptilian creature, tied up down there, doesn't mostly disturb you because of its parallel situation to your Grampa's dying-out effort to finish one last poem, Miss Jelkes?

HANNAH: Yes, I . . .

SHANNON: Never mind completing that sentence. We'll play God tonight like kids play house with old broken crates and boxes. All right? Now Shannon is going to go down there with his machete and cut the damn lizard loose so it can run back to its bushes because God won't do it and we are going to play God here.

HANNAH: I knew you'd do that. And I thank you.

[SHANNON *goes down the two steps from the veranda with the machete. He crouches beside the cactus that hides the iguana and cuts the rope with a quick, hard stroke of the machete. He turns to look after its flight, as the low, excited mumble in cubicle 3 grows louder. Then* NONNO'S *voice turns to a sudden shout.*]

NONNO: Hannah! Hannah! [*She rushes to him as he wheels himself out of his cubicle on to the veranda.*]

HANNAH: Grandfather! What is it?

NONNO: I! believe! it! is! *finished!* Quick, before I forget it – pencil, paper! Quick! please! Ready?

HANNAH: Yes. All ready, Grandfather.

NONNO [*in a loud, exalted voice*]:

> How calmly does the orange branch
> Observe the sky begin to blanch
> Without a cry, without a prayer,
> With no betrayal of despair.
>
> Sometime while night obscures the tree
> The zenith of its life will be
> Gone past forever, and from thence
> A second history will commence.
>
> A chronicle no longer gold,
> A bargaining with mist and mould,
> And finally the broken stem
> The plummeting to earth; and then
>
> An intercourse not well designed
> For beings of a golden kind
> Whose native green must arch above
> The earth's obscene, corrupting love.
>
> And still the ripe fruit and the branch
> Observe the sky begin to blanch
> Without a cry, without a prayer,
> With no betrayal of despair.
>
> O Courage, could you not as well
> Select a second place to dwell,
> Not only in that golden tree
> But in the frightened heart of me?

Have you got it?

HANNAH: Yes!

NONNO: All of it?

HANNAH: Every word of it.

NONNO: It is *finished*?

HANNAH: Yes.

NONNO: Oh! God! Finally finished?

HANNAH: Yes, finally finished. [*She is crying. The singing voices flow up from the beach.*]

NONNO: After waiting so long!

HANNAH: Yes, we waited so long.

NONNO: And it's good! It is *good*?

HANNAH: It's – it's . . .

NONNO: What?

HANNAH: Beautiful, Grandfather! [*She springs up, a fist to her mouth.*] Oh, Grandfather, I am so happy for you. Thank you for writing such a lovely poem! It was worth the long wait. Can you sleep now, Grandfather?

NONNO: You'll have it typewritten tomorrow?

HANNAH: Yes. I'll have it typed up and send it off to *Harper's*.

NONNO: Hah? I didn't hear that, Hannah.

HANNAH [*shouting*]: I'll have it typed up tomorrow, and mail it to *Harper's* tomorrow! They've been waiting for it a long time, too! You know!

NONNO: Yes; I'd like to pray now.

HANNAH: Good night. Sleep now, Grandfather. You've finished your loveliest poem.

NONNO [*faintly, drifting off*]: Yes, thanks and praise . . .

[*MAXINE comes around the front of the veranda, followed by PEDRO playing a harmonica softly. She is prepared for a night swim, a vividly striped towel thrown over her shoulders. It is apparent that the night's progress has mellowed her spirit: her face wears a faint smile which is suggestive of those cool, impersonal, all-comprehending smiles on the carved heads of Egyptian or Oriental deities. Bearing a rum-coco, she approaches the hammock, discovers it empty, the ropes on the floor, and calls softly to Pedro.*]

MAXINE: Shannon ha escapado! [*PEDRO goes on playing dreamily. She throws back her head and shouts.*] Shannon! [*The call is echoed by the hill beyond. PEDRO advances a few steps and points under the veranda.*]

PEDRO: Miré. Allé 'hasta Shannon.

[SHANNON *comes into view from below the veranda, the severed rope and machete dangling from his hands.*]

MAXINE: What are you doing down there, Shannon?

SHANNON: I cut loose one of God's creatures at the end of the rope.

[HANNAH, *who has stood motionless with closed eyes behind the wicker chair, goes quietly towards the cubicles and out of the moon's glare.*]

MAXINE [*tolerantly*]: What'd you do that for, Shannon?

SHANNON: So that one of God's creatures could scramble home safe and free . . . A little act of grace, Maxine.

MAXINE [*smiling a bit more definitely*]: C'mon up here, Shannon. I want to talk to you.

SHANNON [*starting to climb on to the veranda, as* MAXINE *rattles the ice in the coconut shell*]: What d'ya want to talk about, Widow Faulk?

MAXINE: Let's go down and swim in that liquid moonlight.

SHANNON: Where did you pick up that poetic expression?

[MAXINE *glances back at* PEDRO *and dismisses him with 'Vamos.' He leaves with a shrug, the harmonica fading out.*]

MAXINE: Shannon, I want you to stay with me.

SHANNON [*taking the rum-coco from her*]: You want a drinking companion?

MAXINE: No, I just want you to stay here, because I'm alone here now and I need somebody to help me manage the place.

[HANNAH *strikes a match for a cigarette.*]

SHANNON [*looking towards her*]: I want to remember that face. I won't see it again.

MAXINE: Let's go down to the beach.

SHANNON: I can make it down the hill, but not back up.

MAXINE: I'll get you back up the hill. [*They have started off now, towards the path down through the rain forest.*] I've got five more years, maybe ten, to make this place attractive to the male clientele, the middle-aged ones at least. And you can take care of the women that are with them. That's what you can do, you know that, Shannon.

[*He chuckles happily. They are now on the path,* MAXINE *half leading, half supporting him. Their voices fade as* HANNAH *goes into* NONNO'S *cubicle and comes back with a shawl, her cigarette left inside. She pauses between the door and the wicker chair and speaks to herself and the sky.*]

HANNAH: Oh, God, can't we stop now? Finally? Please let us. It's so quiet here, now.

[*She starts to put the shawl about* NONNO, *but at the same moment his head drops to one side. With a soft intake of breath, she extends a hand before his mouth to see if he is still breathing. He isn't. In a panicky moment, she looks right and left for someone to call to. There's no one. Then she bends to press her head to the crown of* NONNO'S *and the curtain starts to descend.*]

THE END

Nazi Marching Song

Heute wollen wir ein Liedlein singen,
Trinken wollen wir den kühlen Wein;
Und die Gläser sollen dazu klingen,
Denn es muss, es muss geschieden sein.

Gib' mir deine Hand,
Deine weisse Hand,
Leb' wohl, mein Schatz, leb' wohl, mein Schatz,
Lebe wohl, lebe whol,
Denn wir fahren. Boom! Boom!
Denn wir fahren. Boom! Boom!
Denn wir fahren gegen Engeland. Boom! Boom!

Let's sing a little song today,
And drink some cool wine;
The glasses should be ringing
Since we must, we must part.

Give me your hand,
Your white hand,
Farewell, my love, farewell,
Farewell, farewell,
Since we're going –
Since we're going –
Since we're going against England.